THE REMARKABLE EXPEDITION

The Story of Stanley's Rescue of Emin Pasha from
Equatorial Africa

BY

OLIVIA MANNING

C . 1

New York   Atheneum   1985

The map is based on one in *The Rescue of Emin Pasha*
by Roger Jones, published by Allison & Busby.

Library of Congress Cataloging in Publication Data

Manning, Olivia.
 The remarkable expedition.

 Reprint. Originally published: The reluctant rescue.
Garden City, N.Y. • Doubleday, 1947.
  Bibliography: p.
  Includes index.
  1. Emin Pasha Relief Expedition (1887-1889) 2. Stanley,
Henry M. (Henry Morton), 1841-1904. 3 Emin Pasha,
1840-1892. 4. Tippu Tip. d. 1905. 5. Africa, Central—
History—1884-1960. I. Manning, Olivia. Reluctant rescue.
II. Title.
DT363.M3 1985   967   85-47607
ISBN 0-689-11627-6

Originally published in 1947 by the Doubleday Publishing Company
under the title *The Reluctant Rescue*

To the memory of my brother, Lieutenant Oliver David
George Manning, A.R.I.B.A., R.N.V.R., killed on active
service October 7th, 1941. He has no grave but the sea.

CONTENTS

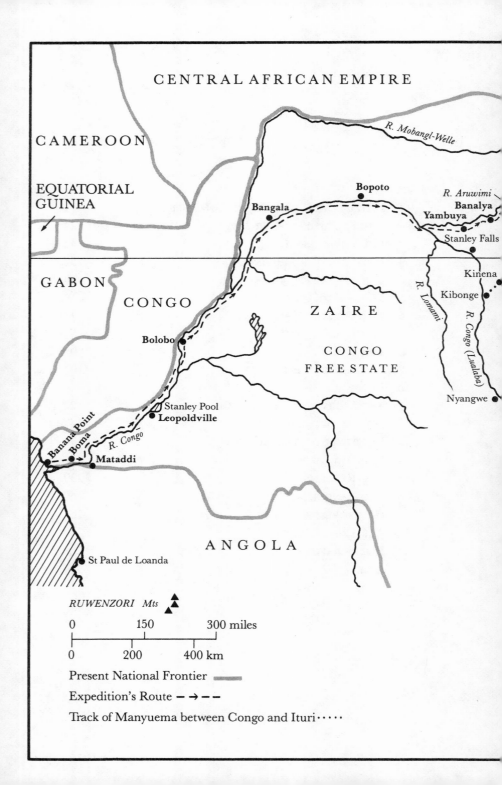

CENTRAL AFRICAN EMPIRE

CAMEROON

EQUATORIAL
GUINEA

Bopoto

R. Mobangl-Welle

R. Aruwimi
Banalya

Bangala

Yambuya

Stanley Falls

GABON

Kinena

Kibonge

R. Lomanni

CONGO

ZAIRE

CONGO
FREE STATE

R. Congo (Lualaba)

Bolobo

Nyangwe

Stanley Pool
Leopoldville

Banana Point

Boma

R. Congo

Mataddi

ANGOLA

St Paul de Loanda

RUWENZORI Mts

| 0 | 150 | 300 miles |

| 0 | 200 | 400 km |

Present National Frontier ━━━

Expedition's Route ━ → ━ ━

Track of Manyuema between Congo and Ituri ·····

The Expedition's route across Africa

Based on a map of 1890 in Stanley's *In Darkest Africa*

PREFACE

Olivia Manning was primarily a novelist and wrote non-fiction only when she had no novel to write. This book, *The Remarkable Expedition* (1947), published in the USA as *The Reluctant Rescue* (1947); *The Dreaming Shore* (1950), a travel book about the coastline of Ireland that she much loved; and a collection of *Punch* funnies, *My Husband Cartwright* (1956), pretty well cover the non-fiction side of her writing. While recovering from a serious illness, she did half a dozen precise radiant watercolours of irises growing in the Judean hills: she may have tired of her painting, for which she was trained, too early.

She began to read about Emin Pasha who was so reluctantly to be rescued, and the explorer Stanley in 1938, immediately after the appearance of her first novel, *The Wind Changes*. War seemed a few months away: evidently, as was her general state after intense concentration on a novel, she was lying fallow but felt she wanted to be writing about something (Mrs Belloc-Lowndes had told her, 'Never a day without a line.').

We were introduced outside Peter's Bar in Southampton Row by my old schoolfriend, Walter Allen, in July 1939, and married three weeks later in Bloomsbury Register Office (Louis MacNeice was best man and Stevie Smith bridesmaid). Four days after the wedding, I received orders to return to my British Council post within thirty-six hours: Olivia, ignoring bureaucratic difficulties, and aware that war would start in a matter of days, said, 'I'm coming with you.' A sailor's daughter, she was taking no chances of possible years of separation. We set out together on an already blacked-out Simplon-Orient Express, leaving trench-digging, tree-chopping, sandbag-filling London for the Bucharest she recorded so vividly in the first part of *The Balkan Trilogy*.

She brought with her maps and her notes on Emin, Stanley and the fatally and grotesquely avaricious Tippu Tib, as well as copies of the diaries and letters of the unnecessarily doomed professional soldiers and amateur explorers who made up the tragic Rear Column.

Semper aliquid novum ex Africa. It all makes a highly dramatic tale,

xi

and one that has appealed to other writers. Graham Greene, in a typically generous review, revealed that he had read the letters and diaries, and recently Simon Gray wrote an interesting play (Harold Pinter directed it brilliantly) about the tensions and terrors of the Rear Column.

Olivia Manning loved a good yarn and had earned her first typewriter by stories of exotic loves and adventures in darkest Cairo, to which she made a spectacular literary return with *The Levant Trilogy*. But looking back on *The Remarkable Expedition*—a book which I had not read since doing the proof corrections—I find it remarkable that the writer, in her portraits of the three main characters, chose three sacred monsters, of the class of Miss Bohun in *School For Love*, and Yaki in *The Balkan Trilogy*. It was not for nothing that she loved Dickens.

R.D. Smith

Introduction

THE EGYPTIAN EMPIRE

"I feel that all these wrongs can only be washed out in blood."
GORDON

B RUCE, the explorer, returning in 1773 through the Sudan—the
Country of the Blacks—from the southern regions where he had
discovered the source of the Blue Nile, wrote of the tribesmen who did
little to help him on his way: "War and treason seem to be the only
employment of this horrid people, whom Heaven has separated by
almost impassable deserts from the rest of mankind."

Even the most ambitious of the pharaohs made no attempt to conquer
the Sudan. At no time before 1820 did the Egyptian frontier extend
south of Wady Halfa. Between Wady Halfa, the southernmost
Egyptian town, and Hannech, the northernmost town of Nubia,
stretches 180 miles of sand. The river, then the only high road, is full of
rock ridges. The first attempt to overcome these natural barriers and
claim the rich lands beyond was made not, of course, by an Egyptian,
but by an Albanian using Turkish and Albanian troops officered by
Turks and Circassians.

It has been said of the fellah, the happy-go-lucky true Egyptian, that
he would make a good soldier if he only wished to kill someone. It is
believed that the victorious pharaohs depended upon mercenaries.
The Egyptians, fortunate owners of the richest country of the ancient
world, loving life and dreading death, could afford to pay others to
fight and risk death for them. The habit of aggression did not develop
in them. From Cambyses through Alexander, the Ptolemies and
Saladin's dynasty to the thirteenth century and beyond, Egypt depended
for her military power upon foreigners. The day came when, with
Saladin's dynasty petering out, the army—composed of virile Caucasian
slaves called Mameluks—realised its own strength. The slaves became
masters and remained rulers until 1517, when Egypt was taken into the
Ottoman empire. Under the Turks the Mameluks continued to hold
office.

Egypt, given over to an Oriental chaos of despotic inefficiency and official dishonesty, began, in the eighteenth century, to assume for Europe something more than an historical interest. Great Britain was acquiring an empire. She had already secured the Cape of Good Hope and Mauritius to ensure the safety of the sea route to India. The safety of the overland route depended on Britain's friendship with the Turkish rulers of Egypt. Napoleon, who saw the situation clearly, wrote: "By seizing and holding Egypt I retain and command the destinies of the civilised world." English residents in Egypt during the recent war were reminded of Napoleon's methods when natives in the delta town of Tanta shewed them the birthplace of the mother of that devout Moslem, Adolf Hitler. Installed in Egypt, Napoleon declared that he and his men were better Moslems than the Mameluks. All men were, he said, equal, and all posts in Egypt would be open to all classes. He was bringing not the sword, but peace and western civilisation. To begin with he pillaged Rosetta for 100,000 francs; Damietta for 150,000 francs; the Copts for 528,000 francs; the damask merchants for 300,000 francs; and ordered the wives of the Mameluks to be plundered of all they possessed. Rich and important people were accused of treason and permitted to ransom themselves for vast sums. The only lasting token of his rule is the mutilated face of the Sphinx, which was used as a target by his troops. Nevertheless this adventurer gave to Egypt its first glimpses of the western world, where ideas and action took the place of the oriental dream of a genie in a bottle.

Britain in 1801 helped Turkey to drive out the intruder and so freed again the route to India. An ambitious Albanian called Mohammed Ali was sent by the Turkish Sultan to help the Mameluks clean up pockets of French resistance. But the Mameluks were finished. Five hundred years of intermarriage and the Egyptian climate had orientalised them. Power passed into the hands of the newly arrived foreigner. By 1805 Mohammed Ali was in a position to declare himself governor of Egypt, but he wisely made no attempt to throw off Turkish sovereignty.

He was known to favour the French, so the English, ostensibly to avenge the cruelty with which he liquidated the Mameluks, in 1807 sent to Egypt a British Expedition, which was miserably defeated. British prisoners in Cairo were forced to walk between stakes on which were exposed the heads of hundreds of British officers and men. Within a few years all the powers had accepted the Albanian as master of Egypt.

Mohammed Ali as a Moslem was only half a European. His

enormous energy and ambitions were limited by the muddle-headedness that results from orthodox Moslem education. His attempts at westernising his country had a certain imaginative breadth, but were carried out with such inefficiency that the lot of the wretched fellah, the eternal victim, was worse than before. Taxes and more taxes were levied to keep open factories that did not pay for years. Twenty thousand workmen died to build the canal from Alexandria to the Nile. The worst blow, however, fell when Mohammed Ali decided to conscript an army of native Egyptians. Some so dreaded the routine and dangers of service that they mutilated themselves to escape it. In spite of its early unpopularity, the formation of this fellahin army was the first cause of the awakening of a sense of nationalism in the Egyptian people. Within its ranks the words "Egypt for the Egyptians" were first spoken. That the fellahin could fight when forced, that they could even win victories, fired them with a desire for independence—for these docile, hardy peasants gained enormous successes in Mohammed Ali's Syrian Wars of 1832 and 1839. But the Turks and Circassians remained in control and half a century was to pass before it was possible for an Egyptian to rise higher than a sergeant.

When it came to the venture nearest to his heart—the conquest of the Sudan—Mohammed Ali fell back on mercenaries. He sought to rule not a vast desert region but the countries beyond, the fabled lands whose soil was carried by the Nile to supply the fertile river banks of Egypt. In those regions, it was said, corn could be produced in quantities that would astonish even the delta agriculturists. But not only corn. A French traveller from the southern Sudan had brought to Mohammed Ali some seeds of an indigenous plant—Pliny's "wool-bearing trees of Ethiopia". Mohammed Ali counted out the grains among gardeners responsible for their success and himself superintended their sowing. So began the great cotton cultivation of Egypt. The name Nubia derived from legendary gold-mines. Small quantities of gold found to the south-east of Sennar at the foot of the Abyssinian hills seemed to promise greater wealth in the interior. Added to all this was the rich caravan trade to the Red Sea. By 1820 his plans were ready. He ordered the first expeditionary force south. It advanced without difficulty into the province south of Berber. The Sudanese chiefs, capitulating with a smile, invited the conquerors to a banquet. The officers were served with poisoned wine. The disorganised troops were trapped and burnt to death.   A*

Mohammed Ali did not give his Egyptian subjects time to react with their usual panic. Before the news of the destruction of the first had spread, he organised and sent out a second force which, warned against treachery, succeeded. Once inside the Sudan, he employed the rivalry of the tribes to his own ends, sowing dissension that prevented their coalition against the invader. Soon he had among the desert population allies who furnished him with transport camels and supplies. All appeared to be going well in the Sudan.

At home the situation was less satisfactory. Law and order had been introduced into the country and attempts made to promote education and the study of medicine, but the price of these advantages was paid by the long-suffering fellahin, who laboured under taxes, monopolies, corvée and conscription. In 1824 rebellion broke out in Upper Egypt. It was easily crushed, but gave the first hint of trouble to come.

Mohammed Ali was steadily building up land and sea forces until by 1831 he was able to make a show of open revolt against Turkish rule. For the next ten years the strained relationship between the Sultan of Turkey and the Pasha of Egypt was to agitate the diplomatic world. British interest in the two overland routes to India—one via the Isthmus of Suez, the other through the Valley of the Euphrates— placed British diplomacy in a peculiarly delicate position. At that time Britain may well have regretted the fact that she did not occupy Egypt, as she could easily have done, after the Battle of the Nile.

The Sultan attempted to smooth out the situation by granting Mohammed Ali the pashaliks of Syria, Damascus, Aleppo and the district of Adena. This small, virtually independent empire he six years later tried to regain. This was the opportunity of Egypt's new fellahin forces. Under the Pasha's son, Ibrahim, they drove back the Turks with such vigour that Egypt might have taken possession of the whole Ottoman Empire had the European powers not intervened.

At the Conference of London in 1840, England neglected another opportunity to occupy Egypt, the grounds this time being that Mohammed Ali's friendship with France threatened Britain's right of way. Instead, although permitted to form a dynasty, the Pasha was forbidden to maintain an army of more than 10,000 men or a fleet of any kind. Although prevented from making further conquests, he still had the Sudan. Almost unnoticed he was widening it in all directions. A small fishing village, no more than a collection of temporary huts in a low, unhealthy position at the junction of the White and Blue Niles, chosen by Mohammed Ali for its defensive possibilities as the site of the capital of the new province, was now growing rapidly without plan or control. Because of a spit of land that appeared between the Niles at low water, the capital was named Khartoum—the Elephant's Trunk.

At home the Pasha concentrated his energies on constructing with unpaid labour vast public works that drained the last milleme from the pockets of the fellahin. He died insane in 1849. Abbas I, who succeeded, let himself be persuaded by the British to build the railway from Cairo to Alexandria to expedite goods exported from the Sudan to Great Britain, but he was by nature a reactionary. He had no wish to imitate the western world and it would seem that the exhausting era of improvements was past.

After a reign of only six years, Abbas was murdered. He was followed by Mohammed Ali's favourite son, Said. Though lacking his father's force of character, Said had all his ambition and admiration for French culture. The French had little difficulty in interesting him in a scheme to construct a canal across the Isthmus of Suez. The English advised him against the idea, possibly because it was French, and the English engineer, Stephenson, condemned it on the grounds that the Mediterranean and Red Seas were on different levels. Said decided to take whatever risk that mistaken belief implied, and granted de Lesseps a concession for the construction of the Suez Canal. The English were to find themselves in the ignominious position of being without rights in the quickest route to their own empire.

Said, by borrowing three million pounds from German bankers, started the national debt. Fresh taxes were levied upon the fellahin. At the same time thousands of lives were being lost that Egyptian territory might be increased in the Sudan. By 1861 the frontier extended sixty miles south of Khartoum. Egypt was encroaching steadily on Abyssinia, and as regions rightly regarded as Abyssinian were being abandoned by nervous natives, they were added to the Egyptian Sudan. When asked by the President of the Royal Geographical Society what were the actual frontiers of Egypt, Said replied that they were very elastic.

He was succeeded after his death in 1863 by his nephew Ismail, who, combining European ideas with oriental opulence, managed to outshine even the extravagance of his predecessors. He was, indeed, to bankrupt his country, but for a while his expenditure purchased an appearance of achievement. He improved the military system. The army—which had dwindled to a mere handful of men—was increased to 100,000 well-equipped soldiers. He completed a number of public works. In 1869 the Suez Canal was opened.

It was the day not of the military but the commercial adventurer. The termination of the American Civil War had loosed on the old world dozens of natural mercenaries. Many of them hastened to Cairo with enticing, impracticable schemes that excited Ismail, who was ready to venture money on anything. European and Levantine sharpers of all sorts were flourishing in the cities. While the Khedive "took from the fellahin the little land that remained to them, despoiling them even of their vessels of brass and the ear-rings of their women; when even the eight-year-old shoe-blacks were required to pay an annual tax of twenty francs", the foreigners who preyed upon the land were exempt from taxation. This state of affairs remained until 1883, when English administration required them to contribute to the country a small percentage of their spoils.

Ismail's ambitions covered the Sudan, the elastic borders of which he was determined to stretch even further. It was at this time that territory visited only by the explorer and the slave trader was becoming accessible to the Egyptian imperialist. In 1863 Sir Samuel White Baker, the explorer, and his wife travelled south to a collection of trader's huts on the White Nile known as Gondokoro. There they met the explorers Speke and Grant, who, destitute and exhausted, were returning from their discovery of the great lake—now known as the Victoria Nyanza—which they believed to be the Nile's source. Information given by the explorers enabled Baker a year later to discover Lake Albert. Gondokoro began to grow important as a setting-off place for scientific and exploratory expeditions. As trade followed discovery, it grew as a trading centre and was soon the main village of a province of indefinite size which was to exist for a few years in history as Equatoria.

Other European explorers made their way through the Jur country and Bahr-el-Ghazal, the Upper Nile, Dar Jertit and Kordofan. Wherever they went, Egyptian troops and officials followed greedily to possess larger and larger tracts of land. Turkey handed over the Red Sea coast with the ports of Suakin and Massowah. By 1865 the irregular frontier of the Sudan ran round Boghos, Cassala, the

Rahad, Dinder and the Blue Nile as far south as Fazoklé. A constant border warfare was being carried on between the Arab tribes and the Abyssinians. Four years later Fashoda had been established on the White Nile and Ismail's empire extended to within one degree of the Equator.

Egyptian rule was at once happy-go-lucky and ruthlessly self-interested. Egypt regarded the province purely as a source of profit for herself. Very little was put back into the enterprise. Mohammed Ali's capital, Khartoum, that had been founded with all the usual resplendent Egyptian intentions, was left to fend for itself with the usual Egyptian indifference. Baker, who visited it first in 1862, described it as the most dirty, miserable and unhealthy place he had ever seen. There was neither drainage nor sanitation; the bodies of dead animals rotted in the streets among the filth of years. In spite of the fact that the population of 30,000 included prosperous Levantine traders, the aspect of the place was one of utter misery. Among the officials dishonesty and fraud were customary. Everyone cheated according to rank. The slave traffic was the main business of the town.

The slave traffic was, indeed, the main business of the Sudan. It had grown with the ivory trade. As the tsetse fly wiped out any horses or oxen introduced into the Sudan, some other beast of burden had to be found to carry the ivory. The negro was the cheapest and most plentiful. He acquired a new value. Slaves were now being captured in such numbers that there were plenty to spare for domestic use. The ivory trade had become a government monopoly, but the Arabs were free to recoup themselves by unrestricted slave-trading. This state of affairs made Egyptian rule tolerable to them. It was not to last.

Ismail's European creditors, to whom he owed vast sums, now demanded that the slave-trade be suppressed. He was forced to put up an appearance of shocked horror as details of this traffic in human beings was revealed to him. He agreed to equip a costly expedition under Sir Samuel White Baker, for which, of course, the fellahin had to pay. The expedition could scarcely have been less popular among the slavers than it was among the Egyptians.

In 1870 Baker, at the request of the Khedive, penetrated beyond Gondokoro into the beautiful, fertile regions of valleys and streams called Dufilé and Fatiko. Slaver-traders were everywhere. To the west lay the lands of the Dinka tribe, which had been reduced to a third of its size by the trade. This devastated country, which Baker had six years before described as "a perfect garden", was now a wilderness. One slave-trader, Zebehr, lived with the magnificence of a prince and his power had grown in the area to that of a dictator. Baker was energetic in winning the confidence of the native chiefs and establishing a number of small military settlements for the protection of the tribes. Unfortunately when he returned, very pleased with himself, to England, the Egyptian officials he had installed set up in the slave-trade for themselves.

In 1874 Zebehr attacked the province of Darfur, and the Khedive, feeling it politic to assist him, claimed the new territory thus won. Egypt now held the entire basin of the Nile from the Equator to the Mediterranean. Zebehr was created Bey and then Pasha, but he was not to be satisfied with empty titles. He demanded the Governor-Generalship of Darfur and, to back his claim, went to Cairo to bribe the Pashas. He was not permitted to return.

Zebehr's son, Suleiman, now broke into revolt on behalf of his father and Baker was sent south again to restore order. It was at this time becoming clear to the outside world that Egypt not only condoned the slave-trade but practised it; that Zebehr, the chief trader, had been created Pasha, and if he were being detained under open arrest in Cairo, it was only because he menaced Egyptian rule in the south. The Press disclosed that from such areas as Bahr-el-Ghazal, Kordofan and Darfur more than 30,000 slaves were supplied each year for what it described as "Oriental luxury and debauch". Ismail was forced to consent to the Equatorial provinces being put under the control of a European officer. Colonel Gordon, who had become known as "Chinese Gordon" in the Far East, and was soon to be made Gordon Pasha, was sent to replace Baker. When, two years later, he returned to Cairo worn out by the miserable intrigues and jealousies of Egyptian officials, he wrote: "I returned with the sad conviction that no good could be done in these parts, and that it would have been better had no expedition ever been sent."

Affairs in Egypt itself were only slightly less wretched. The fellahin, reduced to the extremes of poverty, could pay for nothing more. Ismail, who had repeatedly broken faith with his creditors, could raise no more loans in Europe. In 1876 he was forced to sell his 176,602 founder's shares in the Suez Canal. This opportunity for Britain was seized by Disraeli only against considerable opposition. He bought the shares for £4,000,000. Six years later they had trebled in value, but, more important than that, England had at last acquired rights in the management of the quickest highway to India.

As for the £4,000,000—it was not a sum sufficient to put Ismail's affairs in order. The situation had been clear enough to Gordon when, on his first visit to Cairo, he wrote: "Things cannot last long like this, they are paying 36% for money." It became clearer when on his appointment as Governor-General he studied the situation, that Egypt was spoiling the Sudan and the Europeans were spoiling Egypt. "Duke of This wants steamer—say six hundred pounds," he wrote, "Duke of That wants house, etc., all the time the poor people are ground down to get money for all this. If God wills, I will shake all this in some way not clear to me now." But Gordon was to find himself no match for the money-lenders and financiers who were about to close in on Ismail.

With the £4,000,000 in hand, the Khedive had launched a new campaign—this time on Abyssinia. The fellahin whispered of the traditional curse that the prophet had put on Islam should any attempt be made to subdue these mountain Christians who had once sheltered him from his enemies. Such an invasion would announce the ruin of the invader.

Whatever it was to prelude, the invasion itself was a disastrous failure. The fellahin forces broke before the Abyssinian strength was upon them and trained soldiers armed with Remington rifles were scattered by spearmen. Vast quantities of ammunition, prisoners and treasure fell into enemy hands. It is said that the Abyssinians were so amazed by the quantities of gold they had won that they supposed it counterfeit, and in return for a few silver dollars would give handfuls of sovereigns—the sovereigns that had bought the Suez Canal shares.

Ruin indeed was upon the invader. The Egyptian budget of expenditure had trebled in forty years. Ismail paid interest on the enormous national debt at the rate of 25%. He was forced to face a series of international enquiries. He called upon Gordon, the only man he trusted, to help him. Gordon hurried to Cairo, where he saw with disgust the pack of European money-lenders and financiers who were claiming their dues, and the crowds of officials who were waiting to take over the country at enormous salaries. As a gesture he cut down his own salary as Governor from £10,000 a year to £2,000, putting the difference into the beggared Sudanese treasury. He demanded that the small officials and employees who for months had received no salaries in order that the money-lenders should be paid their outrageous interest should now be compensated. He worked out a simple and reasonable solution of the situation, and was snubbed, ridiculed and intrigued against for his pains. The financiers had everything to gain by complicating the situation. Gordon returned helplessly to Khartoum.

An English official was appointed to superintend the revenue; a French official the expenditure of the country. Another French and British commission controlled the enormous landed property of the Khedive. Ismail still represented the government of Egypt but the public purse was out of his reach. He felt the position to be intolerable. It seemed to him that his schemes for developing Egypt were merely enriching foreigners.

As soon as there was hope that the wonderful agricultural resources of the country might restore the fellahin to prosperity, and Egyptian bonds began to rise in value, Ismail, feeling himself on his feet again, attempted a *coup d'état*. He dismissed both the French and English ministers of the newly appointed Finance Control. Had he insulted only one, the other might have overlooked the incident. As it was, England and France combined in a rage to depose him. France advocated a military occupation. England, more lenient, required Turkey to exile Ismail. In 1879 he was retired to Naples, and his son, Mohammed Tewfik Pasha, was proclaimed Khedive.

Tewfik was willing to co-operate in the effort to pull Egypt together. He refused to take for his personal use the usual large sums from the civil list, and reduced all unnecessary expenditure. He accepted British and French control, but the Egyptian ruling classes were tired of foreign interference. Gordon was to be the victim chosen to allay their discontent.

He had undertaken a mission to Abyssinia which had failed lamentably. He had made enemies among those now in power in Cairo and Tewfik disliked him. He was criticised not merely because he was a foreigner, but because he had appointed other foreigners to control the different provinces. An Austrian, Slatin, was Governor of Darfur; an Italian, Gessi, Governor of Bahr-el-Ghazal; an eccentric German doctor, ostensibly a Moslem and calling himself Emin, had in 1878 been appointed Governor of Equatoria; while such men as Mason Bey, ex-Governor of Equatoria, and the young ex-mate Lupton were in influential positions at Khartoum. Thus at least one half of Egypt was under foreign rule. Now the other half was administered by England and France, employing a host of foreign officials at salaries hitherto unheard-of in Egypt.

Gordon was replaced by the disastrous Raouf Pasha, but his European lieutenants remained. The Egyptians could not see these foreigners as being, however honest and hard-working, better worth the money than their own cheap, if dishonest, speculators. They believed that, now they were secure from the progressive Ismail, they could manage their own country. Jealousy against foreigners in high positions was fanned by other foreigners who had failed to do so well for themselves. Even the fellahin who were being safe-guarded resented the control. There was deep rooted in the Egyptian a love of the old muddle which everyone understood.

The Khedive was now little more than a figurehead. Pressed by his creditors and afraid of the Egyptian "socialists" who would depose him, Tewfik knew that only the British were strong enough to uphold him. As a result, they were seen by the Egyptians to have an unwelcome influence in directing his affairs and policy. France, whose attachment to Egypt was largely romantic, was suspect. Respect for France had failed after Sedan, but since she had established a colony in Tunisia, only three days' sail away, it was believed she was awaiting an opportunity to renew aggression.

The powerful class of senior army officers from whose ranks rose not only generals but chief ministers and other important functionaries now saw the end of its power. Said, and later Ismail, had, as a gesture of independence against the Turks, begun to promote the fellahin both in military and civil offices. The bitter fight made by officers in England against the abolition of purchase and the introduction of promotion by merit was repeated by the Turkish and Circassian officers, who had now to meet on equal terms members of the despised, exploited fellahin. Among the fellah officers, who hated and resented these foreign officers, a strong nationalist movement began to grow. It broke at last into open revolt under a fellah officer calling himself Ahmed Arabi the Egyptian. Arabi was a solid, direct character, not intelligent but having a rough eloquence that moved the common soldiers. His professed aim was to protect the Egyptians against their Turkish and European oppressors.

The outside world merely asked in whose pay Arabi might be. Baker, writing regularly to *The Times*, was convinced that the Turkish Sultan was using Arabi to try and overthrow European influence in Egypt. Others believed that England was behind Arabi with the familiar object of "coming in to keep order". Still others that Tewfik himself had organised the revolt as a gesture of independence against Turkey. Whoever protected Arabi did so effectively. When he appeared before the palace at Cairo to dictate terms to the Khedive, the government granted him one concession after another. He was made a Pasha, then Under-Secretary for War and later a Member of the Cabinet. These honours, however, did not pacify him and many in England began to see Egypt as a second Ireland. To outsiders, it seemed rather a second India.

Egyptians, who saw no advantage to themselves in the present situation, said openly they would be better off as part of the British Empire. They believed that now, were they to declare themselves independent of Turkey, England could not be relied upon to support them. During the Turco-Russian war, Egypt was described in print as a "British interest", by attacking which Russia would rouse British hostility, but England made no move to protect her "interest" against the Turkish demand for 20,000 Egyptian troops. The troops under Prince Hassan were obliged to sail for Varna. England's only action was to bring men from India up the Suez Canal to occupy Cyprus. Cyprus was then described as dominating Egypt and giving England command of the Suez Canal. These statements were translated into Arabic and widely read in Egypt. Baker advocated a treaty of alliance between England, France and Egypt that would guarantee Egyptian independence and safety from attack. Instead, the British and French fleets appeared at Alexandria.

Arabi Pasha, now Minister for War, at once started constructing earthworks to protect the port. The excitement in the town led to a massacre of Europeans, among them British residents who had pointed out some weeks before that they were "absolutely defenceless". A month later, in July 1882, the British admiral bombarded the Alexandrine forts and Arabi's followers prepared to fight. The Sultan refused to suppress them. France refused to co-operate with Britain, so Britain decided to act alone. Troops under Sir Garnet Wolseley were landed at Ismailia and Arabi was defeated at Tel-el-Kebir.

England was, of course, blamed for every move she made. Although it was agreed that only British intervention had saved the lives of many foreigners in Egypt, the bombardment of Alexandria—during which Baker accused the English fleet of meekly standing by and doing nothing—was described in the French Press as an act of unparalleled brutality. The victory of Tel-el-Kebir was said to have been bought with cheques which the traitors were later forced to return.

Lord Dufferin, then British Ambassador at Constantinople, was sent to Egypt to adjust affairs and report on the situation. He prevented the execution of the ringleaders of the revolt and insisted that a new liberal spirit must prevail in Egypt. The Egyptian army was disbanded. A year later a small fellahin force of men was raised for the defence of Egypt. A young lieutenant called Kitchener was one of its first officers.

After the victory of Tel-el-Kebir, Arabi's movement soon degenerated into an excuse for odd murders and robberies. Its nationalist character had faded before that. Nationalism was something of which the Egyptian Arab understood little. The true uniting force was religion and against that force the English were to admit ignominious defeat.

By 1881 those interested in British imperial power in Egypt were talking of the possibility of an insurrection of Arab tribes in the Sudan. To the average Englishman in England such a possibility in that remote region of uncertain frontiers could not mean very much. Tourists went as far as Cairo or, if very adventurous, took the journey to Philæ and the first cataract. But Egypt stretched 2,000 miles south of the capital. Egyptian rule, unsatisfactory enough at home, grew steadily more irresponsible as the heat and distance from Cairo increased.

Arabi's revolt was to prove a small affair when time brought comparison with the holy war now developing in the Sudan.

According to Mohammedan belief a Mahdi or Messiah would appear in human form twelve centuries after the Hegira. His mission would be to redeem mankind. He would be known by a mole on his cheek.

The Hegira—Mohammed's flight to Medina from Mecca, which marks the commencement of the Mohammedan era—took place in A.D. 622. The twelve Moslem centuries ended in November 1882. Mohammed Ahmed, later to be called by millions the Mahdi, appeared out of his retirement a year too soon. Apart from this miscalculation or impatience, he fitted the part as well as another. There exists a photograph which shows him as a young man with classical features, large eyes, a remote glance and a full, firm mouth set in a delicately trimmed Arab beard—a face differing only in its dark skin from the conventional portraits of Christ. He had a mole upon his cheek. He was noted for personal magnetism enhanced by confidence in his cause.

His birth had been low and his trade the favoured one of carpenter. At one time he was servant to the French surgeon-general in the Sudan. His character is hidden from us beneath the reputation for sanctity which he began to acquire when he joined the order of the Ghelani dervishes and which soon placed him beyond criticism, but he appears to have been always a rebel. Years before he was due to reveal himself as the Mahdi, he called an Islamic revolt within the Ghelani order. Gessi Pasha had had him thrown into prison for five months.

When Gordon was replaced by the dishonest and stupid Raouf Pasha, Mohammed Ahmed was able to continue his career unchecked. He went to live on the little island of Abba above Khartoum, where the austerity of his life gained him a reputation for great sanctity. Islam does not demand celibacy from its ascetics and the carpenter of Dongola, growing rich on the offerings of the faithful, acquired a number of wives. These he was careful to select from the families of the most powerful and wealthy slave-dealers in the Sudan.

In May 1881 he publicly proclaimed himself the Mahdi. "Merciful God has put the sword of victory into my hand; and to prove to the world that I am the Mahdi, He has marked my left cheek with a mole. In the confusion of battle, I shall be led by the luminous standard of Azrael, the angel of death, the exterminator of my enemies." He invited every fakir and religious leader of Islam to join him on his island. He gained popular support by announcing that prophecies were about to be fulfilled, and won the richest section of the community by proclaiming the slave-trade legitimate. He called upon all Sudanese to rise against the rapacious and tyrannical Egyptian officials.

For the first time Raouf realised he must do something. He sent a handful of black soldiers to Abba with orders to capture the Mahdi. The poor soldiers, filled with superstitious dread, and helpless before the Mahdi's armed followers, were cut to pieces. This move by Raouf prompted the Mahdi to withdraw with his followers into the mountains of Southern Kordofan. From there in August 1881 he declared open revolt.

The advent of the Mahdi had done no more than detonate the discontent that had long been growing throughout the Sudan. The suppression of the slave-trade had brought poverty to thousands of

Sudanese. The ivory trade had long been lost to them. No attempt had been made to develop other industries. The people, miserably reduced, were forced to pay unjust and oppressive taxes to conquerors who felt no responsibility towards them and who, far from bringing civilisation and enlightenment, devoured the country like locusts. Raouf Pasha, a greedy and easily flattered idiot, had quickly undone all Gordon's work in the Sudan. He had dismissed the Sudanese employees, replacing them with Egyptians who tried to get the slave trade into their own hands.

Egyptian authority throughout the Sudan was represented by scattered garrisons of armed men undisciplined, demoralised and badly officered. Revolt would be easy, but the governor refused to recognise the fact. When ordered to report on the Mahdi rising he sent to Cairo ridiculous wordy letters that completely misrepresented the situation.

Among the first to recognise the gravity of the situation was Emin Bey, Governor of Equatoria. In March 1882 he journeyed from Equatoria to Khartoum to warn Raouf Pasha of the dangers of the situation. Emin offered himself to interview and come to terms with the Mahdi, but his alarm was treated as ridiculous and he was ordered to return to his own province and confine his attention to its government. When he left Khartoum in June, he was never to return.

The Mahdi at this time was generally believed to be no more than another of the false prophets that often caused minor disturbances in the Sudan, but faith in him was growing. He was soon firmly installed in Southern Kordofan. With a brilliance that seemed to prove to his followers that he had miraculous protection, he was evading every attempt to capture him. His next move was to burn the town of Sennar and lay siege to the Kordofan capital of El-Obeid. The Mudir of the Nile station of Fashoda, with 1,500 men, set out against him and was destroyed with all his men. In July 6,000 government troops from Fashoda suffered the same fate, and the station itself was burnt to the ground. The way to Khartoum lay open. Raouf panicked and appealed to the Khedive, who ordered Abdellal Bey's negro regiment to go to the Sudan. The order came at the time of the Arabi pronouncements, and the rebels, supposing the Khedive was planning to get rid of some of them by sending them south, refused to allow Abdellal and his men to go.

The Egyptian Government was now at last aware that this was no mere temporary disturbance. Raouf was withdrawn. The British

Government recommended that Gordon return at once to Khartoum, but the Khedive refused, giving the excuse that the appointment of a Christian at such a time could only make matters worse. Abd-el-Kadar was selected instead. He at once set about fortifying Khartoum and reorganising the Egyptian troops. He was at first successful in turning the rebels out of the main part of Kordofan, but in a furious counter-attack the Mahdi massacred the garrison of El-Obeid and made this town the base of his operations.

At the time of the British victory in Tel-el-Kebir, the Sudanese situation was very serious. Slatin Bey's province of Darfur, to the west of Kordofan, was being threatened, while Bahr-el-Ghazal, where Lupton had succeeded Gessi as governor, and Emin's province of Equatoria had been cut off from Khartoum. The Egyptian troops, suffering heavy losses, were on the verge of rebellion and Abd-el-Kadar admitted the situation was beyond him. The Khedive appealed for aid from Britain. Colonel Stewart was sent to Khartoum to enquire into the causes of the rebellion. Stewart's good sense and some successful attacks by Egyptian and English troops seemed to promise an early end to trouble when a new disaster, more frightful than any that yet occurred, restored and increased the Mahdi's prestige.

In December 1882 Hicks Pasha, the new Commander-in-Chief of the army of the Sudan, a man of great physical presence, after conferring with Sir Samuel Baker and his brother, Baker Pasha, set out to finish the rising once and for all. Hicks himself had thought it better to let Kordofan settle down without interference, but the Egyptian Government had ordered him south with 10,000 fellahin troops. The British Government, having refused to send English or Indian troops with him, declared the campaign foolhardy and refused to accept responsibility for whatever might result. Against Stewart's advice, Hicks and his inadequate, useless army disappeared into the desert towards Kordofan. Heat and shortage of water accounted for most of the 10,000. When the miserable remnants met the Mahdi's forces in the valley of Kashgil, scarcely fifty of them, all wounded, survived to crawl away into the desert. Hicks, who died with his men, was blamed for the whole disaster.

When news of this defeat spread, tribes that before had taken no interest in the situation now declared for the Mahdi. His vast, growing armies began to have things all their own way. By 1883 they had captured 20,000 rifles, nineteen guns and large stores of ammunition. Government troops in the province numbered only some 7,000, and these, unless formed into squares, could not be relied upon, to resist close attack. The need to protect their long-drawn baggage train of 6,000 camels, required to transport not only food but water, made the formation of squares impossible. The Mahdi's men destroyed wells and drove all herds into their own camps, so the Egyptians, forced to consume their supplies, soon suffered from hunger, thirst and fatigue. In confusion, completely demoralised, they were easily destroyed. The highly trained British troops, unable to apply the ordinary rules of warfare against the Mahdi's furiously fanatical attacks, were not much more use than the Egyptians.

Darfur fell. Slatin Bey was taken into captivity. The British Government realised that Darfur and Kordofan, with their useful products of gum arabic, camels, ostrich feathers and tamarinds which were now going to Tripoli instead of Cairo, would have to be regarded as lost. The west bank of the White Nile marked the new Egyptian frontier. In 1883 Dufferin on the question of the Sudan said that Egypt could scarcely be expected to agree to give up the southern provinces but "unhappily Egyptian administration in the Sudan had been almost uniformly unfortunate". The success of the Mahdi was itself "sufficient proof of the government's inability either to reconcile the inhabitants to its rule or to maintain order". But these diplomatic hints meant nothing to the Egyptians, who wished to recover their empire. Sir Evelyn Baring, who succeeded Dufferin, had to point out that they "had neither the soldiers nor the money to do so".

The situation was not improved by an announcement that Britain was going to withdraw her troops. The Mahdi, established in the west, began to plan the extension of his conquests. He intended personally to direct the attack upon Khartoum while his generals, Osman Digna and Karamalla, were to carry the revolt to the eastern and southern areas where Egyptian influence had already been seriously undermined. In 1882 the Dinka tribe of Bahr-el-Ghazal, inspired and supported by the Mahdi's revolt, had risen against the government. Lupton Bey fought brilliantly during eighteen months of savage warfare.

Lupton, a natural adventurer, had been born at Ilford, Essex, in 1853. At the age of twenty-five he was chief officer on a Red Sea steamer plying between Suakin and Jeddah. Gazing from his boat at the coast of Africa, he felt drawn towards its little known interior and offered himself to Gordon. He was called to Khartoum. A young man with a wide brow, a determined, energetic and intelligent face, an impudent

nose, Lupton had the force and initiative for whom Gordon was looking. He sent him with a flotilla to the relief of Emin Bey and Gessi
Pasha, who had been shut in by the sudd, the barrier of floating weed
which often blockaded the upper Nile. When Gessi, whose health was
breaking, retired from Bahr-el-Ghazal to die at Khartoum, Lupton
succeeded him. In a short time the young governor had changed his
province from a burden on the Egyptian exchequer to a source of
profit. By the end of 1883, despite the Dinka war, he had in hand a
surplus of £100,000. This was the early promise of a career doomed in a
few years to end in captivity and desolating misery.

The Dinka revolt had been carried to the Bari tribes and by 1884
the stations of Gaba-Shambe and Bor had fallen with their garrisons
into enemy hands.

By 1884 the population of the Eastern Sudan had risen. The Egyptian
garrisons of Tokar and Sinkat were surrounded and Baker Pasha
was dispatched to Suakin to relieve them. His British troops, after a
first success near the wells of El-Teb, were forced to withdraw.

The discussion whether or not the Sudan should be held dragged
on. The British public was disgusted with the whole affair. Young
Englishmen were being killed. A famous Arabic scholar had lost his
life. Why, after assuming the protectorate of a country, were we
permitting this dangerous internal disorder? Sir Samuel White Baker
was convinced that the Sudan could be held by British arms if—a
familiar cry—the British authorities would wake up and do something.
Were we to lose the road to the heart of Africa? We had only to build
a railway through the Sudan and cotton could be shipped to Liverpool
direct from Suakin; wheat shipped to London cheaper than from
California. Were we going to permit the slave-trade to ravage Central
Africa again? We had only to announce our determined policy to
uphold the Khedive's authority and the allegiance of the Arab tribes
would be regained. "If General Gordon were in command in the
Sudan," wrote Baker, "he would solve the difficulty."

At the beginning of 1884 the Egyptian Government admitted itself
defeated. The Prime Minister, Cherif Pasha, resigned, and a new
cabinet was formed by the Armenian Nubar Pasha. A Christian
himself, his prejudice was rather in favour of the Christian Gordon, for
whom he sent at once.

The situation was now desperate. Khartoum was surrounded. The
Equatorial provinces, on which Karamalla was advancing, were com-

pletely cut off from hope of aid. The war was dragging on near Suakin, where Baker Pasha opposed Osman Digna. In February 1884 Baker Pasha made another attempt to relieve Tokar. His 4,000 Egyptian constabulary, all old soldiers, outnumbered the tribesmen nearly three to one. They did little more than fall on their knees and beg for mercy. They were ruthlessly slaughtered. Eleven European officers died with them.

Britain decided that the Sudan was lost. The Egyptian Government was advised to retire to Wady Halfa. Sixty thousand people— Egyptian officials and soldiers, and Christians of every nationality— remained to be evacuated. This was the job given to Gordon when he arrived in Cairo in January 1884. Only in his hands could the project have even hope of success. When in February he reached Khartoum with his six servants and his white wand of office, he was welcomed as a deliverer.

One escape route only remained open, and this because it passed through a waterless desert where even Mahdi patrols could not exist for long. The river was in flood and could take light craft over the Fifth and Sixth Cataracts. The refugees could make a fairly safe desert crossing from Abu Hammed to Korosko. During the next two months 25,000 widows, children and wounded were got out of the Sudan. It was essential, were the evacuation to continue, that this route should be kept open by posting troops at Berber, Abu Hammed and the well of Mourat, but instead the panic-stricken Egyptians sent soldiers to Luxor and built earthworks at Assuan.

Gordon, unlike those who sent him, saw clearly the difficulty of withdrawing a garrison by this route. As for the Equatorial provinces, the only hope for them would be to declare them part of the territory under the King of the Belgians.

The Khedive had ordered Gordon not only to evacuate the Sudan but to establish, once Egyptian rule was abolished, some other form of settled government. This second requirement gave him the scope he wanted. He did not regard as irretrievably lost the province in which his earlier labours had shown such magnificent results, and he felt it would be cowardly to abandon it. He declared the Sudan independent. He then started to undo the results of the flagrant misrule of the Egyptian governors. Collaborating with Stewart, he completed the defences of Khartoum, reorganised the troops and got in provisions against the probability of a long siege. He suspended the anti-slavery laws throughout the areas occupied by the Mahdi, a diplomatic measure that scandalised the Anti-Slavery Society.

His mind was all the time on Zebehr Pasha, with whom he had come face to face in one of the Egyptian ministries in Cairo and whom he had felt instinctively to be a man of integrity. He began to see Zebehr as the necessary rival to the Mahdi and a solution of the problem.

For three months it looked as though Gordon might hold the Sudan after all. The Mahdi, overawed by the General's reputation and following, made no move. The General, as convinced as was the Mahdi himself that he was the instrument of God, now refused to consider giving up Khartoum. The British Government was willing to let him save it if he could, but was unwilling to risk further troops or money upon it.

Gordon, growing more confident as he remained unassailed, proposed now to visit the enemy camp and negotiate with the Mahdi for the surrender of Kordofan and Darfur. Faced with this proposal, the British Government knew its own mind. Gordon was at once forbidden to make such a move. It might lead to an awkward situation. He next asked that Zebehr Pasha should be sent to the Sudan. Horrified philanthropists in England put a stop to this plan.

Frustrated at every point, Gordon made a last request—that 200 English soldiers be sent to Wady Halfa as a symbol of his authority. He received no reply.

In April Berber fell. A mere 600 men had been left to defend it, while at Abu Hammed there had been no garrison at all. The escape route was closed. Knowing that without British backing his cause must, in the end, prove hopeless, Gordon now decided to resign. He planned to retire with his men and five steamers full of stores to the Equatorial provinces, which he would hold and govern in Leopold's name. This move would, he believed, save the provinces and would also help finish the slave-trade by cutting off the chief sources of supply. But Britain had no wish to see the slave-trade stopped by servants of the Belgian king or to see the provinces in Belgian hands. Gordon was sternly ordered to remain in Khartoum but refused further military aid. The British Government believed he could save himself any time he wished. It was true that a small steamer waited at the Khartoum quayside to take him to safety should he choose to retreat, but it could take him with no more than a few of the city's refugees. The rest would have to be abandoned. "He had," he wrote, been made

Governor-General "in order to carry out evacuation of the Soudan," not "to run away from Khartoum, and leave the garrisons elsewhere to their fate."

The Mahdi's forces encamped on all sides of Khartoum were steadily increasing in number. At last news came through that Baker had suffered a further defeat at Trinkinat, with a loss of 2,000 men. This victory seemed to lift the spell of Gordon's presence from the enemy. The blockade began drawing closer. By the end of April an outlying station in the Khartoum purlieus, with all its ammunition and a steamer, fell into Mahdi hands. Shells were beginning to drop into the centre of the capital. Communications had ceased with the fall of Berber but occasional exasperated requests for information managed to get to Gordon from Shendi. To one of these he replied: "I stay at Khartoum because Arabs have shut us up and will not let us out."

At home people realised it was no longer a question of evacuating Khartoum but of getting Gordon out alive. Public opinion demanded that he must be saved at all costs. After the usual doubts, arguments and official delays, Parliament voted £300,000 for the fitting out of a relief expedition.

Early in September, when the river was at its highest, Gordon decided that the small paddle-boat *Abbas* should attempt the descent to Dongola. He hoped to get Power, the British Consul, and Herben, the French Consul, to safety and sent with them eighteen Greek merchants and fifty soldiers. At the last minute Colonel Stewart, for a reason never known, asked that he might go too. Gordon agreed at once. He overcame any diffidence that Stewart might have felt at leaving him in this way by giving the colonel letters, siege journals, dispatches and a batch of telegrams to be sent from Dongola and telling him he could, when he reached Egypt, urge in person the desperate cause of Khartoum. On the night of September 9th the *Abbas* set out. Gordon was now alone in the palace.

On the 19th he was writing in a tone familiar to anyone who has spent war years in the Middle East: "I have the strongest suspicion that these tales of troops at Dongola and Meroe are all gas-works and that if you wanted to find Her Majesty's forces you would have to go to Shepheard's Hotel in Cairo." There he was wrong. The troops had not even left England, but at the end of the month Gordon sent four steamers loaded with provisions to Metemmeh to aid and hasten them on their way.

Early in October General Wolseley with a volunteer camel corps of English officers and men reached Dongola. There the relievers split into two columns, one continuing overland under General Stewart; while Wolseley's column attempted to shoot the rapids in whale boats.

Rumours were now reaching Khartoum that the *Abbas* had been lost. They proved to be true. She had been forced to shell and destroy Berber before she could pass; she had then successfully negotiated the Fifth Cataract north of Berber, but at the Fourth was caught in a current and wrecked upon the rocks. The Arabs of Monasir, persuading the party ashore with false promises, slaughtered it to a man. Gordon's official papers were sent to the Mahdi, who saw from them how little hope remained in Khartoum.

The river column rowed with great labour and heavy loss of life as far as Abu Hamed. There it learnt that it need continue no further. The overland rescue column made good progress until it again touched the river; then it met with Mahdi troops. In the battle that followed General Stewart, a number of his officers and two newspaper men were killed. The column continued under Colonel Sir Charles Wilson.

Fighting was now furious around Khartoum. The Mahdi was at the city gate directing the siege himself. The survivors of the garrison were starving and on the verge of revolt. Gordon, who had still a hold upon the situation, fought with a superhuman appearance of confidence against the despair and mutiny of his men, but his own hope was failing. On December 14th he terminated the journal he had kept during his weeks alone: "Now, mark this, if the Expeditionary force— and I ask for no more than 200 men—does not come in ten days, the town may fall and I have done my best for the honour of my country." He added final farewells to old friends. Expecting Khartoum to fall daily he sent a steamer to Shendi with last messages. The dead were heaped unburied in the streets. The soldiers, emaciated, will-less, swayed on the battlements, yet the garrison—living on rats, mice, the leather of boots, mimosa gum and palm-tree fibre—somehow still held out.

In January Wilson met the provision steamers at Metemma where they had been waiting 112 days. The column boarded them and started upstream for Khartoum. The desolate city came in sight on January 28th. The Egyptian flag was not flying from the palace. The silence filled the rescuers with apprehension.

Two days earlier the city had been betrayed into Mahdi hands. The besiegers silently took possession by night and at dawn the mob surrounding the palace began howling, flinging insults and firing at the gates. Gordon was making his way at the head of a small party of soldiers and servants towards the Church of the Austrian Mission, the reserve magazine of the town, where they hoped to make a final stand. Turning the corner, they came, in the first light of day, face to face with a body of Mahdist Arabs. Gordon, in his uniform, wearing all his decorations, paused, folded his arms and gazed at the Mahdists with a serene expression. For some moments there was complete silence. Then a shot was fired. Gordon, hit in the brow, died instantly. His head was cut off, stuck on a pole and placed at the entrance to the Mahdi's tent. His body was thrown in the river. The Mahdi, after giving thanks for victory in the mosque, handed the town over to one of the bloodiest massacres in history. During some six hours, 4,000 persons were hacked to pieces. The 6,000 surrendered and disarmed men of the garrison and police-force were later killed in cold blood. The surviving townswomen were distributed among the Mahdist generals; the men stripped and turned adrift.

Wilson pressed on. An Arab cried from the banks that Gordon was dead. Unwilling to believe this, Wilson continued until stopped by increasing fire from the shore. Nothing remained for him but to make his difficult and dangerous way back with the news that the frontiers of Egypt were again what they had been in 1819.

Chapter One

THE SOUTHERN PROVINCES

"Find me the man and I will take him as my help, who utterly despises money, name, glory, honour; one who never wishes to see his home again; one who looks to God as the source of good and the controller of evil; one who has a healthy body and energetic spirit; and who looks on death as a release from misery; and if you cannot find him then leave me alone. To carry myself is enough for me—I want no other baggage."

GORDON

"DEAR EMIN, It is all up with me here; everyone has joined the Mahdi, and his army takes charge of the Mudireh the day after to-morrow. What I have passed through the last few days no one knows. I am perfectly alone. The man who brings you this will give you all particulars. I hear that an army was never so totally defeated as was that of General Hicks. Out of 16,000 men only fifty-two are alive, and they are nearly all wounded. Look you out; some 8,000 to 10,000 men are coming to you well armed. Hoping that we shall meet, Yours truly, F. Lupton."

This letter, written on April 25th, 1884, and received by Emin a month later, was the last word to come out of Bahr-el-Ghazal. Lupton was taken prisoner to Kordofan, then to Omdurman, where, laden with chains, half-starved, filthy, his frustrated spirit eating in upon him, he died in 1888 of privation and despair.

The two governors, Lupton and Emin, had had little news from the outside world for a year. The last steamer to sail up with provision from Khartoum, the *Telahuin*, had in March 1883 told them of the event then being discussed—the bombardment of Alexandria. Hicks's defeat, so slowly did information travel, was still no more than a rumour. The possibility of the loss of Khartoum was never for a moment considered.

In 1884 the rising of the Dinkas in the Southern Provinces was known to be the work of a new trouble-maker calling himself the Mahdi, but that the Mahdi was victorious in west and east and was already sitting at the gate of the besieged and helpless Sudanese capital were facts of which the two governors were completely ignorant. The undisciplined, hysterical, braggart mob that swept almost without warning over

24

Bahr-el-Ghazal arrived at the frontiers of Equatoria a month later.
At that time Equatoria extended along both banks of the Nile from
Lake Albert to Lado and included the Shuli, Madi, Bari, Lattuka,
Makraka and Moru countries, and the northern part of Unyoro. The
province was large, but what was known as the settled position was
some 200 miles long and 150 miles wide with 2,000,000 inhabitants.
Baker's old capital of Gondokoro had, because of its unhealthy
locality, been abandoned in Gordon's time and the new seat of government was at the northern frontier town of Lado.

When Emin first appeared at Khartoum in 1875, a slender, delicate,
young-looking man with a pallor enhanced by dark eyes and beard,
he gave his name as Hakim. He said he was a Turk who had been
educated in Germany and he was seen praying in the mosque, but it
was soon generally known that according to his passport he was a
Prussian, born in Silesia, a qualified medical doctor named Schnitzer
who had been christened Edouard. No one in Khartoum in those days
was likely to care what reason Schnitzer had for hiding his identity.
He was welcomed as a new diversion in a small community where
amusements were few. His skill at chess, his remarkable knowledge of
Arabic, Turkish, Albanian, French, Italian, Latin and modern and
ancient Greek, his ability to play on the pianoforte such romantic
composers as Chopin and Mendelssohn, delighted the little European
community. He had also a natural gentleness and kindliness, and a
gaiety that led Junker, the Russian explorer, to write of him: "He was,
on these occasions, the merriest and maddest of the party." His friends
subscribed to set him up in a small house where he could practise as a
physician. He seemed contented with his earnings. He did his own
housework and shopped in the market-place. He had arrived penniless
and he was never to grow rich. His generosity, his inability to hold on
to money, became a joke in the city. If he made any large sum by
performing an operation he at once distributed it among others poorer
than himself. Giegler Pasha, later deputy Governor-General of the
Sudan, said it was sometimes necessary to make collections for Emin.

Emin, like most romantics, was unreliable on the subject of his own
past. Probably no one in Khartoum at that time ever learnt why he had
made his way to Central Africa. His own hints about being mixed up
in political and amorous intrigues were smiled at, yet they had some basis
in reality.

He had been born in 1840, the son of Lutheran parents. His father, a prosperous wool-stapler, died when Emin was five. The delicate, sensitive boy, deeply interested in natural history, a little spoilt by his mother and sisters, was one of those who, though physically smaller than their fellows, regard them with fatherly and indulgent understanding. He never throughout his life guarded against the possibility of his own friendliness being met with anything but equal friendliness. In his student days he was hurt when he found that those who had been attracted by his open-handedness lost interest in him when his money was spent. He began to prefer to be alone. Probably the sharp disillusionments of early life led him, like other disappointed perfectionists, to believe that an ideal world existed anywhere but at home. In 1864, as soon as he had qualified in Berlin as a surgeon, he hurried from his own country. He went to Turkey, where he became involved with the "Young Turk" Party and wandered about until his money was spent. He later said he learnt Arabic while attached to an expedition sent from Constantinople to Saudi Arabia, but it is doubtful whether he ever went to Saudi Arabia. After his arrival in Turkey he was employed as tutor to the children of Ismail Hakki Pasha and taken with the family to Janina when the Pasha was appointed Governor of Western Albania.

Writing home to his mother and sister, Emin described the old Pasha, "still very robust and attached to me", and his young, pretty wife, "very kind and amiable", and their life in the large house, filled with children and servants, situated on a hill half an hour's distance from the town. "We are," he said, "content to confine ourselves to our own premises and the surrounding mountains." Albania was, as usual, in revolt, and while "the bullets were whizzing round", the young tutor, in an emotional atmosphere heightened by danger, fell in love with his employer's wife. Madame Hakki Pasha was a Transylvanian, not a Moslem; a woman of character who had grown up with the outlook of a European. Without much difficulty she gained considerable influence over the romantic young German, who found himself, when the Pasha died, adopted as protector of the widow, children and servants. All thirteen of them travelled aimlessly about Europe until Emin, growing desperate as his money disappeared, brought all of them to his family at Neisse. For a reason that some believed to have been prudence—although it would have been more prudent and safer not to have brought her at all—he introduced the widow as his wife. If the small, interested town of Neisse had any suspicions about the relationship, these were soon to be confirmed.

Emin, reduced almost to beggary, his love for Madame Hakki Pasha worn very thin, began to travel to near-by towns to visit museums. In an effort to escape the responsibility he had shouldered, he fled to the study of natural history, going farther and farther afield until one day he disappeared altogether. Before he turned up with Madame Hakki Pasha, his family had not seen him for eleven years. Much longer was now to elapse before they were even to hear of him again. They were left with the hysterical widow and her eleven followers. She did not take the desertion well. She complained loudly and bitterly throughout Neisse that Edouard Schnitzer had cast her off without marrying her.

Emin—thirty-five years of age, without work, without prospects, completely penniless—arrived in Alexandria to start life again. By practising as a doctor among the poor, he made just enough to pay his fare to Khartoum. There, having put sufficient distance between himself and his past, he remained. Much of his affable sociability at that time may have been the hysteria of relief.

Gordon had reached the Province of the Equator—a name not yet condensed to Equatoria—on April 13th, 1874. When he heard from Junker of this latest arrival in Khartoum, he called the German to Lado. Lado's Egyptian doctor had just returned to Cairo. The newcomer took not only his position but his name. As Emin, "the Faithful One", Edouard Schnitzer, happy in anonymity, settled down at Lado.

Equatoria was twenty-six days' journey from Khartoum. When Gordon first saw the province, he wrote: "No one can conceive the utter misery of these lands, heat and mosquitoes day and night all the year round," and later: "The only possessions Egypt has in my province are two forts, one here at Gondokoro, the other at Fatiko; there are 300 men in one, and 200 in the other. You can't go out in any safety half a mile."

The slave-traders, and the looting, cattle-thieving Egyptians, had turned the natives into enemies and the countryside into a wilderness. In September, when the rains came, the land became a swamp. The English members of Gordon's staff died off one by one and Gordon described himself as "a shadow".

A few miles above Gondokoro, at a rapid in the river, he built the station of Rejaf. This site was less unhealthy, yet the deaths among the staff continued. Gordon worked to wipe out the slave-trade, to win the

B

natives and reclaim the land. By the end of the rainy season, in spite of disease and desertion, the province was taking shape. New stations were being built to form a chain up the river to the great lakes. He asked for two steamers and these arrived in sections to be assembled somewhere above the rapids.

He wrote: "The whole of the original staff except Kemp have gone down, eight in all. I will have no more fellows up here." He decided that only a European of over forty, already accustomed to tropical climates, could survive Equatoria. Of the Egyptians he soon wrote: "Oh! I am sick of these people." Gordon, in disgust, knowing he risked dismissal, wrote frankly to the Khedive his opinion of the civilising influence of Egyptian rule. Ismail was no ordinary Eastern potentate. He appreciated Gordon, listened to him rather than to his enemies, but could do little to change the nature of his people.

Gordon said his whole sympathy was with the natives, whose attitude was: "This land is ours, and you shall not have it, neither its bread nor its flocks." He knew that he and his men were merely intruders.

After the rains came the fierce sun and "the moment the sun goes down a cold damp arises which enters one's very bones. There is not an interval of five minutes from the setting of the sun and the rising of this dreadful damp, and you feel the danger as it were, at once."

The steamers *Khedive* and *Nyanza* were at last ready to be launched. When the first made its way among the papyrus-covered islands to the point at which lake and river met, Gordon refused to explore the lake. He said: "I wish to give a practical proof of what I think regarding the inordinate praise which is given to an explorer." His lieutenant, Gessi, was the first man to circumnavigate the Albert Nyanza that Baker had discovered ten years before. It proved disappointing—a mere 140 miles from north to south, and fifty miles from east to west, with a depressing swamp at the southern end.

Emin, like most men who came into contact with Gordon, felt Gordon's approval necessary to his self-respect. In less than two years the Governor had raised the province out of a chaos of corruption. The slave-traders skulked in exile, the officials could find no opportunity for dishonesty, debts were paid, the country was at peace. Gordon moved among his people as though there could be for him no question of their dishonesty or treachery, but they knew him to be alert; a man not only beyond self-interest, but one they could not deceive. This combination of intellect and integrity was outside the range of their experience. It intimidated them by seeming to have the quality of the supernatural.

Gordon knew that only his own tremendous will had been able to prevail against the sloth, incompetence, indifference and ingrained dishonesty of the officials he had to use. If the results of his labours were not to be destroyed the moment his back was turned, he must, he knew, find men to whom he could delegate his work. This was made more difficult by the fact that so few could survive the Equatorial climate. He had assessed Emin before he appointed him. The two men became friends. Friendship with Gordon was not easy. It called for uncriticising devotion and unquestioning obedience. Emin eagerly gave both. He toured the province in Gordon's train.

Lado still received its wheat supply from Khartoum but the country itself was becoming a long valley of rich pasture and forest land promising great fertility. South of Lado was a marsh where grass and reeds rose twenty feet from the river's edge. Beyond was the Eighth Cataract, where the tree-grown island of Bedden stood in the midst of magnificent scenery. Still farther south, in the lovely districts of Dufilé and Wadelai, the thick woods opened into grass stretches as tranquil as English parkland. The whole formed the basin of the White Nile, the Bahr-el-Jebel, enclosed in a semi-circular range of mountains. Gordon was still adding to his stations, so that within a year of Emin's arrival they formed a network in which no one was more than three days' march from another.

Emin, whose inclination was towards research rather than practise, enquired into every wonder his wanderings revealed. Eastwards they came into what Gordon had described as "a dead, mournful land, with a heavy damp dew penetrating everywhere; as if the angel Azrael had spread his wings over the land". In the south, tramping through down-pouring rain, breaking through thick entanglements of wild vine, they felt the ground beneath them shake as they approached Murchison Falls, where, unable to speak above the uproar, they watched the water topple from the table-land into the canyon's depths. At one time Emin says he saw chimpanzees, on their way to rob native orchards, lighting the road for themselves with flares.

With his delicate features half hidden by a black beard, his penetrating and humorous dark eyes disguised by the heavy lenses of his spectacles, Emin was beginning to look like the typical German professor. But his one classical German characteristic was his thoroughness. He had had as a student a sensitive vanity, morbidly condemning his own faults but quickly taking offence at criticism and enjoying the praise of his masters. These qualities mellowed as he aged, but there remained throughout his life a pride in his appearance. He would be extravagant in dress if he could afford to be, but even in poverty he had been scrupulously neat and clean, and treated his clothes with the extreme care that was natural to him. His friend Dr. Felkin of Edinburgh wrote of him: "Marvellous minuteness and accuracy characterise all his work and are shown not least in his letters, which are written in elegant language, with exquisite neatness, and in an almost microscopic hand."

These letters that he was then beginning to send abroad to interested societies were acquiring for him a certain fame. Students were delighted by the minute detail of their information and it was said "one can even hear the buzz and feel the sting of the insects about which he wrote".

Gordon condoned these interests until there seemed danger of their becoming too absorbing; then Emin was sharply reminded that he was employed not as a gardener or photographer, geologist or botanist, but as an army medical officer. Emin would reply humbly that he only wished to do his duty.

Gordon, however, was willing to put to the test whatever other abilities Emin might have. He was sent to try his powers of diplomacy on the formidable M'tesa, King of Uganda. The year before, an explorer named Stanley believed he had converted M'tesa to Christianity. This was quickly followed by a second conversion when the missionaries of the Khedive Ismail expounded the advantages of Mohammedanism. Three hundred Egyptians, avid as ever for new lands to exploit, had followed the missionaries to annex the new Mohammedan province. They failed to do more than get themselves imprisoned and condemned to death. Emin was sent to rescue them and returned with the 300 safely at his heels.

When on October 6th, 1876, Gordon left Equatoria, Emin remained as Surgeon-General to the Forces. First Prout, then Mason, became Governor. Each was forced by illness to retire. Emin seemed unaffected by the difficult tropical climate. He remained to see the province, under a succession of native governors, deteriorate rapidly. In 1878 Gordon returned to the Sudan as Governor-General and at once appointed Emin as Governor of Equatoria. Emin, who had studied Gordon's methods, could now follow his example and restore the province for himself.

Gordon wrote to him: "I appoint you for civilisation and for progress sake." He set to work with a will. The natives, become used to the indolence of the Egyptian governors and their officials, were astonished by the energy of their new governor. Gordon they had recognised as superhuman, but Emin, a man kept apart from them by his absorption in an incomprehensible study of birds and insects, had as medical officer shown little of Gordon's cunning. Now, conscious of the responsibility of his position, he changed. In a few days he would journey from Lado to Wadelai, visiting every village on the way. He would then go south to Fatiko, a pretty station standing among millet fields, and to the great lake; or pass into the Rohl country, or east to Shuli, administering, advising, seeing everything with his own eyes, enquiring into and himself righting every cause for complaint. The officials, recognising the awful spirit of Gordon come again among them, automatically started to mend their ways.

Emin tackled the problem of governing natives, who were to him like children, by treating them like children. In Lado he instituted a roll-call, a lock-up at nightfall and a curfew; a morning hour after which fires could be lighted; a signal for going out to work in the fields, another for midday rest, another for coming home. He required strict punctuality and discipline. As for the slave-trade, he was as effective against it as Gordon, who in the end had had to write: "I declare I see no human way to stop it."

The natives responded like children, glad to have their lives simplified in this way. With the Egyptians it was a different matter. Added to their indolence there was their Semitic self-esteem, which resented in another the authority they were not competent to wield. Instinctively they knew that Emin, although inspired by Gordon, was no Gordon himself. He was a milder, weaker character, lacking a faith—which in Gordon amounted to genius—in his own invincibility.

They were, also, the worst of their kind. The Egyptian Government used Equatoria as a penitentiary colony for civil servants who had been flagrantly dishonest. These remained "permanent officials" and once their sentences were served, employment had to be found for them in Equatoria. Emin could not dismiss them. As usual with colonial civil servants, the Egyptians in the Sudan assumed the airs of a ruling caste. They acquired tastes, needs and whims that would have got them only jeers at home. In Equatoria the natives were forced to supply both officials and soldiers with concubines, slaves, beasts and grain. When these gifts did not come up to expectation, the soldiers would raid the native villages and carry off everything of value.

During his first year of office Emin returned the province to the state of order in which he had first found it. As even Gordon himself might have discovered had he remained longer, it was easier here to introduce a regime than to maintain it. After the first startled activity of the officials had worn thin, they slipped back into their old habits. In 1879 Gessi Pasha, then Governor of Bahr-el-Ghazal, complained to Gordon of the lack of discipline in the Equatorial provinces. At that time Emin had Gordon behind him. To the officials—among whom there was a belief that one day the great white Pasha would sail up the Nile to reward and punish them—the threat of Gordon's wrath meant much. But when Gordon, after only one year of office, was recalled by Tewfik, Emin had to face the situation alone. The new Governor-General, the imbecile Raouf Pasha, was not interested in the development of the southern provinces. The central government quickly slipped back into its old state of indifference, and Emin, forced to refer to it for sanction for his every plan and project, would wait months, even years, for an answer, or receive no answer at all. Frustrated though he was, he laboured on. If he equalled Gordon in nothing else, he equalled him in courage. His authority was very limited, yet his energy produced results. By 1880, in spite of the expense of new roads, his budget showed, instead of the usual yearly deficit of £3,000, a surplus of £8,000. He now planned to develop his territory on a scale no one before had ever attempted.

He encouraged wheat-growing, so it became unnecessary to beg supplies from Khartoum. He organised a postal service and began enlarging the stations. Lado, which was burnt down in 1878, doubled its size when rebuilt, while the village of Dufilé grew into a strongly blockaded town of regular streets lined with neat grass houses, government offices of sunburnt brick and a dockyard where river craft were built. Public gardens were laid out in all the bigger towns.

Emin introduced the cultivation of coffee, rice, tobacco, nutmegs and indigo, and promoted cotton-growing to an important industry. He planned to increase to a vast commercial scale the export of india-rubber and gum arabic. He managed to obtain camels and oxen, and experimented in the hope of breeding species that would be immune to the tsetse fly. He asked the Egyptian Government for specimens of the buffalo that in Egypt takes the place of the cow, but these, of course, did not arrive.

The Egyptians, with their old attitude of "not possible" when faced with any problem not instantly and easily soluble, were soon bored by Emin's activity. Febrile and feather-pated, they plotted to get rid of him but were defeated by their own inability to act. They were delighted by the advent of Raouf Pasha. While Emin waited for his sanction, opportunities were lost, criminals escaped and projects failed. The officials had always these delays as an excuse for doing nothing. Emin relied on them less and less. He had won the friendship of the native chiefs, who knew that he, like Gordon, would protect their tribes against the slave-traders. He began to form an army of native soldiers and by 1882 the government report on his territory could state: "The soldiers at the stations are mostly Makaraka men of fine physique and cheerful temperament; they are well armed with Remington rifles. The artillerymen are Egyptians and their health is very unsatisfactory. Even the officers are now, in many instances, natives." It could also state: "Crime is unknown."

A traveller on the Nile met Emin during his first year as governor and described him: "I well remember going aboard his steamer and the warm reception he gave us. Dressed in a white uniform and wearing a fez, he presented the appearance of a tall, thin man of military bearing. The lower part of his face was hidden by a well-trimmed, black beard, and a moustache of the same colour partially veiled a determined mouth. His eyes, though to some extent hidden by his spectacles, were black, piercing and intelligent; his smile was pleasing and gracious; his actions graceful and dignified, and his whole bearing that of a man keenly alive to everything passing around him. Courteous but reserved, he was distinguished as a thorough gentleman. He addressed us in English, but subsequently finding I spoke German, we conversed in that language. Emin is a remarkable linguist, having a knowledge of most European languages, and of several of those spoken in Asia and of many African dialects."

As the first success of his province excited his hopes, he planned to interest European investors and believed that were they to subsidise his purchase of seeds and agricultural instruments, he would, in a few years, show an annual profit of £20,000. He said he could supply the zoological gardens of Europe from among the wild beasts of his province, he could manufacture soap from its many oils and it was possible that new foods and medicaments might be produced from trees and plants known only in Equatoria. Of the iron found everywhere, he wrote: "We are rather inclined to believe that great treasures of this kind are hidden under the earth, principally in the East."

At the time the Mahdi was declaring open revolt in Kordofan, Emin was looking to the day when the government would help him open a trade route to the east coast. Then the potential wealth of Equatoria—a country that even in its primitive state was noted for the hardest ivory and finest ostrich feathers in Africa—would cease to be handicapped by geographical position. With a safe and regular postal service established, he would receive from Europe all the latest books on agriculture and new medical text-books. Meanwhile he did what he could with those he had. Although he had been sent a Tunisian Jewish doctor to take over the medical practice of the province, Emin still at six o'clock every morning attended the Lado hospital. At this time he wrote: "A sick man is no subject, but a feeling and suffering being whose sensibility is greatly heightened. Be to your patients in the first place friend, then doctor. Our mission is a high and holy one, and the murmured thanks of a poor man is of far higher value than a few guineas, and the knowledge that one has saved a sick child for its mother is a far more beautiful reward than can ever follow a brilliant but risky operation or the humbug of the so-called 'scientific medicine'. Do not laugh at my words. I have grown old and grey in the battle of life, but it is just this Idealism which has helped me over many a bitter hour." Emin knew only too well what work had to be left undone for want of equipment and modern knowledge. He dreamt of the day when the province, grown rich, could afford a magnificent modern hospital.

Three months after the *Telahuin* in March 1883 had brought news of the bombardment of Alexandria, Emin began looking for its return. The province depended on the outside world for medical supplies, clothing, especially footwear, and some foodstuffs. All its small luxuries came from Khartoum. To Emin the arrival of the steamer meant letters, new books, periodicals, contact with the scientific world that was beginning to respect him for his research and discoveries.

Six months passed without sign of the steamer. A year passed. During the early days of Emin's governorship, the Nile had been blocked by the sudd and Lupton had had to cut a passage through. Emin thought it likely that another sudd block was holding up the steamer. The "block" was actually Fashoda, which in Mahdi hands had become a fortress preventing the passage of river traffic. Its loss early in the war had kept the southern provinces in ignorance of the extent of the Mahdi's successes. The two governors could not know that the disturbances with which they had to contend were only part of a major upheaval that was to overthrow Egyptian power in the Sudan. They could not understand why their plea for help, sent north in the *Telahuin*, was being ignored. Hopelessly incompetent though the central government might be, this was a matter it could not neglect.

Bahr-el-Ghazal was now in a state of open warfare. Although the settled area of Equatoria was peaceful enough, the tribes of the wild surrounding country, remote from Emin's influence, were being affected by the atmosphere of revolt. Early in 1883 Junker, who was seeking the source of the Welle—later found to be a tributary of the Congo but then believed to flow from Lake Tchad—was warned by Lupton that the countryside was unsafe. Lupton, however, was confident that help would come with the next steamer. Junker, deciding to wait until the natives calmed down, made his way to Lado, where he was to remain for many a long day.

The Mahdi revolt was tending northwards, westwards and, later, eastwards, leaving the south free. The full force of attack came upon Lupton in the south-west. On April 12th he wrote to Emin: "I will fight to the last. If I am conquered they will march upon you, therefore be on your guard. This letter may be the last I shall send you! My position is hopeless; my people have surrendered to the enemy in great numbers. Either I win the day or die." When his province fell, Equatoria, alone of Egypt's vast possessions, remained to be conquered.

The first news of the true state of affairs came to Emin from the enemy. The Mahdi general, the Emir Karamalla, having one trophy in the shape of poor Lupton, expected to acquire another even more easily. So hopeless did Emin's position appear that Karamalla did not think him worth attacking. Instead a letter was sent urging him to give himself up without bloodshed.

Emin did not believe Karamalla's boasts, but he realised that even if help were on its way it would not come in time. In his first bewilderment, he called a general meeting of the officers and employees at Lado and read aloud Karamalla's letter. They unanimously decided to surrender, and even Emin at first seriously considered going with his staff to Dem Soliman, where Karamalla was awaiting his decision. He probably supposed that such a step would entail no more than exchanging Raouf's government for one that could scarcely be worse.

B*

Fortunately, before any move could be made, refugees brought the news that the Egyptians captured in Bahr-el-Ghazal, far from living in the happy freedom described by Karamalla, had been sold into slavery, while Lupton, as guest of the Mahdi, was loaded with chains. The Lado officials at once changed their minds. After further squabbles and arguments they agreed to send to Karamalla a deputation offering surrender on condition that the *Telahuin* be permitted to come from Khartoum to take the Egyptians to safety. The deputation left on July 3rd, 1884, and nothing more was heard of it.

At this time an Italian named Casati, who had, at the request of Gessi Pasha, been sent in 1879 by the Italian Government to seek the source of the Welle, was wandering on the outskirts of Equatoria. Panic among the natives made him realise that some calamity had occurred and he decided to make his way back to a settled area. He followed the Dongu river up to Makaraka and, learning the situation, hurried to Lado. There he joined the little band of Europeans—Emin, Junker, a Greek merchant named Marco and, possibly one might include by courtesy, the Tunisian Jewish doctor Vita Hassan—and began to play a fairly prominent part in Equatoria's affairs. In his own memoirs, written some time after the events they describe, he appears as the wise, far-seeing adviser of a besieged governor, but no other references to him confirm this self-portrait.

Several months passed and Karamalla made no move. He occupied himself by sending letters inciting the officials to revolt and trying to disturb the faithful with the Mahdi's tenet: "The tree casts shade and the Koran is mine; it is the light. There is no other god but God, and Mohammed Ahmed is the real and last envoy. I have given my blood, my wealth and my children to God; for it is His will." Mahdi pro-paganda circulated freely among the fellah and Sudanese soldiers. It was said that the bullets of those aiming at the Mahdi's followers turned in the air and plunged into those that fired them. One Mahdi officer had been seen to display a sackful of locusts which he declared were the souls of infidels.

The native chiefs, realising the government's weak position, began to revenge themselves on the Egyptians by pillaging State property. They also took the chance to seize as slaves the women and children of other tribes, while the old slave-traders, for long out of business, began rounding up panic-stricken natives for sale to the Mahdi.

At Amadi, a frontier town, Karamalla's propaganda had worked well among the natives. Incapable of realising that they had as much to lose as anyone by the invasion, they were convinced that a Mahdi victory meant no more than the overthrow of Egyptian authority and assisted Karamalla as soon as he attacked the town. News came to Lado that seventy Egyptian officials had been killed and eaten by Amadi cannibals.

The Lado officials began to panic. In a disturbed moment—so Casati states—Emin tried to reassure them by saying: "We white men shall escape—I answer for it. We will give our black soldiers to my good friend Kabba Rega, King of Unyoro, and he will permit us to cross his boundaries." These words, whether they had been spoken or not, were repeated until they reached the native soldiers themselves. They were terrified by the thought of becoming slaves of the notorious Kabba Rega. The whole population of the province, filled with mistrust and fear, was near revolt. Things were not improved by an eclipse of the moon, an event held to presage bloodshed, misfortune and ruin. Every day crowds of natives crossed the frontier to join the Mahdi forces.

Casati advised abandoning the province. Although there was little hope of taking a long train of refugees safely through the wild, hostile lands of Unyoro and Uganda, a small party composed of, say, Emin, Casati, Junker, Vita Hassan and Marco, with bearers to carry food and water, might get through to the coast. Emin refused to consider making such an escape. The province was his responsibility. He knew what would be the fate of his native people once he abandoned them: the women and children would be taken as domestic slaves, those men that survived the slaughter would be yoked two and two like oxen to carry ivory to the coast. He said he had not lost hope that help would come from Khartoum, but a new year began and there was still no news.

The province had been cut off now for twenty-one months. Three battles had been fought at Amadi without results, but Emin's losses were mounting. He could not replace his casualties, while Karamalla could draw upon the whole Sudan. In February word came from the frontier town that if fresh troops and provisions were sent, the line would hold. Emin tended, like most kindly, gentle natures, towards the circular madness of alternating despair and hope. During a spell of high optimism, he sent the greater part of his military resources to Amadi. This enabled it to hold out for one more month. Ammunition ran short, food failed and at the end the men were gnawing the leather of their sandals. They began dying off from starvation. Some went crazy beneath the strain. The rest, in a panic, begged their officers to yield, but the officers dreaded slavery more than starvation. In desperation and against orders, the men rushed from the fortress and tried to cut a way through the besiegers. A number, banded together, did manage to escape.

Amadi was lost, but its defence had been heroic. Emin sat down and wrote to Felkin in a last hope of rousing the outside world to help him: "Ever since the month of May, 1883, we have been cut off from all communication with the world. Forgotten, and abandoned by the government, we have been compelled to make a virtue of necessity. Since the occupation of Bahr-el-Ghazal we have been vigorously attacked, and I do not know how to describe to you the admirable devotion of my black troops throughout a long war, which for them at least, has no advantage. Deprived of the most necessary things, for a long time without any pay, my men fought valiantly, and when at last hunger weakened them, when, after nineteen days of incredible privation and sufferings, their strength was exhausted, and when the last torn leather of the last boot had been eaten, then they cut a way through the midst of their enemies and succeeded in saving themselves. All this hardship was undergone without the least *arrière-pensée*, without even the hope of any appreciable reward, prompted only by their duty and the desire of showing a proper valour before their enemies. . . . As I once more repeat, I am ready to stay and to hold these countries as long as I can until help comes, and I beseech you to do what you can to hasten the arrival of such assistance."

Karamalla, now only five marching hours from Lado, was at the same time writing that if Emin did not surrender within ten days he would continue his advance. Emin, to gain time, replied that his soldiers were preventing him from going to make his submission at Amadi. He then, in deep despondency, prepared to evacuate the capital.

The ten days passed, but Karamalla chose to attack Makaraka first. There the chief had been pillaging the State warehouses and restoring the countryside to its old disorder, but, in spite of sabotage, the garrison drove the Mahdi forces back to Amadi.

Karamalla's next letter enclosed one from the Mahdi that described the death of Gordon and fall of Khartoum. Emin was heart-broken by the news. The officers and officials, their confidence gone in a moment, agreed to make an attempt to escape southwards. The two steamers *Khedive* and *Nyanza* were to take all the refugees across the Nile.

The steamers would then be destroyed and the Nile would form a moat between the refugees and the enemy. The Lado officials agreed enthusiastically to these plans. Next morning Emin left the capital to prepare the officials in the villages. Casati says that only himself and the commander of the Lado garrison were on the landing-stage to see him off; and that, as the ship hoisted sail and slid away down the river, a murmur rose among the townspeople: "The governor has fled."

Next day the Lado officials, who were supposed to follow Emin south, suddenly decided to stay and defend the capital. Casati tells us: "I at once wrote to Emin about this state of affairs, and begged him to stop at Gondokoro in order to prevent further dissension. He did not listen to my advice and by a hurried march to the southern countries caused the ruin of his own authority and prestige, and drew a series of misfortunes upon himself."

Emin, however, even if he gave rise to misunderstandings, was moving with no selfish purpose. He stopped at Khor-Ayu, south of Laboré, and ordered supplies of corn to be sent to Lado against the possibility of its suffering a long siege. He had no great faith in the heroics of the officials and he probably believed they would soon choose to follow him. His "retreat" ended at Dufilé, where the officials rejected the plan of escape on the grounds that they could not countenance the destruction of the two steamers and their loss to the Egyptian treasury. Casati, in his eagerness to prove that he alone in the province had a grip on the situation, contradicted his earlier implication by expressing a suspicion that Emin, unwilling from the first to retreat, had induced this absurd refusal.

Casati now hurried to Dufilé to act as Emin's adviser. He arrived in time to witness an attempt by Major Hawashi, the Town Commander, to murder Emin. Hawashi obviously hoped that the Dufilé Egyptians, who were unwilling to leave their privileged lives in Equatoria for the hardships of poverty in Egypt, would be glad to remain under his authority if Emin were out of the way. Emin discovered the plot but did not take it very seriously. He dismissed two officials who were implicated but, for want of a better man, left Hawashi in office. Hawashi, who had been exiled during the Abyssinian war for selling ammunition to the enemy, was unusually well educated for Equatoria. This fact, combined with a smooth manner and an ability to lie his way out of almost any situation, had saved him a number of times before. Emin and Casati continued to Wadelai.

The decision of the Lado garrison to defend the town was now strengthened by the fact that Karamalla suddenly and mysteriously withdrew from Amadi. Some supposed he had been discouraged by his defeat at Makaraka; others that he had to quell a rising inside Bahr-el-Ghazal. Later it was supposed that Wolseley's attempt to relieve Gordon, leading to a widespread rumour that white forces were advancing from the north, had led the Mahdi to withdraw troops from the south. It is equally probable that Karamalla found himself in the predicament that has paused generals in greater wars. It is known that his troops were finding little sustenance in Bahr-el-Ghazal and he had no reason to suppose he would find more in Equatoria; he had stretched his line of communication too far.

The Lado garrison, the Rejaf garrison and the whole of the 1st Battalion, the battalion stationed in the north, greatly heartened by this negative victory, now declared a state of revolt against the government. They protested they would never leave Equatoria. Emin was sure that Karamalla's retreat was no more than postponement of attack, but even if not, the situation of the province, cut off from supplies and isolated in the midst of hostile country, was intolerable. Some means of communication with the outside world must be found.

In Wadelai, Emin settled down to a daily routine much like that he had followed in Lado. He had there a beautifully constructed reed house, domed and oval in shape, of an unusually large size, where he kept his library, his scientific apparatus and his charming little daughter Farida. Farida was the child of an Abyssinian woman, now dead, to whom Emin usually referred as his wife. He had still 1,500 regular troops armed with Remington rifles, all, except for forty Egyptian artillerymen, negro. These, commanded by ten Egyptian and fifteen Sudanese officers, were divided over ten stations. He decided that while Lado remained in revolt, Wadelai would be the centre of government.

Emin now asked his friend, the kindly Russian Dr. Junker, to try and open a road to the coast. He gave him letters and begged him to make on his behalf an appeal for help to the countries of Europe, especially England. As he had now carried his worship of Gordon over to the English as a whole, he was convinced that once they knew of his plight they would send an army and annex Equatoria to the British Empire. He could think of no more satisfactory solution of the situation.

Junker set out, but towards the end of 1885 had to return with the news that the King of Uganda would permit neither white men nor their correspondence to pass through his territory. A little later Junker, with a small escort, made a second attempt, this time by way of Unyoro, and reached Zanzibar nine months later.

Chapter Two

PLANS FOR RESCUE

"A full-faced, stubborn, self-willed, round-headed, uncompromising, deep fellow."

Early description of STANLEY.

EMIN'S letter on the siege of Amadi got through to the coast. It was the first cry from out the sea of savagery that was believed to have swamped the whole Egyptian empire.

Dr. Felkin of the Royal Scottish Geographical Society, with whom Emin had been corresponding in code ever since their first meeting at Lado in 1878, published this letter and many others, drawing a picture of the besieged governor that could not but capture the world's imagination. It was rendered the more pathetic by the fact that side by side with the letters was published the last letter from Bishop Hannington, who had recently been murdered in Uganda by the insane King Mwanga, son of M'tesa, who had taken to persecuting Christians.

Gordon was dead; Khartoum taken; Baker defeated; Lupton, Slatin, Mason and many other Europeans were prisoners, some slaves, all horribly degraded; the whole Sudan was abandoned to massacre, slavery and misrule—all had seemed lost until now, from beyond the barrier of chaos, there came this news of one man holding out miraculously against the very forces that had overwhelmed Gordon. People were deeply stirred, but they could see Emin's position only as hopeless. Even if help were sent, even if it could get through to Equatoria, he must be destroyed long before it could reach him.

A year later Junker reached Zanzibar. He went at once to Cairo to make his appeal on Emin's behalf. His story, his description of Emin's position, decided people that something must be done. The British public, believing firmly that Gordon had been lost by official incompetence, demanded that this man, the last of Gordon's lieutenants, should be saved. The situation had, as usual, its difficulties. The Egyptian Government said it could not afford to send an expedition. The British Government felt that for political reasons it could not do so. Emin was not an Englishman and not officially connected with England. It was also felt that England's association with the Sudan had cost

42

the taxpayer enough. Equatoria, an inland country about the size of Ireland, hopelessly hedged in by unfriendly savages, did not at that time offer much to British imperialists. Although Emin was a German, he did not hold a commission for Germany, so his own country felt no interest in him.

It was soon evident that if help were to be forthcoming it would be only through private enterprise that might make a profit from its services. Emin was known to have in his province large stores of ivory— enough to guarantee a dividend to his rescuers. Investors might be found in both hemispheres, for by now people throughout the civilised world were writing and asking about this mysterious European with the Oriental name. It was rumoured, as is so often rumoured about remarkable newcomers before the public eye, that he was a Jew. Anti-Semitic circles in Germany were said to be preventing his rescue by his own countrymen.

Resolutions were being sent daily to the Foreign Secretary. Many blamed England for the Sudanese catastrophe and held her responsible for this heroic man now fighting with his back to the wall in Central Africa. The Press took it for granted that some sort of expedition would be sent. The British Government agreed to give all possible assistance behind the scenes. No other government offered aid, but many months later, having slowly laboured towards the conclusion that Britain's efforts could not be purely altruistic, the German Government indignantly complained that it alone had had a right to rescue this great German.

Felkin had received through Junker more letters from Emin: "I am," he wrote, "almost the last of those who knew the Sudan. Most of my friends have gone to their last rest, having finished their fight. But I must remain here." "If I die, who will take this work up? I think only of that." "I am too much needed here to think of leaving my post. My life will probably end in Africa."

Pondering these sentiments, Felkin advocated a small scientific expedition that would take Emin ammunition and clothing. Sir William Mackinnon offered to organise the expedition, and used his considerable trade connections with Zanzibar and the Congo Free State to raise some £9,000. The Egyptian Government added £10,000 and the Royal Geographical Society £1,000. Thomson, the Scottish explorer, was first chosen to lead an expedition from Mombasa. Three routes were planned—the first, known as the Karagwe route, started

from Zanzibar and, keeping south of the Victoria Nyanza and north of
the Albert Edward Nyanza, reached the Albert Nyanza up the Semlila
River. A similar expedition had once done this journey in 156 days.
The second route saved time by crossing the Victoria Nyanza but led
through the hazards of Unyoro and Uganda. The third route started
from Mombasa and, passing through Masai, kept north of the Victoria
Nyanza. This had been previously covered in 154 days. Once it had
been decided which of these three routes was best, there seemed no
reason why this unpretentious scientific expedition should not set out
straight away.

But the Press, voicing, so it said, the will of the people, called for
bigger things. The relief of one hero was surely a job for another hero—
indeed for Henry Morton Stanley, the man who had discovered Livingstone in 1870; who had mapped the Congo river in 1876 and had
formed the Congo State. Big newspaper owners in Britain and the
United States were prepared to contribute generously to the expedition
in return for exclusive rights in Stanley's letters, diaries or reports.

Felkin and his friends were not enthusiastic. They were aware that
once Stanley took charge, the expedition would grow beyond their
influence—but the public had now rallied to the idea of employing
Stanley. The promise of large contributions could not be overlooked.
Felkin decided he must do the best he could for his friend. Stanley was
approached.

Stanley had been following the "Emin Story" in the Press and had
decided, he tells us, "that if assistance could be rendered at a reasonable
cost, there would be no difficulty in raising a fund to effect that desirable
object". Emin he imagined to be a mixture of Cromwell, Francia of
Paraguay and Gordon.

Stanley had been about to start on a United States lecture tour which
would, he said, have brought him in £10,000. In spite of this he was
willing to give up his engagements and, without fee or reward, plunge
back into the Africa he now knew so well.

He had been born in the same year as Emin, but in circumstances so
different that it is doubtful whether any opportunity or event in after life
compensated him for his beginnings. He was a Welshman, native of
Denbigh in North Wales, the son of poor parents called Rowlands, and
had been christened John. When he was two his father died and his
mother, forced to take service in London, left him in charge of his
paternal relatives. They had disapproved of the marriage and had no

use for the child. When he was four one of his uncles beguiled him with lies to the workhouse school of St. Asaph and left him there. He says that as the door closed on him he experienced "for the first time the awful feeling of utter desolation". He realised how he had been deceived and there entered into his infant spirit a bitter distrust of humanity that was never to leave it. He later wrote: "I must have been twelve ere I knew that a mother was indispensable to every child." The headmaster of the school was a sadist who was to die in a madhouse, but not before he had confirmed into morbidity Stanley's natural pride, vanity and ambition. It is said that at this school Stanley showed the first signs of his powers of leadership. He was a good scholar with an unusual understanding of geography and arithmetic. When he was fourteen he felt strength and confidence enough to do what he must have burned to do for years—he thrashed the headmaster and ran away from school. He was described then as a boy with a strong body and short legs who "could stand no chaff, or the least bit of humour".

He went to his grandfather who refused to let him in and was adopted at last by a cousin, a teacher, who employed him as a pupil teacher. During the months he lived with his cousin, Stanley developed a passion for books and was not unhappy, but his aunt saw him as a drain upon her son's slight income and got him promise of work from an uncle at Liverpool. In Liverpool Stanley met, for the first time in his life, genuine affection and kindliness from a relative. The uncle was a decent fellow but the job existed only in his good intentions, and so desperately poor was the family that the aunt pawned Stanley's clothes. The boy joined as cabin-boy on a sailing ship bound for New Orleans and there found work with a merchant. This merchant, named Stanley, took a fancy to him, adopted him, promised to leave him a fortune and gave him the name he was to make famous—Henry Morton Stanley. Even now, had circumstances proved kinder, it would not have been too late for the workhouse boy to settle down comfortably as a nonentity, but instead they were to sting him to further efforts. The merchant died before he made a will and Stanley was left penniless. When the American Civil War broke out, he joined the Confederate Army under Johnstone and in 1862 was captured at Shiloh. He escaped by plunging into a river and crossing it under heavy fire. He worked his way back to England and returned at once to Denbigh, where the door of his mother's house was shut in his face. Whether the scandal of his attack on the house-master or whether his unmistakable air of poverty made him unwelcome, there is no knowing, but when that door shut, the last bond broke and Stanley was finally confirmed as an individual against the world. He returned to the United States and, landing in New York, joined the Federal Navy as willingly as he had joined the Confederate Army. He was a mercenary, an adventurer, but when the war was over he had to look for a job. He found one for which he had been made. He became travelling correspondent of the *New York Herald* and was at once ordered to Abyssinia to report on the activities of Napier's Army. He could bring to his work a ruthless intelligence and determination to succeed that soon put him ahead of all rivals. He was the first to send news of the fall of Magdala. The New World was undoubtedly his and he became a citizen of the United States.

In 1869 came his most important assignment. The *New York Herald* sent him to find Livingstone, of whom nothing had been heard for two years. The paper was willing to spend unlimited money but there must be no question of failure. Stanley, among the discoverers of the "scoop", was the man to succeed. He did so. Livingstone refused to leave Africa before he had traced the Lualaba to its main river, which he believed to be either the Nile or the Congo. Stanley returned to write the story of his almost superhuman endurance on the journey and his meeting with Livingstone. It was ridiculed and disbelieved, but when it was proved to be true in every detail, Stanley's reputation was made.

Livingstone's humanity and natural greatness must have touched Stanley as the qualities of few men had ever done. When Livingstone died with his project unachieved, Stanley felt the Lualaba mystery to be his inheritance. He returned to Africa and succeeded in solving it. He became known as the "Congo King" and he was regarded as having peculiar rights in Congo territory. As a free American citizen, secure from the squabbles of Europe, he was pleased to assist the King of the Belgians in the management of the Congo State.

By this time the virile, aggressive Welshman was no longer very young. Someone described him then: "The rich, black hair had become tawny and tow-coloured, the bright, fresh, clear complexion had become sallow, and the skin was pitted almost as if from smallpox, but the eyes were still those of fiery youth and energy." So he looked when approached by the Emin Pasha Relief Committee.

He was asked which of the three east coast routes he preferred to take. He replied that if he agreed to lead the expedition he would do so through the Congo. The committee was dumbfounded. Such a possibility had never before been considered.

Stanley gave his reasons in a manner that did not encourage argument. The west coast route would prevent the French and Germans from suspecting the expedition of any territorial ambitions. The country between Emin and the Congo was very rich in ivory and caoutchouc, so an expedition might hope to pay its way. The east coast routes were impracticable for different reasons—on the first the expedition might face a food shortage; on the second the hostility of Uganda; on the third the hostility of different native tribes. Then there was the possibility of the Zanzibari carriers deserting back to the coast. Stanley's idea was to go to Zanzibar for carriers and supplies, sail round to the Congo and proceed as far as possible by river, then march to Lake Albert. He believed that some 900 miles could be done by steamer and the whole journey should not take more than 157 days.

The Relief Committee was not impressed. On the Congo route the expedition might do 900 miles by water, but that meant that on land it would have to march instead of going on mule- or donkey-back. Seven hundred miles would have to be done under the Equatorial sun, with heavy loads to be carried, through country much of which was unexplored. The men, faced with no one knew what hardships, were likely to desert anywhere, and were more likely to meet with starvation, disease or death by violence. Taking them round the Cape to the Congo would be an added expense. There was no precedent for supposing the journey could be done in 157 days. Aruwimi could be reached in two months but beyond lay the unknown forest, the legendary heart of darkness; and beyond the forest were regions under the influence of the fearful Mwanga, murderer of Bishop Hannington.

Stanley thrust aside every obstacle, but it was less easy to thrust aside public opposition and hints that he had some ulterior motive in insisting on taking the expedition across territory in which his old employer, the King of the Belgians, was so interested. Stanley lost his temper. He said if the committee members were determined on the east coast route they could find some other leader. He packed his bags and went off to the United States.

Time was passing. The committee realised that without Stanley, whose arrangements had by now gone far, they would have to start from the beginning again. They cabled asking him to return. He tells us his agent was in despair. His first lectures had been a great success, his audiences adored him, his receptions were ovations—but, as he was fond of quoting, "the path of duty led the way to glory". It led him back to London. His annoyance must have been extreme when he discovered that the committee was still hankering after the east coast route.

He at last agreed on the route but said he so disliked it he would rather solve the problem by dropping the ammunition to Emin from a balloon. He had already sent 200 loads of rice inland from Zanzibar and bought pack and riding animals for the east coast, when a message from Brussels declared that King Leopold could lend Stanley's services to the expedition only on condition that he took the west coast route. The king, who had apparently not objected to the American lecture tour or to the fact that Stanley had been absent from Africa since 1883, felt he would be failing in his duty to the Congo State were he to deprive it of Stanley's services for any length of time. He would, however, not only lend Stanley for the Congo route but would lend some river steamers. The Relief Committee was forced to give way.

Stanley crossed at once to Brussels and had a satisfactory audience with the king. For some time before, their relationship had been strained. Stanley had been unable to obtain from Leopold any definite appointment in the Congo and had felt himself neglected. He had probably realised that the question of his leading an important expedition through Congo territory must reawaken the king to his existence. The interview appeared to clear up all past misunderstandings and Stanley undertook to carry out for Leopold a number of "little commissions".

By now there had been selected from among the crowds of adventurous Englishmen who had begged for a place in the expedition a number of young men, mostly military, who were sent ahead by sea to Zanzibar. Stanley himself was going by the faster overland route and would visit Cairo *en route*. Before he left England he was presented with the freedom of the City of London and given a banquet. He spent his last day at Sandringham describing to the Prince and Princess of Wales the plans for the expedition.

When he arrived in Cairo, Stanley had to convince the Egyptian Government and the explorers Junker and Schweinfurth that the Congo route was best. He appeared amused by their protests. If the members of the Relief Committee, among them experienced African explorers, and all distinguished and level-headed men, had decided upon the west coast route, who was competent to criticise? Junker and Schweinfurth were dissatisfied but silenced. The Egyptian authorities had to agree that the English always knew best.

During these discussions there must have been many who, wondering what led Stanley so firmly to insist upon the west coast route, remembered his book describing the Lualaba exploration. On that occasion he had set out on behalf of the *Daily Telegraph* to learn the character of Lake Albert. He had taken with him three young Englishmen and a number of Zanzibar porters. The column had suffered acutely from hunger and had met at first hostility from, then sharp attack by, the natives. It eventually reached not Lake Albert but Lake Victoria. There, while attempting to circumnavigate the lake, the party was persuaded ashore by cannibals and only escaped destruction through Stanley's skill in diverting the natives while he got his own men back into the boat. Two of the Englishmen died of exhaustion. With his remaining white companion, Stanley made his way to the Lualaba that he had long intended to explore. When he reached the river he was in Manyuema country, north of which was the vast area controlled by an Arab slave-trader called Tippu-Tib. With some idea of what lay before him, Stanley decided to increase the strength of his column. He persuaded Tippu-Tib to supply him with 700 men in return for £1,000. With these he passed the verge of the great, unknown forest. The natives, bitterly alienated by the slavers, were hostile. A chilling note, unlike any other the two white men had ever heard, sounded from village to village. It was the war note of the tribes. Poisoned arrows were shot at the party as, exhausted, sick, low-spirited, it was urged on by Stanley. Smallpox broke out. One man after another died and was thrown overboard.

"What a terrible land!" Stanley had written in 1879, "both banks shrouded in tall, primeval forests, were filled with invisible savage enemies; out of every bush glared eyes gleaming with hate; in the stream lurked the crocodiles to feed upon the unfortunates; the air seemed impregnated with the seeds of death!"

Tippu-Tib soon had enough of this. In spite of his bargain and the large sum he had accepted, he abandoned the harassed little party to its fate. Stanley, with his one white companion and the remnant of his Zanzibaris, went on. They managed successfully (to the disgust of the natives gathered on the banks to enjoy their destruction), to navigate the seven cataracts later called Stanley Falls and reached the confluence of the Lualaba and the Yambuya. Here they were pursued by a thousand shrieking cannibal warriors in fifty-four fast canoes. One of the canoes required as many as eighty paddlers and eight steersmen and carried a band of capering, howling spearsmen. The Zanzibaris were terrified. Weakened by starvation and disease, they would have thrown themselves overboard had it not been for Stanley's threats. He forced them to fire back at their pursuers. One volley of rifle fire was enough to silence the wild chanting and to put the whole lot to flight. The Zanzibaris, delighted by their own prowess, now became the pursuers and Stanley revenged himself by burning huts and ivory fetish temples, and setting canoes adrift. This, though satisfying, did not improve matters. The war continued all the thousand miles to the pool now known as Stanley Pool. Here the last of the three young Englishmen was drowned trying to shoot the rapids. Stanley went on alone. As the party neared the coast, the natives, demoralised by the traders, would exchange food only for gin. Stanley had none. With his men weak, emaciated, suffering from dysentery, ulcers and scurvy, he at last reached the sea. The Lualaba had been proved part of the Congo.

Stanley had solved the mystery which had taken Livingstone to his death, but he had not yet touched on Lake Albert. In an essay on the *Dark Continent* published in 1886, he wrote: "To know the extent of that lake would be worth some trouble." He was now not only going to reach Lake Albert at its extreme west tip, but he was going to pass on foot through the great forest that, starting at Aruwimi, stretched an unknown distance to the east. In one of his letters home, Stanley said he supposed he could get through the forest in a fortnight. He had no reason for such a supposition and to another man it would have seemed scarcely a fitting occasion for experiment. To Stanley the hazards of the route were irresistible. They gave the expedition the dignity of an exploration. He would again be first—this time through the forest.

At Zanzibar Stanley found awaiting him the officers and baggage of the expedition. The senior in rank among the men was Major Barttelot of the 7th Fusiliers, who had been to Aden to engage carriers. He had in the past distinguished himself by an aggressive courage on active service and his square face, with its thin mouth tending to twitch at one corner, had a pugnacious, critical look that soon began to get on Stanley's nerves. Jameson, a wealthy young Irishman with an unaffected charm of manner, a delicate face and agreeable expression of helpfulness, had contributed £1,000 to gain the privilege of joining the expedition and, as he said, doing some good in the world. There was a lieutenant in the Royal Engineers called Stairs, and a South African army captain called Nelson, useful and ordinary, who would have been handsome had he not been prematurely bald. Probably the most obviously attractive of the men was the youngest, Jephson, whom the selection committee had considered too well bred and would have rejected had not his cousin, the Countess de Noailles, contributed £1,000 on condition that he be included. The doctor, Parke, a good-looking, dark young man with a short energetic face and intelligent eyes, had offered his services to Stanley in Alexandria. Stanley, who had a prejudice against doctors, told him gruffly that if he were serious he could come and offer himself again in Cairo. Parke followed Stanley to Cairo and was engaged. A hospital steward of the Army Medical Association called Bonny had been engaged earlier as a paid medical assistant. When his first applications were ignored, he presented himself in person with a "breast covered with medals" and so there he was—a middle-aged man with a heavy moustache, protruding ears and the look of the N.C.O.—at Zanzibar. Two other paid members of the expedition—Ward and Troup—had already been sent to West Africa to buy stores.

The officers had brought a large cargo of provisions, a Maxim gun and the parts of a steel boat to be assembled and launched on Lake Albert.

Zanzibar, an island about twenty miles from the shore, was then ruled by Prince Barghash, who received flattering attention from those major powers who were interested in the East African mainland. It was described by Stanley as tropical Africa in miniature. Every creed from jungle idolatry to fanatic Christianity was practised. Every colour from the cream of the octoroon to the rich black of the negro could be seen in the bazaars where Stanley bought guns, ammunition, ropes and tools for the expedition, and the cotton cloths, beads and coils of wire necessary for barter.

Here he took on 620 Zanzibaris to carry loads. These men swore to follow him wherever he would wish; to stand by him in time of trouble, and to die with him if necessary. He swore to be a father, mother, brother and sister to each, and to protect them all from harm. God was called upon to witness these pledges.

At Zanzibar also was an old acquaintance of Stanley—none other than that Tippu-Tib who had deserted him on the Lualaba in 1877.

Tippu-Tib's wealth, power and notoriety had increased immensely. He had dominated the ferocious Manyuema people and their chiefs had become his vassals. Hundreds of interbred Arabs and Manyuema had become his followers and the Stanley Falls area was now a vast slave-trading centre. After Stanley left the Congo in 1883, the officer in charge of the Stanley Falls station made a treaty with one of Tippu-Tib's sons by which the Arabs agreed to abstain from slave and ivory raiding, and to remain at peace with the white men. A year later Tippu-Tib himself repudiated the treaty. An open quarrel resulted and the Arabs attacked the station. After three days' hard fighting, when the ammunition had run out, Deane, the English officer, was forced to make his escape. The station was taken over by Tippu-Tib as a slave-raiding office. He was at Zanzibar disposing of the slaves and ivory he had for sale when the expedition arrived.

Stanley's young officers, knowing nothing of Tippu-Tib, were impressed by his romantic appearance. One of them described him as having, with his smiling courtesy, his spotless white draperies, his dagger of filigree silver, the air of a well-bred Arab. They saw in his broad, snub face energy, strength and intelligence. He was half-Arab, half-negro. His famous and curious nickname, Tippu-Tib, referred to the nervous twitching of his eyes.

Leopold had required Stanley to come to terms with this powerful slaver. On Stanley's first approach, Tippu-Tib produced three Krupp shells that had been used by Deane in his attempt to protect Stanley Falls station, and, with much indignation, described them as trophies of Belgian aggression. It took Stanley "some time to quiet his spasms of resentment". When calmed down, he explained that the attack on the station had been made during his absence and without his knowledge. He repeated his often given assurances that he had nothing but the best of intentions towards the white settlers.

Stanley said he was glad to hear this, for he had been instructed by the Congo Government to offer Tippu-Tib service with the Congo State. In return for his undertaking to uphold governmental authority and oppose the other Arab slave-traders, Tippu-Tib would be appointed Stanley Falls Commissioner at a salary of £30 a month. Tippu-Tib decided to accept the offer on condition he and his ninety-six relatives were conveyed free of charge back to Stanley Falls.

Leopold, when cabled, agreed enthusiastically to the appointment and the terms. The members of the Anti-Slavery Society were furious but their opposition cut no ice with the King of the Belgians.

This "little commission", as Stanley described it, successfully completed, there was one other matter to be discussed with Tippu-Tib. Emin Bey, Governor of Equatoria, whom Stanley was setting out to relieve, had in his province seventy-five tons of ivory. Would Tippu-Tib supply 600 porters from the Stanley Falls area who would help carry goods to the province and from there bring the ivory back? Tippu-Tib would, at the price of £6 a head.

Stanley later admitted that he knew the choice between Mwanga, King of Uganda, and Tippu-Tib to be merely that of the frying-pan and the fire, but he did not let the fact worry him in Zanzibar. There were other duties to which he must attend. He had to send off word to Emin saying that he hoped to reach the end of Lake Albert by August 8th—a date some six months ahead. He advised Emin not to attempt escape without "the ample means of causing yourself and men to be respected" which was being brought to him.

To everyone then, Stanley included, the object of the expedition seemed clear. Stanley wrote: "It is the relief of Emin Pasha that is the object of the expedition, the said relief consisting of ammunition in sufficient quantity to enable him to withdraw from his dangerous position in Central Africa in safety, or to hold his own if he decides to do so for such length of time as he may see fit."

So now, as it was believed that Emin's position grew daily more desperate and the Tippu-Tib commission was completed, there was no reason why the expedition should not set out. It did so in February 1887.

Two years had passed since the outer world heard of Emin's plight, a year since Junker's arrival at the coast proved that Equatoria was accessible. For four years Emin had been cut off completely from the outside world. During three of those years his province had been open to attack.

Chapter Three

HOPE FOR THE PROVINCE

"The death of Gordon has been a great blow for civilisation in Africa."
EMIN: Letters

ON June 22nd, 1885, the Mahdi died, but by then his regime was established. He was succeeded by a Baggara Arab called Abdullah el Ta'arsha.

British seamen and troops were still holding Suakin and in the year of the Mahdi's death one last attempt was made by the British Government to regain a hold upon the overland trade route between Egypt and the Red Sea. A force was sent to Suakin under orders first to break down the power of Osman Digna, then to construct a railway supply line to Berber. Before it could do anything it was withdrawn and sent to quell a rising on the Afghan frontier.

As the last of the British and Egyptian troops retreated, Abdullah seized the remaining stretches of northern Sudan and so held the whole vast province which for fifteen years he ruled with despotic cruelty. He constantly threatened Egypt, but internal disorder kept him too busy to plan an invasion. Possibly for the same reason, he gave little attention to Equatoria.

An attack was made on Lado by the allied Bari and Dinka tribes; this failed and a quarrel between the allies brought the revolt to an end. By 1886 the Equatorial province was calm. The northern stations of Rejaf and Lado remained in revolt, but in the south Emin felt sufficiently confident to start building five new stations, three of which were on the river.

Still there were mysterious disturbances here and there to remind him of his abnormal situation. Unusually good grain crops had just been stored at Laboré and Dufilé when fires broke out and destroyed them. Another fire destroyed all but fifteen of the Lado huts, so the rebels had to take themselves north to Rejaf. Fires also broke out at Wadelai and Muggi. Although these might easily be accidental in the dry season, this year they were so frequent that Emin realised the agents of the Mahdi must still be at work. Attack was merely delayed, and when it came at last he would be almost defenceless. Although his ammunition could, if conserved, last a year, a few hours' serious fighting would leave him unarmed. He had little faith in the Egyptians and many of the Sudanese must sympathise with the enemy. At moments, when he realised that his position was desperate, he saw his work in the province destroyed, his people enslaved and himself carried off like Lupton to be paraded as a prize by Karamalla. He would then dash off a letter to the coast, crying "help us quickly, ere we perish!" But when no attack came, as the new stations grew, as one or other of his projects succeeded, his determination to hold the province strengthened.

Early in 1886 he received from Nubar Pasha orders to abandon Equatoria and return to Egypt via Zanzibar. Egypt had resolved in May 1885 to give up all her Sudanese possessions. Whether Emin had been willing to obey or not, any hope of escape southwards had by now been destroyed by a declaration of war between Uganda and Unyoro. Emin would have tried to send away small batches of Egyptians, but the native troops, remembering the rumour that they were to be handed over to guarantee the safe conduct of their masters, contemptuously refused to help any of the officials to safety.

At last Emin received a letter from Junker. A relief expedition was being organised. Long before it set out, he had time to range repeatedly from hope to despair, and to decide: "The work that Gordon paid for with his blood, I will strive to carry on, if not with his energy and genius, still according to his intentions and with his spirit." He wanted only a safe supply route from the coast that the needs of his province and his correspondence might not be at the mercy of "childish, disreputable Arabs". "All we would ask England to do is to bring about a better understanding with Uganda, and to provide us with a free and safe way to the coast. This is all we want. Evacuate our territory? Certainly not." He was grateful that an attempt was being made to bring him ammunition: "If, however, the people of Great Britain think that as soon as Stanley or Thompson come I shall return with them, they greatly err. For twelve long years I have striven and toiled and sown the seeds for future harvests, and laid the foundation stones for future buildings. Shall I now give up the work because a way may soon open to the coast? Never! No, never!"

Emin's friends and the other English subscribers to the fund hoped he would hold his province, but the government, seeing it as inaccessible and more nuisance than it was worth, hoped he would give it up. The

Khedive wrote to tell him he might do as he pleased, but if he refused
Stanley's escort to safety, he must expect no further help.

Emin planned to evacuate the Egyptian officials under Stanley's
protection. "I shall indeed be glad when I succeed in getting rid of the
Egyptians," he wrote, believing that with those indolent, dishonest
trouble-makers out of the way, there would be nothing to hinder the
construction of a perfect state over which he would rule like a kindly
father.

The Egyptians themselves, some of whom were unwilling to go, others
afraid to stay, were caught in a chaos of plots and counterplots. The
news that an expedition was being planned to relieve them from the
south was received with suspicion. They knew the only road to Cairo
was downstream via Khartoum. Would the Khedive suggest their going
south? It was not possible. The letter must be a forgery, a trick.
Rumours flew round the volatile, nervous companies—Emin was
planning to sell them as slaves to Uganda; or he meant to abandon
them, and they, out of touch with Egypt, leaderless and disorganised,
would be slaughtered by the waiting Mahdists.

Emin, who probably saw them now as only a temporary nuisance,
scarcely bothered to remonstrate with them. When he was shown a
letter from Hawashi urging the rebels in the north to depose the
governor and elect another, he did not rebuke the writer. The rebel
1st Battalion began to seethe with plots to capture Emin so he might not
escape without them. The officers of the 2nd Battalion in the south,
seeing no advantage to themselves in Emin's possible imprisonment at
Rejaf, begged him to take precautions. He shrugged his shoulders,
saying: "I am not afraid of death; let them come—I will await them".
The Sudanese, forming an overwhelming force with grievances of its
own, planned to seize Emin and the whole of the rebel battalion, and
march with the prisoners to Khartoum. Should the capital be indeed
fallen, they would turn the prisoners loose and disperse to their tribes.

Nothing came of these plots, but the atmosphere was disturbed.
Ruling as he did, without Egyptian authority, a province filled with
unco-operative Egyptians, he realised he might soon be in danger. He
tried to crowd out awareness of this fact by incessant activity. He
planned his day so that from six in the morning, when he arrived at the
hospital, until twilight, when he could settle down at his table to work
on his natural history collection, he had no leisure to think of the
future. His past hours of work were justified now by the fact that only

his development of the country was saving it from famine. These present hours must also be rewarded.

The clothing situation was a little better. Junker, on his way to the coast, had, with the aid of Mackay the missionary, been able to buy for Emin 2,000 dollars worth of stuffs. A Turkish merchant called Biri managed to get the bales to Wadelai. Emin at once ordered a new uniform for himself and saw that his men were neatly dressed.

News came from Felkin that the expedition was on the point of setting out. He replied: "Is it not altogether curious that whereas people in England in such a noble way spend thousands of guineas to send us help and assistance, I have not even received a single letter from Germany, with the exception of one from Dr. Hartlaub who is concerned to get new birds. . . . If I bore a celebrated name or had much money—but why complain!"

In later letters Felkin discussed the future of the province with an enthusiasm that led Emin to expect much from the expedition. As Egypt had abandoned the province, anyone was free to come to terms with its governor. Felkin and others in England were working to obtain for Emin a lucrative agreement with a British company that would maintain and protect him in his position, give him the means to develop the country further, yet leave him independent. The company would pay in money and goods for the large accumulation of ivory in Emin's care. Emin became very excited by these plans. He saw his province a second Sarawak; himself another Rajah Brooke. But Felkin, while rousing Emin's hopes in this way, saw fit to caution him against Stanley, who would, he knew, expect to dominate the situation. Emin must think twice before signing any agreement with the Congo State or a private company. He must maintain his independence at all costs.

Meanwhile the months were passing. There was no further news of the expedition. Emin decided that while waiting there was one thing he could do. He could ensure a safe passage for Stanley to and from the province by coming to terms with Kabba Rega. His possible diplomats were the Italian Casati and the Greek merchant Marco. He picked on Casati. Casati despondently agreed to undertake the mission.

"It was a Calvary," he said, "but I did not hesitate to ascend it." He went south on the *Khedive*.

Chapter Four

THE "RELIEF HURRICANE"

"In some respects the most remarkable expedition that ever entered Africa."

Librarian of the Royal Geographical Society

WHEN the expedition steamer left Zanzibar on February 25th, 1887, it carried the eight white officers, 623 Zanzibaris, sixty Soudanese armed as soldiers, four Syrians, 13 Somalis, Tippu-Tib gorgeously clad in silks, a jewelled turban and jewelled kriss, his ninety-six relatives, stores supplied to the expedition as an advertisement by different manufacturers, the machine gun, the steel boat in sections, and Stanley's Madeira.

Trouble started at once. The Zanzibaris and ninety of Tippu-Tib's men crowded the Soudanese into a stifling space between decks. Bullied and outnumbered, the Soudanese fell into a panic and made wild accusations against the Zanzibaris and Arabs. A free-for-all fight resulted. Stanley's orders could not be heard above the din and, in a rage, he armed the officers with shillelaghs and sent them into the fray. The officers hit out right and left, and Stanley, watching them, noted with satisfaction that Jephson, whom he had suspected of effeminacy, was "actually fierce when roused". He had already summed them up: Nelson and Stairs were satisfactory; Jameson was always "sociable and good"; but Barttelot was too eager, he did not always remember to ask Stanley's permission before taking action. Stanley wondered if it were possible that Barttelot lacked a proper respect for him. Bonny, on the other hand, was sadly submissive and lacking in initiative, as though at some time he had worked under a martinet.

The Congo mouth was reached on March 18th. The steamer anchored off Banana Point, where traders of different countries flew their flags outside their huts. An unusually large number of naval and trading vessels lay in the harbour that day. Stanley rowed ashore to discover what transport for his party he could find among them. The traders were astonished to learn from him that he had not only brought Tippu-Tib back from Zanzibar but had appointed him an officer of the Congo State. Stanley did not remain to argue about the matter. Next day the party embarked on five small steamers and started the journey up the river.

The Congo, the seventh largest river in the world, was not the magnificent waterway it had at first appeared to be. A hundred miles upstream, rapids and falls made it unnavigable. The expedition disembarked at Mataddi, where Stanley terrified the inhabitants by practising on the machine-gun. Here, for the first time, the column was placed in marching order. Stanley, with his terrier Randy at his heels, took the lead on a brilliantly caparisoned donkey. His boy, marching beside him, carried the Stars and Stripes and the standard of the Emin Pasha Expedition. On March 28th, at 10.30 a.m., Stanley's piercing whistle— a kind of marine fog-horn with a huge gong and worked by a piston —cut through the camp. There lay before the column a journey of 2,000 miles, the distance from Mataddi to Wadelai.

The next stage was the overland journey to the upper river. The first enthusiasm of the officers began to fade when they found they had to keep going a train of exhausted and unwilling carriers. The caravan road was no more than a rough path leading them up mountain-sides and down into marshy hollows. The heat was intense. Barttelot wrote home to his sister: "Stanley expects us to hit the men though he always took their part when they complained. We have been nothing but slave-drivers since we started."

Stanley tells us that in order that they might become experienced in the difficulties of conducting an expedition, he left most of the work to the younger men. As a result, the carriers ran wild. As soon as they had pitched their tents, they rushed off to loot the native villages. The officers had no knowledge of how to control them. Now was Stanley's opportunity to point the moral that discipline produces more satisfactory results than forbearance. In his next letter home, Barttelot's tone had changed: "Stanley as rear-guard got on A.1. He flogged loafers and they all kicked amazingly." At the same time the gentle Jameson was writing of his leader: "How he did lay his stick about the lazy ones, and the Somalis whacked away too! It was a sight for sore eyes to see the lame, the sick, the halt and the blind running with their loads as if they were feathers; and I was delighted to see some of my men catch it hot, after I had been told by Mr. Stanley himself not to strike them."

Stanley feared that any leniency on his part would lead the column to suppose him too old to supervise the march. He saw to it that such a

c

supposition could enter no one's head. He forced the column relent-
lessly on until at the end of the stage he could reflect: "There is nothing
more agreeable than the feeling one possesses after a good journey
briefly accomplished. We are assured of a good day's rest; the remainder
of the day is our own to read, to eat, to sleep, and be luxuriously
inactive, and to think calmly of the morrow."

Although the officers quickly overcame their reluctance to bully the
carriers, they remained sensitive to Stanley's bullying of themselves.
Barttelot was particularly resentful of it. Stanley threatened to ruin
him in the service if the Sudanese revolted. The retorts of Barttelot,
who could see no reason why he should be held responsible for the
behaviour of the Sudanese, were as sharp as Stanley's temper, but
Stanley, in command, could have the last word. The Major found
himself in charge of seventy men noted for their laziness and in-
capacity for carrying loads, and was told if he lost one he was "to look
out".

While the carriers remained within easy distance of the coast, they
too could make threats. The Sudanese, having gorged all their
rations in the first fifteen days, announced their intention of deserting
the expedition if not given more. Stanley said it was too early yet to be
other than patient, and more rations were served. When conflicts
between the blacks and officers got out of hand, Stanley enjoyed acting
as the calm, judicious mediator. "Provided," he wrote, "one is not
himself worn out by being compelled throughout the day to shout at
thick-headed men, it is most agreeable work to extenuate offences
and soothe anger."

However adept Stanley may have been at soothing the tempers of
the men, he had no control over his own. It was always leading him to
make furious, ridiculous threats that the young officers took seriously.
He would accuse them of any crime that happened to come into his
head. Barttelot complained in a letter that he and the others "were, at
any rate, gentlemen and not accustomed to be accused of that sort of
thing". They converged instinctively against the Yankee journalist,
who, however experienced as a rescuer, was in their opinion no
gentleman.

Stanley's easily injured self-esteem must have felt their criticism
acutely. He, the individualist, found himself up against the solid self-
righteousness which is the backbone of the English public school team
spirit. It was to him the most irritating of hindrances and he hit out

against it indiscriminately. He had the advantage of knowing what he was doing. His officers were inexperienced. He understood the unreliable nature of the carriers. He knew there lay ahead dangers of which the young men could not dream. He believed that, considering everything, he was displaying superhuman patience towards both officers and men.

The expedition became known as the "Relief Hurricane" throughout the lower Congo.

It was now passing through the beautiful Falls region, where the river, between steep banks, rolled wildly down a staircase of rock from a height of 800 feet. Some 235 miles of uphill country led to Stanley Pool, which had been discovered by Stanley during his Lualaba trip in 1877. The column journeyed in an atmosphere of impolite misunderstanding.

There were already eight European settlements of traders and missionaries on the lake-shore. The chief of these were the Free State settlement of Leopoldville and the French settlement of Brazzaville. The whole area was elaborately picturesque and richly cultivated. But—Stanley now learnt for the first time—the region stretching beyond was suffering a severe famine.

It was too late to turn back. Stanley later said that had the expedition set out seven months earlier, the Congo route would have been ideal. During that seven months unceasing slave raids had devastated the country. Village after village had been wiped out. The women and young men were kept as slaves, the rest ruthlessly slain and their bodies, hacked into pieces, hung up on trees to terrorise other villages into submission. Those natives that had escaped the slaughter were in hiding and a rapid growth of tropical weeds was quickly destroying the village plantations. Stanley realised he could only continue.

At Leopoldville Ward and Troup, who had been sent ahead for different reasons, joined the expedition.

While a camp was being set up behind the American Mission, the Commissioner, who had served under Stanley at Bolobo, rode out to find his old chief "standing with the most undisturbed coolness, and with an air that might be said to betoken indifference" as though he had never been away from Leopoldville. Stanley was indeed in his own regions. He had opened them to traders and settlers of all nations, who could lead a free life outside the dominion of any European power. A conference held in Berlin under the auspices of King Leopold had resulted in the formation of the Congo Free State in 1885. Since then it had developed under a Governor-General, administering in Leopold's name, with a staff of 150 Europeans, an army of 1,000 men and a service of six steam-boats on the lower river and five on the upper. There was a court of justice and eighty-five factories.

Stanley's coolness was not to remain for long undisturbed. The new steamers promised by the King of the Belgians were not ready. The steamer *Stanley* on which Stanley had been relying was in dock. He refused to consider waiting until these vessels were usable. He looked round for others and his eye fell on the *Peace* belonging to the Baptist Mission and the *Henry Reed* belonging to the Livingstone Island Mission. The *Peace* was lent as a great favour, but the owners of the *Henry Reed* refused to part with a vessel that was, they said, their only means of transport to missions on the upper river. Stanley at once ordered an officer and some soldiers to take possession of the *Henry Reed* and sent a letter to *The Times* accusing the missionaries of ingratitude for past services. At last the area Commandant took the matter up and, together with Stanley's violent outbursts of temper and remarks about the uncharitableness of Christians, persuaded the missionaries to hire out their steamer for £100 a month. This sum Stanley worked out as being 30% per annum of her value.

At last the expedition could embark again. The *Peace*, as flag-ship, towed the steel boat, now assembled, and a government launch. The *Stanley*, hurriedly put in order, preceded another steamship, the *Florida*, while the *Henry Reed*, towing an English Mission whale boat and a hulk called the *En Avant*, brought up the rear. The *En Avant* was filled by Tippu-Tib and relatives. Even this flotilla was inadequate. So many stores remained on the quayside that Troup had to be left behind to look after them. It was decided that the *Stanley*, when it reached Aruwimi, would return for him and make a second journey upstream.

Stanley's party left at dawn. The ships slid away between the dark mountains and out to the narrow river beyond the pool. Here the hills sank until the banks were no more than a few feet above the water. Stanley, in an easy chair on deck, gave himself up to enjoyment of the tranquil, repetitive view of earth green woods, the prismatic glitter of the waving grass, and the strong perfume of tropical flowers. He wrote: "Everything is going on infinitely better than could be expected."

The officers wrote home disconsolately. Stanley had chosen to travel in the *Peace* that headed the procession upstream at less than a knot an hour. Every forty-five minutes a halt had to be called to oil her up, to clear the cylinders of her propellers, to raise steam which promptly fell again, or to clear the grate of charcoal. A day was lost when her rudder broke. As one mishap after another impinged upon Stanley's mood of calm, the spell was broken. He leapt out of his easy chair into the arena. Squabbles followed. He accused Stairs and Jameson, perhaps not without reason, of being tired of him. He told them to get into the bush out of his sight for he was finished with them. Leaning over the rail of his chosen steamer *Peace*, he offered to fight Jameson, who was standing on the shore. Only the dividing water prevented blows from culminating what Jameson described as a "most disgraceful row". Two missionaries who overheard it were shocked by Stanley's swearing and said they had never heard the like before.

Endless quarrels were caused by the inability of the officers to manage the carriers. Stanley had ordered them to flog culprits, but when a sentenced man made a flattering appeal to Stanley's power and mercy he would be released. Stanley preferred to believe the men rather than the officers, whom he accused of tyranny. On one occasion he called Jephson a "goddamn son of a sea cook" and threatened to have him thrown overboard. Some of the officers were very young. Some still retained their schoolboy faith in the taciturn efficiency and comradeship of men of action. All felt outraged.

The river now was full of islands. As many as ten or more channels might open before a ship. Very careful navigation was necessary. The islands, covered with woods and creepers, were reflected in the clear water. The beauty of this stretch of river was exceptional but the officers had little time to admire it. There was not only trouble with the *Peace*; the *Stanley* went ashore with her stern stove in. The alarm was great but she was patched up within two days.

The young Englishmen were enduring this climate for the first time. They had to accustom themselves not only to the failings of their leader, but to the smothering heat that kept them sodden with sweat, the light that disturbed the nerves and the stinging, tormenting insects. The deceits of the carriers bewildered them, and when they looked to Stanley for guidance their bewilderment was increased. They found his behaviour unpredictable. He had charming moments of tact and discretion, but these failed at once when some trifle disturbed him. In anger he flung aside all his poses in which he was reformer, civiliser, missionary, rescuer and man of God, and displayed nothing but an unashamed determination to get his own way. His worst enemies admitted that he got things done, but with a fury that upset everyone and delayed everything. In his overriding of obstacles, he overrode ruthlessly all the scruples of his officers, declaring them to result merely from stupidity and inexperience. They were resentful. He resented their resentment. Barttelot, now burnt black by the sun, roused his especial irritation. He was convinced by nothing more than his dislike of the man that the Major was influencing the others against him.

Stanley had decided that when the expedition reached Bolobo, some 440 miles inland, the sick and useless men should be put ashore in charge of an officer. Those that recovered could be picked up by Troup when he came up on the *Stanley* with the excess stores. Stanley now announced that Barttelot would be the officer who must remain at Bolobo.

It would have been well for Barttelot had he accepted this decision. As it was, he protested bitterly against it. He had no doubt at all why Stanley had made it and he refused to submit. He was giving his services voluntarily to the expedition and should be permitted some say in disposing of them. At last Ward and Bonny, both salaried men, were chosen to await Troup.

Bolobo was reached on May 8th. It was a large native settlement, and the expedition rested for six days while the *Peace* was at last repaired. A better pace could now be made down the long, curving stretch of river between Bolobo and Aruwimi.

At Aruwimi the river forked. One branch, the Lualaba, dropped south to Stanley Falls, where, on a fortified island, Tippu-Tib had his stronghold. The other branch, the Yambuya, continued east towards Lake Albert, and this the main body of the expedition would follow. Someone, however, must remain at Aruwimi until Tippu-Tib delivered the 600 carriers. It was clear that no one wanted the job.

During the three months in their company, Tippu-Tib had courteously appeared unaware of the incessant altercations between the officers of the expedition and their civilising leader. If he smiled, his smiles were hidden. He had now to go south to take up his new office. Barttelot was ordered to take him and his family in the *Henry Reed* to Stanley Falls. Tippu-Tib departed with promises that the 600 carriers would be dispatched to Yambuya as soon as he arrived.

Stanley did not even pretend to believe him. He knew that whoever waited for the 600 carriers would wait a long time. He had no intention of waiting himself. That job would be for Barttelot and this time Barttelot would not be permitted to refuse. Before he left for Stanley Falls, the Major was told that when the expedition reached the Aruwimi Rapids and navigation ceased, it would be divided into two guards— an advance guard that would strike for the first time into the great forest, and a rear guard of sick and wounded that would remain under his charge to await Tippu-Tib's 600 and Ward, Troup and Bonny with the stores.

Stanley, prepared this time for Barttelot's protests, was unmoved by them. Barttelot, as the senior officer, was the best fitted to take charge of a second column. If he disliked the job—well, he would later be rewarded by being given a more interesting part to play in the work that lay ahead.

Barttelot, who had distrusted Tippu-Tib from the start, asked Stanley why he had ever chosen to associate with such a man. Stanley patiently explained that his intention was not only to placate a dangerous man, but to obtain for Barttelot the 600 carriers he would need to transport the 500 loads Troup would bring up from Stanley Pool. Did Barttelot suppose that these could be carried by the 200 sick men Stanley proposed to leave behind with him?

Barttelot was floored for the moment, but during the months that followed he must many times have asked an imagined Stanley why, if 600 more carriers were needed, they could not have been hired with the others at Zanzibar? or, if he wished to save the cost of their transport, why had he not accepted Leopold's offer of Bangala men who were, he said, "excellent soldiers" and "did not fear the Arabs like the Zanzibaris"? These Bangala men and the steamers that were not ready had been used by Stanley as strong arguments in favour of the west coast route. The steamers would have been large enough to take all the provisions and any number of carriers. Their failure had resulted in Troup being left with the loads at Stanley Pool, Ward and Bonny being left with the sick to wait for him at Bolobo, while Barttelot had to remain at Yambuya, a desolate spot, 1,400 miles up the Congo, to await the three of them. All these contingents, amounting to 300 men, would then be held at the whim of Tippu-Tib, who might or might not send them porters.

Barttelot, deeply despondent, accepted his position without much complaint. He had been half expecting it. He did, however, wonder what he had done to earn Stanley's antagonism. In the end he brought himself to ask Stanley if anyone had been warning him against him. He was, he knew, hasty and on one unfortunate occasion his temper had led him to use his fists against some coloured troops. He was afraid this incident may have been remembered. Stanley reassured him at once. He said he knew nothing of Barttelot's past and it was Barttelot's face alone that had warned him of the young officer's lack of forbearance. Now Barttelot had only to remember the words:

> "Not once or twice in our fair island story
> Has the path of duty been the way to glory."

"There," said Stanley, "shake hands upon this, Major. For us the word is 'Right Onward', for you 'Patience and Forbearance'. I want my tea. I am dry with talking."

The others were so eager to proceed that Stanley preferred not to order one of them to remain with Barttelot. He allowed the Major to choose his own second-in-command. Barttelot asked for the sensitive and gracious Irishman, Jameson, who had become his friend and who was probably the only one good-natured enough to stay behind willingly.

Kavalli's on Lake Albert, the point for which the expedition was making, was on the same latitude as Yambuya, 326 miles ahead. The expedition had now to journey less than a quarter of the distance it had come from the coast, but through a forest that was an unknown quantity. Map-makers usually indicated it by a blank. The natives swore it went on for ever. The horrors it might contain were unimaginable. Stanley was to be the first to face them.

In a sublime mood he approached the village of Yambuya, beyond which the forest rose like a black wall. As always seemed to happen, Stanley's mood was interrupted by the recalcitrance of humanity. The Yambuya natives refused to admit the white men into their village. Neither bribery nor persuasion would move them. Stanley argued until his throat was dry and the sun hot, then he damned restraint and ordered an attack. The steamer sirens screamed, the Zanzibaris and Sudanese leapt yelling ashore, and the startled natives took to their heels. The expedition possessed an empty village.

Stanley saw that the men settled in quickly. Next day they were busily collecting manioc from the fields, chopping fuel for the steamers, and constructing a palisade and trench as a protection round the village. Some of the Zanzibaris were set to guard the paths and prevent the others from wandering out to the dangerous areas where the natives waited to take revenge. The Zanzibaris were volatile, good-natured creatures who forgot orders as quickly as they received them, and their friends, passing with a nod and a smile, strayed out unhindered. A number were killed.

Stanley found the villagers cowardly, mean, untruthful and vicious. They were certainly disgruntled by his seizure of their village and it was a long time before they became reconciled to its new occupants.

When Barttelot returned from Stanley Falls he brought with him letters from Tippu-Tib, one of which, addressed to the King of the Belgians, "assured his Majesty of his devoted allegiance and earnest desire for the maintenance of peace in the district entrusted to his charge".

Stanley now had an idea. The villagers were, he knew, awaiting an opportunity to attack, and as Barttelot had to be left alone against them, some sort of truce must be arranged. Barttelot would be wise to go through a ceremony of blood-brotherhood with the native chief. Both Barttelot and the chief were reluctant, but agreed. The ceremony revolted Barttelot and merely gave the chief a chance to insult him. In return for his fine gifts, he received a fortnight-old chick and a plaited cane bonnet—expressions of native contempt.

Before he left, Stanley impressed on Barttelot the need to get the 500 loads—which contained half the ammunition for Emin, food to sustain the expedition at the barren lakeside, much private baggage and Stanley's Madeira—safely to Lake Albert. If by any chance Tippu-Tib did not deliver the men, then the Major must try and make the march without them. The carriers were, of course, ailing and incompetent, but even slow progress would be better than staying at Yambuya. The loads would have to be taken in double or even triple stages, but Stanley was sure Barttelot would prefer that to complete inactivity. Barttelot fervently agreed.

The *Stanley* with her crew now turned round and started back for Leopoldville, where Troup awaited her. The rest of the fleet went with her. Barttelot watched them go.

Now, free to move on unhampered, Stanley began urging the need for haste. He remembered by how short a delay Gordon's rescuers had

c*

failed. He tells us the words: "Too late, too late" repeated themselves in his ears, and he wrote: "Looking at the black wall of the forest which had been a continuous bank of tall woods from Bolobo hitherto, except when disparted by the majestic streams pouring their voluminous currents to the parent river, each of us probably had his own thoughts far hidden in the recesses of the mind. Mine were of that ideal governor in the midst of his garrisons, cheering and encouraging his valiant soldiers, pointing with hand outstretched to the direction whence the expected relief would surely approach if it were the will of God, and in the distance beyond I saw in my imagination the Mahdist hordes advancing with frantic cries and thrilling enthusiasm crying out 'Yallah, Yallah' until from end to end of the swaying lines the cry was heard rolling through the host of fervid and fanatical warriors, and on the other side multitudes of savages vowed to extermination biding their time, and between them and us was this huge area of the unknown without a track or path."

As Emin had been in this heroic attitude for months that were becoming years, haste was indeed essential. Stanley's whistle sounded once again and the 389 men of the advance guard took up positions. Stairs was weak with fever but so dreaded being left behind that he insisted they should take him with them in a hammock. He, Nelson, Jephson and Parke followed their leader with excitement and curiosity into "that region of night and fable which proved to be the grave of so many of our band".

As Stanley hurried to the head of the column, he turned and waved to Barttelot and Jameson standing gazing unhappily upon the departure.

"Good-bye, Major," he shouted. "I shall find you here in October when I return."

Chapter Five

MISSION TO UNYORO

"Captain Casati, on the other hand, though younger in years, looked
gaunt, care-worn, anxious, and aged."
STANLEY: Letter describing Emin and Casati.

CASATI, the son of a doctor, had been born at Lesmo, near Brianza,
in 1838. As a young man he entered the Bersaglieri and rose to the
rank of major before resigning his commission to pursue an early
dream of fame as an African explorer. Gessi Pasha was asking for a
young Italian to explore the Welle basin. Casati applied, asking if at
the age of forty-one he was too old. His superior officer was not
encouraging: "But you know that Africa is like the beautiful siren that
often kills her lovers?" He was willing to risk so delightful a death.

"When can you be ready for the journey?" he was asked.

He replied: "To-morrow."

He was to spend ten years in Central Africa, most of which time he
was cut off from the civilised world.

The forebodings that oppressed him on his way to Unyoro were to
be more than justified. The kingdoms of Uganda and Unyoro had
been at war, off and on, for years. Each was suffering the devastation of
war and its attendants, famine and pestilence. In Unyoro, when Casati
arrived, an epidemic of smallpox was at its height. The sick lay raving
in the fields. Corrupting corpses were strewn by the roads. Each
kingdom was ruled over by a king, unscrupulous, ambitious and
ruthlessly cruel, who was virtually a dictator. Each was a neurotic
who would have felt at home among the most degenerate coteries of
civilisation. Mwanga of Uganda, murderer of Bishop Hannington, was
a pervert verging on insanity. Kabba Rega of Unyoro, who had gained
the throne by the murder of his brother, was a cowardly hypocrite. His
pretence of friendship towards Emin was no more than an attempt to
persuade out of Equatoria the refugees who would bring with them the
ammunition and ivory he coveted. The fate of Emin and his people
might in the end be entirely in the hands of these two men.

Casati, when he reached Kabba Rega's court, was received with
suspicion. The king, deceptively normal and athletic in appearance,

69

was handsome, and his pleasing manners added to the difficulty of dealing with him. He agreed at once to Casati's proposal that he should permit a transit of correspondence through his territory. This, Casati hoped, would be a first wedge to help open a road to the coast. He began at once to correspond with Mackay and other missionaries in Uganda, but he soon found that their replies were going astray into Kabba Rega's hands.

Casati's next move was to ask if Emin might send small bands of troops through Unyoro to the coast. Kabba Rega again agreed willingly but at once started plotting with Mwanga to seize and disarm the troops when they arrived. Casati soon began to fear that Kabba Rega's perfidy combined with persuasive charm would prove too much for him. His one friend at court was an honest old minister, Kategora, who was soon to pay for his support of the stranger. Kabba Rega had him poisoned and, as the old man lay dying in agony, ordered boys to sing outside his hut a canticle: "He dies! He dies!"

Kabba Rega, however, was not the confident deceiver he may at first have seemed. He was consumed with doubts and suspicions and saw everyone as an enemy. He plotted and counter-plotted; planned a war with Uganda which he was afraid to declare; and attempted with human sacrifices to propitiate his father's spirit, which he believed was tormenting him. When he had got rid of Kategora he began systematically to deprive the ruling families of their rights, boasting that soon he could say "I reign alone, since my ministers are the low and weak".

Casati, no diplomat, was helpless before this neurotic, unmotivated cunning. Attacks of one kind or another were made almost nightly on his hut and he began to suffer from insomnia. Every attempt was made to force him to leave the country of his own free will, but he stayed on stubbornly. At last he was accused of plotting against the king's life and his letters to Uganda were seized. At the same time he learnt that Kabba Rega planned to invade Equatoria across the river and attack Wadelai. Casati warned Emin by messenger and prompt action was taken. As soon as the Unyoro force reached the river, Emin's steamer appeared and shelled the invading canoes. The loss to Unyoro in men and canoes was considerable, and Kabba Rega, imbecile with rage, accused Emin and Casati of designs upon his territory. Casati countered with accusations against Kabba Rega, who, uncertain of Emin's strength, at last agreed upon a peace.

The next disturbance came from outside. Uganda, which Kabba Rega had so long planned to invade, suddenly and without warning invaded Unyoro. Kabba Rega, for all his ostentatious preparations for attack, put up a poor resistance and was soon fleeing into the forest. Casati remained in the main village, and when the conquering chiefs arrived, was approached with respectful invitations to visit Uganda. Actually, he later learnt, these chiefs had been ordered by Mwanga to murder him. His life had been saved by the Christian missionaries, who, for all the fact of their persecution, had gained a remarkable influence over the chiefs.

The Unyoro forces, however, were not yet beaten. Uniting in a counter-attack, they drove out the invader, and Kabba Rega swaggered out of the forest. Secure once more from real dangers, he was free to enjoy further imaginary ones. He at once made plans to murder Casati. Casati wrote begging Emin to send gifts to propitiate the king, but Emin, he tells us, appeared to be offended, as though the Italian had meant to blame him or usurp his power. "I will not give a single piece of ivory," he replied, "nor a cartridge, before blood-brotherhood has been concluded." The situation was not improved when Biri, the Turkish merchant, who had been forbidden the country, suddenly appeared and paid Casati a visit. Illegal entry into Unyoro was held to be an affront to the sacred majesty of the king, and one that Kabba Rega was peculiarly liable to resent. He announced that Casati and Biri were plotting to dethrone him.

It was now early January 1888. A year had passed since Stanley set out from Zanzibar and rumours of his approach began to reach Unyoro. Casati heard them with relief. He felt he was now safely past the worst dangers of his position. Actually they were about to present themselves. He and Biri were seized, tied to trees and left unsheltered through the heat of the day, while the king's vizier searched the Italian's house for evidence of treachery and for certain armed men he was accused of concealing. Nothing was found. His personal possessions and the government ivory in his charge were confiscated and he was accused of causing the recent invasion by Uganda. Casati bore all with exemplary courage, but when he was dragged off to an enclosure reserved for criminals awaiting execution, he realised he had been courageous enough. The time had come to bolt. He managed to disappear into some long grass and, once away from his captors, made for the frontier. The fate of the unfortunate Biri, left tied to a tree, is not known.

When Casati reached the lake he found Emin's steamer awaiting him. Emin had not been much impressed by Casati's appeals for help and had set out to rescue him much as he might to get a small boy out of a scrape. If the Italian had hoped to be received as a hero, he was to be bitterly disappointed. Kabba Rega had been sending to Wadelai false reports on Casati's conduct in Unyoro and not only the credulous officials but Emin himself had believed them. As soon as Casati came aboard, Emin accused him of making chaos of the whole situation by his stupidity and blamed him for losing the government ivory in his care. Casati suggested that Emin should send a letter ordering Kabba Rega to give up Biri and the ivory within fifteen days, but was sharply told that he had been lucky to escape with his life. It was now no occasion for high-handed letters. Instead it was necessary to rebuild the friendship which Casati's folly had destroyed. He tells us that, thinking of "the advice given and slighted, and of this additional wrong inflicted on me after the many already suffered", he kept a dignified silence.

Even Casati's news of Stanley's approach could not soften Emin's manner towards him, but when, at the end of January, Emin set out for the lake end in the vain hope of contacting the expedition, he met with so many proofs of Kabba Rega's hostility that he realised his diplomat could not be entirely to blame. Casati was at last received back into favour.

Within the province the usual intrigues—the "deleterious intrigues" as Casati called them—had been going on. Hawashi appeared to be to blame for most of them, but nothing would persuade Emin to get rid of him.

Undermined as he was by years in a destructive climate, Emin seemed now to depend on the mere habit of a rule that had never been completely effective. It was as though some private religion persuaded him that faith in an object made it worthy of faith, and a show of authority could maintain authority. While fearing open rebellion, he denied its possibility and gave orders he knew would not be obeyed. He refused to be made aware of disobedience.

There had so far been no attempt towards reconciliation by the revolted 1st Battalion. At last it came in October 1887. Peace was offered on a number of conditions, one of them that Hawashi be removed and a new commander appointed. Emin started to hurry north, but when he landed at Dufilé, Hawashi gave such a display of zeal, and was so bewildering in his insinuations and hints of plots he had uncovered, that Emin got no further. Instead he turned against a number of old soldiers who had been his loyal supporters. The Rejaf officers became alarmed, and Emin, told that the rebels were plotting to arrest him, started south again. On his way he received, via Uganda, the firman that bestowed on him the title of Pasha.

Six months later, on March 27th, 1888, a letter arrived from Stanley. It was described by Casati as "an Odyssey full of the vicissitudes, sufferings and misfortunes undergone by the expedition".

Chapter Six

THE FOREST

"In debating within myself as to what distance the forest we were about
to enter would extend inland from the Congo, it never entered my mind
that we should find, at this altitude, a duplicate of that of the Amazon."
STANLEY: Lectures

STANLEY had written in his diary: "We march to-morrow into the
absolutely unknown." The forest started five miles outside
Yambuya. It rose like a dark, dense colonnade before the expedition.
The monstrous, closely growing trunks of the trees were festooned with
creepers, some merely delicate tendrils, others fifteen-inch ropes, all
so massed they choked the spaces between the trees. A way had to be
cut with bill-hooks before Stanley could make his historic advance. He
noted that for the first time an African expedition journeyed into the
unknown, day after day, without a single day's halt.

He was able to keep the men to this pace for a month; then even his
own enthusiasm began to wane. The forest did not remain unknown
for long. All too soon the expedition became familiar with its discom-
forts. The march was often dragged on long beyond the halting time
by the difficulty of finding anywhere where a camp could be pitched.
Space was needed on which to erect not only the canteen and sleeping
quarters, but storage tents for the tons of perishable goods that had to
be protected from damp. When Stanley's whistle sounded at last from
a suitable spot, the men would collect and set about trimming back
branches. Firewood had to be cut and large phrynia leaves found to
make a water-tight covering for the tents. There would come into
existence a sort of guarded village resounding with the cries of the men,
lighted by hundreds of fires and having for centre the noisy, brilliant
canteen.

The uproar kept away dangerous beasts but it also frightened any
small game that might have been shot for food. The bulk of the stores
had been left with Barttelot and the column was to be dependent on what
it could find to eat on the way. The villages were not proving helpful.

News of the forcible landing at Yambuya had been rushed from
village to village and the natives prepared as for the advance of an
enemy. They cut enticing avenues up to each village and planted the
ground with poisoned skewers which they hid beneath leaves—but they

74

gave the game away by standing in warlike attitudes at the end of the avenues. Stanley, coming upon the first of these traps "halted, reflecting and remarking somewhat after this manner: 'What does this mean? The pagans have carved a broad highway out of the bush to their town for us, and yet there they are at the other end, ready for a fight! It is a trap, lads, of some kind, so look sharp.' "

Under a barrage of shots from the Sudanese, the Zanzibaris crawled forward plucking up the skewers. Most of them were incapable of doing this without treading on a skewer or two. Septic wounds would result that often turned gangrenous. The natives fled into hiding from which they showered the carriers with assagais, poisoned arrows and threats. Stanley retaliated with rifle fire and burnt down the villages. After a while villages were often evacuated before the expedition arrived. Relations were not improved but the men found camp and food free for the taking.

The Uganda natives were notorious but their worst qualities were human. The forest natives were of such a low mental development it was impossible to come to any understanding with them. They were of two kinds—the tall villagers and the pigmy nomads. Some were ape-like, others remarkable for their beauty and air of candid innocence, all could turn cannibal when warfare or accident gave them a victim. Stanley tells us: "They had absolutely no idea of a God, nor anything approaching to our soft sensibilities, such as tenderness or pity, and their gratitude is so short-lived, it might be compared to that of a fierce bulldog restrained from throttling you while eating the morsel of beef which has just been thrown to him."

The cunning and skilful pigmies were the greater danger, but no great skill or cunning was needed to catch a Zanzibari and more than one disappeared into a cooking-pot. The remarkable incompetence of the Zanzibaris kept Stanley in a constant state of irritation. If there were calamus spikes on which to stub his toes or ooze into which to sink, some Zanzibari would do it. "Their heads," sighed Stanley, "were uncommonly empty." When hired they boasted of their great courage but at the slightest alarm took to their heels and threw away any such useless burden as a rifle. "Rather than try to protect themselves they would lie down and die." Yet Stanley, who chose to hire them in spite of past experience, must have discovered that their very simplicity made for endurance where wilier breeds would have revolted.

Few of the Congo carriers would have been willing even to enter the forest. It was the last remnant of the primeval jungle that had once covered all dry land. In other parts of the world the great forests had been destroyed at different times and replanted. Only here the trees were direct descendants of the prehistoric trees that had stood on the same spot, and they grew with the same luxuriance. Some rose to a height of 200 feet. Some, still standing, were white with age, their earliest saplinghood dating back perhaps to classical times. Trees fell hourly with a rushing crash that shook the ground. Trunks of fallen trees were quickly bored hollow by ants and would crumble at a touch. The standing trees were clothed in moss from root to tip, while from their forks hung giant ferns, orchids and lichens.

In the dense, misty, hot-house air the perfume of flowers and of stagnant waters was overpowering. The sun could scarcely penetrate the canopy of leaves, but the heavy, icy raindrops broke through like bullets. Everyone agreed that this must be the wettest place on earth. Stanley recorded 569 hours of rain during their five months under trees. Day after day was spent in an exhausting atmosphere of damp heat. There was always thick white mist, dripping dew, torrential rain or storms that set the whole forest shaking and adazzle with purple fork lightning.

It was a natural forcing-house in which the plants grew with monstrous abundance. "The absence of any sign of decay, the general healthfulness of the plants, their lustrous green leaves, their enduring youth and their passionate struggling for pre-eminence, excites wonder. There is no languor or drooping, no sickliness anywhere, but thick glossy leafage—above all the mighty branches of stately trees, rugged teak, shapely bombas, incorruptible greenheart, towering African mahogany, unyielding ironwood, tall, mastlike Rubiaceæ, the butternut tree. . . ."*

The forest was always loud with its own noises—the hum of insects and the screams and cackles of parrots, cockatoos, touracoes, sunbirds, ibis and fish eagles. Clouds of butterflies flew daily upstream, some taking hours to pass. As for the insects—in this ideal atmosphere they had become giants fighting for living-space with highly developed weapons. "Lean but your hand on a tree," said Stanley, "measure but your length on the ground, seat yourself on a fallen branch, and you will then understand what venom, fury, voracity, and activity breathes around you. Open your note-book, the page attracts a dozen butter-

* Stanley: Lectures

flies, a honey-bee hovers over your hand; other forms of bees dash for your eyes; a wasp buzzes in your ear, a huge hornet menaces your face, an army of pismires come marching to your feet. Some are already crawling up, and will presently be digging their scissor-like mandibles in your neck. Woe! Woe!"

The bees that attacked ears, eyes and nostrils were no bigger than gnats and swarmed in the same way. The donkeys, whose legs were stripped bare by bites, suffered most from them. There were some beetles that burrowed beneath the skin, others that bored into the tent-poles and sent clouds of sawdust into the soup, others, two and a half inches long, that blundered into the tents whenever a light was lit and bumped around until driven away. The ants got into the food and, if swallowed by accident, ate through the stomach membranes. A sleeper covered with ant-bites would awake to find himself writhing with a burning itch as though he had been flogged with nettles. Then there were the mosquitoes, gad-flies and tsetse flies with their different poisons, and the "jigger" that laid its eggs in the toe-nails of active men and made the slow ones "a mass of living corruption".

The virulence of the insects was beaten by that of the snakes which lay unseen in the deep undergrowth, and that of the natives who hid in the trees to drop their arrows down on the men below.

The expedition in a file, treading softly on a thick carpet of leaf mould, moved slowly forward in twilight with necks and backs bent. If the trees cleared, it would be merely to reveal a wilderness of quagmires on whose green surfaces lay lilies and lotus flowers. The mud beneath had a sickening stench and men would sometimes sink into it up to the neck.

Stanley exhorted everyone forward with long speeches of a religious nature. To Parke, who after announcing his belief that the forest bees had no sting was badly stung by one on the neck, he remarked: "Just so, nothing like experience to stimulate reason."

The carriers were becoming wretched with apprehension. The rain soaked their thin cotton clothes so that they marched in shivering misery. The Zanzibaris were Moslem only by courtesy. They had grown up in a muddle of legends, descended to them from the ancients, one of which told of a region of increasing darkness at the end of which a gigantic serpent encircled the earth's rim. Here, they began to believe, must be that region. Where else would they encounter these heavy, black rain-clouds, these tremendous thunders, this lightning, and the tempests that brought trees down across their path.

At each dawn, when a white mist drowned the camp, the carriers were roused to new fears. For a while the trumpets, the shouts of the officers and the preparations for the march would give them new heart, but they soon lost it and would frighten everyone, even the young Englishmen, with stories of the horrors they had glimpsed in the depths of the forests.

After the first month sickness began to deplete the men. They had been born to heat and sunlight. The darkness, the icy rain, the unvarying diet of manioc and bananas, continuous effort and their own terror weakened them. A bite, scratch or sting, any puncture of the skin developed into an ulcer that would often eat its way to the bone. The men became gaunt, listless and covered with sores. Even Stanley could not rouse them to life. He became so irritated by their lack of spirit that he scarcely protested when their headmen flogged them or the natives speared them. They scarcely protested themselves. A fatal desolation had come down on them.

Stanley had decided to follow the river to north latitude two degrees in the hope that riverside settlements would provide food. There were oyster fisheries on the island groups and occasionally the expedition ate well, but the food situation was getting steadily worse.

At last the river became navigable. The steel boat was fitted together and Stanley, lying in it, could be paddled in comfort upstream. As he went he could hear the others still carving their way with bill-hooks and axes through the forest, and his old glow of self-satisfaction returned. He sketched the course of the river. He began to make observations of a scientific nature, and when at a riverside village he discovered that no track led from it into the forest, he noted in his diary: "This fact made me think, and it suggested that if tracks were not discoverable by land, and as the people were not known to possess the power of aerial locomotion, that communication was maintained by water." This leisure for speculation so contented him that he wished he had brought his fleet of fifteen whale boats so that the whole expedition might have travelled by water: "What toil would have been saved and what anxiety would have been spared me." He began to see the officers in a new light: Stairs was alert and intelligent, Nelson resolute and obedient as a Roman centurion, Parke enduring and gentle. To Jephson went the highest praise: Stanley likened him to himself in youth.

Those who could get native canoes joined Stanley on the river. Soon there was a whole river column that could leave the weary landsmen with their bill-hooks and axes far behind. The comparative silence of river travel now permitted some of the officers to get glimpses of the many sorts of beasts, in size from rats to elephants, that lived among the trees. Monkeys swung in hundreds over the water, baboons howled within the darkness, crocodiles haunted the sandy points and inlets; herds of hippopotami grunted thunderously as the canoes disturbed them. Armies of parrots screamed over the river surface. Aquatic birds passed in a whirr of wings, and here, as everywhere, the air vibrated with the hum of insects.

At Panga Falls, where the steel boat had to be carried overland, some of the Zanzibaris tried to shoot the rapids and, as usual, came to grief. The carriers could swim but their loads of rifles and gunpowder went to the bottom, and when swimmers reached the shore they had to face Stanley's wrath. "The Zanzibaris," he says, "were so heedless and lubberly among rapids that I felt myself growing rapidly aged with intense anxiety while observing them. How headstrong human nature is prone to be, I had ample proof daily. My losses, troubles and anxieties rose solely from the reckless indifference to instructions manifested by my followers."

The natives were still evacuating their villages. This was "an excellent arrangement", and while there were orchards to be plundered the men need not face the worst of the sufferings before them. It overtook them at last. They reached an area that had been depopulated by slave-raiders. The villages had been burnt down, the plantations maliciously destroyed, the natives killed or taken into slavery. The silence of desertion and utter desolation lay over everything. The food Stanley had brought was scarcely sufficient to feed the officers. The main bulk of provisions was with Barttelot. As the column passed from one hopelessly despoiled village to another, the men's hunger increased until it became unendurable. For miles not a fruit tree had been left standing, not a grain of corn could be found in the dead fields. When at last they came upon some plantains or manioc that had escaped destruction, they gorged madly.

This alternate starving and over-eating killed many of them. Stanley tried to teach them to reserve rations of the food they found, but at the end of another day's march each had eaten all he carried and was looking for more.

At Panga they found a village that had not been evacuated and had still in it the remnants of a population left by the Manyuema slavers.

This was in the centre of a famine-stricken district. The natives put high prices on their food. At Bangala one of the brass rods used for exchange could buy a man five days' provisions. Here four brass rods were asked for one fowl. Stanley saw this as inexcusable profiteering and, losing patience with the haggling that was going on all round him, ordered the Sudanese to drive off the natives with rifle fire, so that the men could help themselves to food. They did so willingly. The whole caravan was able to feast on the natives' stores at no cost whatever. This method of obtaining food, once proved successful, was often repeated. It saved time even if a great deal of ammunition was wasted.

The storms grew worse, the downpours heavier. The black water of the river rose and lapped drearily into the black forest. When lightning and falling trees made progress difficult, the men would crouch beneath large leaves, chilled to the skin and shaking with fright. Nearby stood the terrified asses, their eyes cast up, their ears back and the water rolling from their backs. They were no more than skin and bone. Two of them had already died from starvation. The men were now in little better condition. One went insane and his cries disturbed the camp for days before his death. Some fell behind and were abandoned by the caravan, but usually the friends of a sick man would support him until he was beyond hope.

Those struck by poisoned arrows were in danger of developing tetanus. One man slightly injured in the wrist died within five days. Stairs, wounded below the heart by an arrow, the poison on which was dry and stale, suffered three weeks' painful illness. Parke nursed him back to health but the arrow wound did not close for months. The officers speculated as to what the nature of the poison could be, but none came near guessing right. The mystery was solved when Stanley found in a deserted hut a packet of dead red ants. The ants, he later discovered, were ground to powder and cooked in palm oil. Warriors were forbidden to cook poisons near a village and had to take their pots and ingredients into the depths of the forest. There they smeared their arrows and, in self-protection, covered them with leaves.

These unhappy savages had discovered a weapon so deadly none dared be without it. It had made life hideous for everyone. In some districts, where poisons of a peculiar power had been evolved, native families lived barricaded within huts made like small feudal castles. Fear filled the villages.

As the months passed and the forest continued as before, a feeling of desperation came down upon the expedition. Stanley began to admit the possibility of their being held up for months, even years. Natives were captured and asked where were the grass-lands. Stanley plucked one of the few blades that grew near the river and tried to describe a vast tract of land where only such grass-blades grew. Where could it be found? The natives shook their heads in bewilderment. They knew only trees, trees, trees. The forest was without end. The whole world was forest.

The Zanzibaris whimpered with terror. They knew now they were indeed journeying to the end of the earth. Parke worked unceasingly among those that were sick but they had little spirit left to keep them alive. In his diary for August 18th, less than two months after the expedition had entered the forest, Stanley noted that only eighteen men were still fit to face a day's march. He had started out with a sound 389. Sometimes a thought was spared for Barttelot left on the forest's edge with 250 sick and incompetent, but not often. The advance guard found its own worries enough.

At almost every bend in the river there would be a village of conical huts. Above the Nejambi Rapids the nature of the huts changed. It was here that man's inventiveness had made life a burden for himself and each had immured himself in a square hut, detached from its fellow and hidden behind a tall, thick palisade of logs.

Past these rapids it was possible to take to the river again and the sick could be carried in canoes. There was tremendous excitement one day when a carrier came rushing up from the river to the camp to say he had just seen a canoe flying an Egyptian flag. It must be the Pasha! Stanley got himself into his frogged coat and hurried down to the bank. There, indeed, was the flag but it was flown by men from Tippu-Tib's territory —the notorious Manyuema slavers. The canoe was careful to keep out of the white men's way.

Despite the reputation of the Manyuema and the fact that the expedition had been passing devastated villages and the brutally hacked bodies of natives, five of the incorrigible Zanzibaris made off with the slavers, securing a welcome by taking with them as much ammunition as they could carry. After that desertions became frequent. Not only were the men demoralised by the long, dreary, hungry march but they had lost faith in Stanley. They had ceased to believe in the existence of the lake he was seeking. They saw nothing ahead but death.

Again came rapids and cataracts and the river transport had to be carried. Sixty sick men followed the column at a crawl. Some were able to catch up with it when it camped for the night, others died on the road. There was a pause at Navabe, once a prosperous village, now possessed only by a few scattered skulls. Clearings that had been deserted only a few months were already dense bush through which the leaders had to carve a tunnel. The expedition found what food it could and took a short rest. When it continued it left five men unconscious and dying among the dead.

The forest closed after the expedition like water after a ship's stern. Everything grew at a nightmare speed so within three days of its passing, the column's track was almost obliterated. Some of the abandoned clearings were already young forests hung with creeper and densely choked with undergrowth. Here was an overwhelming force of life in which the white men and their carriers were alien, unwanted and without part.

Suddenly, when things seemed most hopeless, the expedition came upon a magnificent household standing amidst orchards and fields of grain. The tattered, haggard, wondering column passed into a tree-shaded courtyard from which other courtyards opened with vistas of extraordinary luxury and beauty. Everywhere they saw stores of food. Well-fed slaves moved through the gardens. This was the home of Ugarrowwa, the chief slaver of the district. He welcomed the expedition courteously. It had ammunition—the one thing he needed.

When the men had eaten their fill, Stanley met Ugarrowwa's account with an order on Barttelot, who was said to be a few days behind. It was agreed that fifty-six very sick men were to be boarded for $5 each a month, the total sum also to be paid by Barttelot in ammunition.

After four days' rest, with bellies filled and relieved of the invalids, the expedition returned unwillingly into the forest. A canoe followed soon after, in which Ugarrowwa handed back three Zanzibar deserters. For this he was rewarded with a revolver and 200 cartridges.

Stanley decided that an example must be made of these men. He called together the carriers and asked them were they not justified in killing anyone who tried to prevent their advance or retreat? The men agreed that they were. If a man stole their rifles was he not preventing them from advancing or retreating?—"for if you have no rifles left, or ammunition, can you march either forward or backward?" Cheerfully the men said "Yes" or "No" as required, then learnt that they had themselves condemned the three deserters to death. They watched without enthusiasm as the first of the three was hoisted up and hanged from a tree. They were ordered on at once and filed out of the camp before his struggles were over.

Stanley had announced that the condemned men would die one a day, but even deserters are more use alive than dead and he arranged that when all were gathered for the second execution, the headmen should beg the lives of the two prisoners. The little play was effective. Stanley pardoned the men, who wept and vowed to die at his feet. The Zanzibaris, pale with emotion, shouted that never again would they leave him. Almost three days passed before they began deserting again.

The men had regained some of their strength at Ugarrowwa's, but already fifty more sick men were dragging after the column. The food situation was more serious than before. Days were spent in searching the countryside for anything that could be safely eaten. The men devoured arum rhizomes, pineapple flowers and occasional passion fruit—all acid and bodiless, whetting the appetite instead of satisfying it, leaving a bitter taste on the tongue. The officers had little enough and one day Stanley himself had only two bananas.

After the 1886 rise in the price of ivory, the slavers had penetrated farther and farther into the forest in search of slaves. Within five months they had laid waste villages over an area of about 44,000 square miles. The expedition was approaching the trading centre of another notorious slaver, Kilonga-Longa. Some Manyuema told Stanley that the household was only a few days' journey up the river, but Nelson and fifty-two of the men were so crippled by ulcers they could go no farther. It was decided to leave them until help could be sent to them. A camp was pitched for them on a ridge of sand by the river edge and there they were left with eighty-one loads and ten canoes. On one side of them the forest rose to a height of 600 feet. On the other shelving black rocks divided the waters into two cataracts that fell against one another in an uproarious froth. The sick men, with their fears and suffering nerves, had to bear with this noise day and night.

The others limped on. Fungi, banana stalk, bitter amoma berries—anything served as food. The officers had each as daily ration two bananas and a cup of sugarless tea. They must have thought longingly of the Fortnum & Mason tinned dainties left with Barttelot. Jephson asked Stanley if he had ever experienced such grievous conditions before. He admitted he had not, adding: "The age of miracles is passed, it is said, but why should they be? Moses drew water from the rock of Horeb for the thirsty Israelites. Of water we have enough and to spare. Elijah was fed by ravens at the brook Cherith, but there is not a raven in the forest. Christ was ministered unto by angels. I wonder if anyone will minister unto us?" As he spoke a guinea-fowl swooped to his feet and was caught by his terrier Randy. "There, boys," cried Stanley. "Truly the gods are gracious. The age of miracles is not past."

It was, unfortunately, an isolated miracle. Next day Stanley was poisoned by strange fruit that looked like pears, and all afternoon lay in pain in his tent. The officers spent the time inventing menus for imaginary meals. One planned:

> Filet de bœuf en Chartreuse.
> Petites bouchées aux huîtres de Ostende.
> Bécassines rôties à la Londres.

Equally distant was the more homely menu:

> Ham and eggs and plenty of them.
> Roast beef and potatoes unlimited.
> A weighty plum pudding.

The next day a donkey, on the point of death, was shot for food and the meat shared among officers and men. The men were savage with hunger. They fought for the skin, crushed the bones, boiled the hoofs and devoured every fragment. They went on with renewed energy and with high hopes of the comfort awaiting them at Kilonga-Longa's. When they came at last to the track leading to the settlement, they raised shouts of praise and thanksgiving. As they marched between orchards and fields of standing corn, they wept with delight.

Kilonga-Longa was not at home but his chiefs greeted the caravan with enthusiasm. The skeleton carriers passed out of the wilderness into the midst of plenty. They were surrounded by sleek and lusty Manyuema who smiled and waited for Stanley to produce fine cloths, beads, ornaments and ammunition. He had none. That which he had brought had been lost or used up on the way. He produced what was left—some cheap beads and rolls of cheap cloth. The Manyuema looked at these things with disgust. They were rich. They had expensive tastes.

They were not just then in need of ammunition and they had no faith in the rear column that was said to be bringing fine goods and fire-arms a short distance behind. They said they had heard no news of a rear column. They openly doubted its existence. When they realised that they were to be paid with nothing but promises, their smiles faded. They sharply refused to supply the expedition with food.

The starving men wept and pleaded like children. They exchanged their clothes, knives and belts for a few handfuls of grain. They would have gladly given their rifles but Stanley sternly ordered them not to part with them. When all their possessions had been handed over to the greedy Manyuema, they were still frantically hungry. When they attempted to steal the food that was all around them, they were flogged so brutally by the slavers that one of them died. When they wept and begged for food, the Manyuema offered it to them in exchange for their rifles. Hunger easily overcame their fear of Stanley. He discovered that eleven rifles and 3,000 rounds of ammunition had disappeared. His angry accusations caused the Manyuema to drive the whole expedition out of the settlement. He would have been glad of an excuse for a fight had the men been fit to put up any sort of defence, but he knew they were useless. They had been broken by hardship and hunger. They would have sold themselves into slavery for food.

Knowing that once they had lost their arms, the officers would be murdered and the men enslaved, Stanley made one last desperate attempt to frighten the Manyuema. His one strength was the rear column. For an hour he stormed with such vigour that the Manyuema were almost convinced that Barttelot would any minute appear with an army to avenge his leader. To the surprise of everyone, five rifles were returned and a little corn doled out to the men.

Eight days of argument passed before Stanley could persuade the chiefs to sign a contract. In it they agreed to send help to Nelson, to board him, Parke and the sick carriers until Stanley returned for them, and to guide the rest of the expedition out of the forest. In return they were to receive from the rear column one and a half bales of fine cloth.

Jephson returned for Nelson. He had been eighteen days on the bleak ridge of sand and he had lost all hope. He was huddled on a camp stool, his head buried in his arms, when help arrived; and as he caught Jephson's hand he burst into tears. His servants had found him some fungi and berries in the forest that overhung them. The carriers who had not strength to search for food themselves had died one by one. Five only rejoined the expedition.

When the column continued on its way, it left behind with the Manyuema Nelson and twenty-nine sick carriers. Parke remained to attend them. Stanley also left the steel boat that was to have taken the party across the lake to Wadelai.

Six Manyuema guides with their attendant slaves had been hired to lead the expedition out of the forest. They took it through the Balessé country which Kilonga-Longa claimed as his own. His subjects, in an attempt to protect themselves from this unwanted ruler, had felled the trees into an abattis round each village. The members of the expedition had to crawl, climb and leap a way through the wild confusion of tree trunks. The Zanzibaris naturally came to grief. Many were injured; one broke his neck. Even Stanley showed little skill against this new hazard and in one hour took six falls.

This defence had proved poor and the villagers were completely cowed by the slavers. A few shot arrows but hit nothing more harmful than a Zanzibari. The rest mumbled servile greetings as the Manyuema, with swaggering contempt, led in the expedition as they might lead a string of slaves.

Food was still scarce. The men were still hungry, but the Manyuema, afraid of missing some small article they might like for themselves, refused to permit the carriers to trade with the villagers. One carrier who disobeyed was flogged by the Manyuema's slaves. The others submitted. Stanley reviled the men for their meekness, but while they remained on territory claimed by Kilonga-Longa the Manyuema, "cruel, perverse and niggardly", had things all their own way. As soon as this territory was passed, Stanley took a stand. When the slavers came to him with complaints about the "vile Zanzibaris", he silenced them coldly. Now, he said, their day was over and he would give the orders. They retired in silence.

The expedition had arrived at Ibwiri, a village that was not only prosperous but generous. The men crawled in gaunt and naked. They had stripped themselves to buy food. The bones stood out from cracked flesh, for they had suffered seventy-three days of famine and thirteen days of absolute want. "Their native colour of oiled bronze had become a mixture of grimy black and wood ashes; their rolling eyes betrayed signs of disease, impure blood, and indurated livers; that beautiful contour of body, and graceful and delicate outline of muscles —alas, alas!—were all gone. They more befitted a charnel-house than a camp of men bound to continually wear fighting accoutrements."

Perhaps from a natural kindliness, perhaps from fear of the Manyuema, the chief gave them lodging and feasted them on fruit, corn and vegetables. They were told that a few days' march would take them out of the forest into open grassland.

When they left a fortnight later, plump, glossy and in high spirits, they probably thought their troubles were over.

Chapter Seven

THE LAKE

"A more heartless outlook never confronted an explorer in wild Africa, than that which was now so abruptly revealed to us. From the date of leaving England, January 21st, 1887, to this date of December 14th, 1888, it never dawned on us that at the very goal we might be baffled so completely as we were now."

STANLEY

A FORTNIGHT later a break in the forest showed distant pasture land stretching in waves until the eye was checked by a peak that Stanley named Pisgah. The men dropped their loads and, openmouthed, stared before them. One asked did they gaze upon a mirage.

No, Stanley assured them, the grass-land was really there. "By the mercy of God we are well nigh the end of our prison and dungeon."

The men held their hands out towards the distant, brilliant glimpse of open country, then lifted their eyes to the sky. "They recovered themselves with a deep sigh, and as they turned their heads, lo! the sable forest heaved away to the infinity of the west, and they shook their clenched hands at it with gestures of defiance and hate. Feverish from sudden exaltation, they apostrophised it for its cruelty to themselves and their kinsmen; they compared it to Hell, they accused it of the murder of 100 of their comrades, they called it the wilderness of fungi and wood-beans; but the great forest which lay vast as a continent before them, and drowsy, like a great beast, with monstrous fur thinly veiled by vaporous exhalations, answered not a word, but rested in its infinite sullenness, remorseless and implacable as ever."

The path they had cut through it was marked by skeletons of men who had died from starvation or sickness. Others lay dying at Kilonga-Longa's. Stanley, writing his account with the Manyuema, debited them with the deaths of sixty-nine carriers and "mischief incalculable".

He himself had done his best in the lamentable circumstances for which he was responsible. His courage and vanity, not easily separable, occasioned in him the strength that prevails. There could have been for him no turning back, for to do so would be an admission not only of cowardice but his own error in choosing the route. He had won through, even if at a high price in other men's lives, and the forest was no longer unexplored.

But they were not yet out of it. They passed through a piebald of woods and clearings. Here the natives, mistaking the expedition for Manyuema, disappeared as it approached. The guides had been dismissed. The villages were deserted. The expedition lost its way. After days of wandering in forest-land, the carriers began to doubt if they had ever seen the plain. Then one day one of them, climbing to repair the roof of a hut in which he intended passing the night, shouted excitedly that the grass was in sight. His friends called to him mockingly: "Don't you also see the lake, and the steamer and the Pasha whom we seek?" But they, too, climbed to the roof and at once shouted that he spoke the truth. The pasture-land was scarely an arrow's flight away.

On December 4th they emerged from the dark, hot-house atmosphere to see before them the great plain, the grass moving in the breeze and adazzle with sun. They had been in the forest for nearly half a year.

"Judging of the feelings of others by my own," wrote Stanley, "we felt as if we had thrown all age and a score of years away, as we stepped with invigorated limbs upon the soft sward of young grass. We strode forward at a pace most unusual, and finally, unable to suppress our emotions, the whole caravan broke into a run. Every man's heart seemed enlarged and lifted up with boyish gladness. The blue heaven above us never seemed so spacious, lofty, pure, and serene as at this moment. We gazed at the sun itself undaunted by its glowing brightness."

The grass had been burnt a few weeks before. Now it was newly-grown, soft and a bright, pure green. Birds, of species unknown in the forest, took flight before the noisy caravan. The antelopes lifted their heads, then made off, their legs flashing rhythmically. Buffaloes snorted and blundered out of sight. Soon the sward lay like deserted park-land as far as the eye could see.

The natives as well as the beasts took to their heels before the column, leaving fowls, vegetables and fruit for the taking. The men became so heartened that when they saw a cow they called out gaily: "Beef, beef——aye, beef, how are you? we have not seen you since we were young!" The officers lost their haggard looks. "A little wine would have completed the cure," said Stanley, whose thoughts frequently returned to his case of Madeira left under Barttelot's special care.

Only the Zanzibaris remained troublesome. Remembering their long hunger, they stole every edible they saw. Juma, a sly, handsome, young man, would disappear to return with some such trophy as twenty fine goats. Stanley was annoyed and often quoted the favourite proverb of the industrial age: "Honesty is the best policy." But he found it "useless to reason and expostulate; only downright severity restrained them, and as yet, so fresh were we from the horrors of the forest, that I had not the moral courage to apply the screw of discipline." He silenced his conscience with the thought that some avenging native would probably finish Juma off before long.

The expedition was still wandering without direction. Eventually two natives, a woman and a boy, were captured and asked the way. The terrified couple, who "had never heard of Shakespeare, Milton, or even Her Majesty the Queen", were so anxious to answer Stanley's questions that they "smothered comprehension by voluble talk in their dialect, and so perplexed us that we had recourse to silence and patience".

This unusual expedient put Stanley on the right road at last.

The expedition came to a large village, unusually clean and well-built, that stood among rich plantations. The villagers stood in silent groups over the surrounding hills and Stanley supposed they "had been cowed by exaggerated reports of our power". Unfortunately this was not so. As the men were about to make camp and select a supper from the fowl-runs and orchards, a vicious, defiant shout rang out from the hills. The natives intended war.

Stanley, who had been looking forward to a quiet night, was very annoyed. As his scouts fired shots to clear the way, he hurried the column up to an advantageous position on a hill-top and formed the men into a circle. The natives, crowding below, shouted threats. Four Zanzibaris descended cautiously with rifles raised. Four natives bounded towards them and the Zanzibaris fled. Shrieks of derision followed them. A half-hearted exchange of shots and the theft of a cow, which quickly became roast beef, kept the carriers busy until night-fall.

Very disgruntled, Stanley retired to his tent to read his Bible. He had read it through once in the forest and was back again at Deuteronomy. Brooding upon Moses' words to Joshua: "Be strong and of a good courage; fear not, nor be afraid of them; for the Lord thy God, He it is that doth go with thee; He will not fail thee, nor forsake thee", and thinking with disgust of his cowardly Zanzibaris, he seemed to hear a voice exhort him: "Be strong and of a good courage; fear not, nor be afraid of them." He tells us: "I could almost have sworn I heard the voice. I began to argue with it. Why, do you adjure me to abandon the Mission? I cannot run if I would. To retreat would be far more fatal than advance; therefore your encouragement is unnecessary." It replied, nevertheless: "Be strong and of a good courage. Advance and be confident, for I will give this people and this land unto thee. I will not fail thee nor forsake thee; fear not, nor be dismayed."

Next morning the natives sent overtures of peace and Stanley was obliged to reply, not with fiery words inspired by Moses, but with two yards of cloth and a dozen brass rods. After these gifts had been seized, Stanley was rudely informed that the peace overtures had been a mistake and the natives preferred to fight after all.

One hundred rifles were handed out and Stairs led a fierce attack into the valley. This time the natives fled. The day was spent in skirmishing. Stanley, who decided it would be more cruel than kind to leave the natives in any doubt of his ability to defend himself, burnt every village and hut for miles around. One unhappy cow, burnt with her village, supplied more roast beef. A flock of goats was divided among the men. A few natives, who tried to explain how it had all started, were told that if they wanted peace they could buy it with cattle.

The night was quiet but trouble started again next morning. The natives followed the column shouting: "We will prove to you before night that we are men, and every one of you shall perish to-day." This so exasperated Stanley that he set fire to every sort of dwelling he passed. He observed: "The instant the flames were seen devouring their homes, the fury ceased, by which we learnt that fire had a remarkably sedative influence on their nerves."

Unfortunately the natives still buzzed about the caravan like a swarm of wasps. Stanley tried to experiment by leaving the huts standing. It was ineffectual. This generosity was mistaken for cowardice and he abandoned it. Every few hours the natives had to be frightened off by bursts of rifle fire.

For the last few days the column had been marching up an incline with the expectation of finding the lake in the next valley. At the brow, 5,200 feet above the sea, the men found themselves standing on a plateau. Nothing seemed to lie ahead but miles and miles of table-land which rose to a great height and was lost in cloud. A cry of disappointment arose. The men complained that the lake kept going farther and farther away.

D

Stanley knew it must lie hidden in a rift in the table-land not far distant. He shouted: "Keep your eyes open, boys! You may see the Nyanza any minute now," but this remark "like many others tending to encourage them was received with grunts of unbelief".

Yet the Nyanza was there. Suddenly the land fell sharply down 2,800 feet into an immense valley of grey rock where the lake lay under a grey mist. The men, brought to a standstill, stared in silence. Some minutes passed before they realised they were looking down on to water —then they broke into cheers and shouts. They surrounded Stanley and congratulated him on having "hit the spot so well".

As their enthusiasm grew, his failed. Looking at the lake, he realised it was deserted. No steamer awaited them there. No camp had been pitched on the barren, desolate shore. Not even a canoe broke the waters. Of the few gaunt trees clinging to the lakeside slopes, there was not one big enough to be hollowed into a canoe. The steel boat was at Kilonga-Longa's. What were they going to do now?

The expedition started a long climb down the rock face. The natives followed screaming: "Where will you sleep to-night? Don't you know you are surrounded? We have you now where we wanted you." The men, who had twice put them to flight, answered confidently: "Wherever we sleep, you will not dare to come near; and if you have got us where you wanted us to be, why not come on at once."

The endless threats and shouts of the natives so got on Stanley's nerves that he decided to try and improve relations. When they came upon an old woman cutting fuel, he greeted her with extreme politeness. She replied with such gross and obscene abuse that, profoundly shocked, he continued in a more vengeful state than before. He was rather disconcerted to find the lakeside natives timid and uncommunicative and not giving "a single legitimate excuse to quarrel with them". This produced in him "almost unhappy feelings". He made enquiries about the white Pasha and his steamer, and was told that neither had ever been seen at this end of the lake. The unhappy feelings vanished and Stanley gave way to one of his more memorable fits of indignation.

In his letter sent from Zanzibar, Stanley had told Emin to expect him about August 8th. It is doubtful whether Emin ever received this letter, but, having some knowledge of the west coast route, he had himself calculated that the expedition should arrive about December 15th. It actually arrived on December 14th.

On November 2nd Emin wrote to Felkin: "All well; on best terms with chiefs and people; will be leaving shortly for Kibiro, on east coast of Lake Albert. Have sent reconnoitring party to look for Stanley, which had to return with no news yet. Stanley expected about December 15th. Don't have any doubt about my intentions. I do not want a rescue expedition. Have no fears about me. I have long made up my mind to stay."

Stanley used this letter later as a proof of Emin's indifference to the expedition that had suffered so much to relieve him, and as an excuse for not remaining a short period by the lake. For all Stanley knew, Emin might have been expecting him on August 8th and the governor of a besieged province would have more to do than spend four months coasting the desolate lake-shore. Emin had sent out a party of Egyptians to circumnavigate the lake—which was nearly a hundred miles in length—but these were so afraid of Kabba Rega they did not go far. They had been sent merely as a guard of honour, for Emin, knowing Stanley was bringing the steel boat, had expected the party of officers to continue to Wadelai, some fifteen days' journey from the lake-end. When they did not arrive, Emin set out himself towards the end of January, but by then Stanley had been and gone.

Stanley had ordered the note for retreat on December 15th, the day after the expedition reached the lake. The officers were shocked and grieved to go. He had presented them with a stirring picture of Emin's plight—now they were to desert him because he was not at the lakeside to meet them on the day they arrived four months late. Stanley was determined to go. He explained that as Emin "could not or would not assist in his own relief", "the various matters thrust aside for his sake required immediate attention". To the officers these matters seemed merely incidental to the object of the expedition.

Not only was Stanley's pride injured, there was the question of the ammunition. Only forty-seven cases remained with the advance guard. Stanley reckoned that at the rate he used it, it would take him another twenty-five cases to get the expedition round the shore to Wadelai. If he handed over to Emin, say, twelve cases, he would be left with a bare ten to take him back to Kilonga-Longa's. Then there was the problem of food. The lakeside villages had little to offer. They lived by trading salt for their own needs. The forty carrier-loads of Fortnum & Mason goods especially presented to the expedition for consumption by the lake had been left with Barttelot. Were the column to wait without boat or food until Emin cared to appear, it might starve to death.

Disheartened, it started the 2,800 feet climb back to the table-land. Three stragglers were killed by the natives and the warfare went on. Stanley decided that decisive proof of the column's strength must be given to the natives. When the expedition reached the table-land he selected eighty men and sent them out to collect every cow, sheep and goat on which they could lay their hands. Delighted by this lapse in their leader's principles, they went about this business with a will and returned with a whole herd of cattle. A feast followed.

The move was effective. Next day the natives approached with offers of friendship, merely requiring Stanley to kill the chief who had ordered them to make war. The villages were still deserted. The natives stood silent on the hill-tops. The huts had all been newly built, and as the temperature had fallen to 52°, Stanley thought it a pity there was no excuse for burning them down again. He was particularly irritated when on reaching the prosperous village of Ibwiri at the end of a day's march, it was found that the miserable natives had burnt every hut themselves.

Here Stanley ordered his men to clear the ground. He had decided to put the Pasha from his mind and give himself to a work after his own heart. Here he would build the perfect village and call it Fort Bodo— the "Peaceful Fort".

Chapter Eight

THE PASHA

"Stanley is on the heights of Namasi, awaiting me. My hopes are not rose-coloured but—my resolution is taken; go I will not!"

EMIN: Diary, 27.ix.1889

ON June 23rd, 1887, five days before he left Yambuya, Stanley wrote home that for a few months England need not expect to hear from him. Fifteen months were to pass before, on December 21st, 1888, his next letter arrived home. Meanwhile his death had been reported and denied, and the possibility of his or anyone's surviving such a journey repeatedly debated in the Press. It was rumoured that a fresh expedition was being organised to relieve the relievers.

News of this probable failure was received with delight in Germany, where Britain was now suspected of the worst possible motives for sending such an expedition forth. A Dr. Carl Peters at once planned to organise a rival expedition, a German one, that would have all the imperialistic intentions of which the first was accused.

Stanley gave three months to the building and organising of Fort Bodo. Houses, store-rooms, kitchens and corn-bins were built and whitewashed with a mixture made from wood-ash. Charcoal fires were lit to dry them out. The Ibwiri natives had hidden their corn in the bush. It was discovered and stored in the bins. The stolen herd supplied milk and meat. All would have been well had not nature proved, as usual, vile. Rats ate the corn, bit toes and played over the officers' beds. Mosquitoes, fleas and the noise of lemurs kept everyone awake at night, but these were as nothing compared with the red ants.

The ants arrived in wide, orderly columns, guarded by soldier ants, and ate a path through everything that stood in their way. One such column would attack the kitchens, another the officers' mess, another the huts. Their coming would be announced by a rustle of movement as rats, mice, beetles, crickets and even snakes fled before them. Any creature too slow or caught asleep would be devoured to the bones. It was rumoured that a man unconscious from drink or illness would suffer the same fate. At night they would eat a way through the roofs and, dropping to the beds, would awaken sleepers with hundreds of venomous bites. The men screamed, danced and writhed with pain. Later the burning itch of the bites would give way to agonising pustules. The only effective safeguard against the ants was to place burning embers in their path.

The natives were equally trying. They planted poisoned skewers in the paths, blew poisoned darts from the trees and stole anything left for a moment unguarded.

Stairs, with 100 Zanzibaris, returned for the men left at Kilonga-Longa's camp. He found twelve had died—nine of them from starvation—and the rest were little better than skeletons. Those who could have been allowed to work for a wage of three heads of corn a day. The others had had to crawl about in search of herbs. If one were found stealing he was flogged or speared.

Parke and Nelson had been treated with little more consideration than were the men. Nelson, very ill on his arrival, had tried to win the sympathy of the chiefs by giving them gifts to the value of £75. When they had received everything, they told him no provision had been made for him and they could give him nothing. The officers and their boys were allowed a ration of three cups of meal every eight days. They bartered all their personal possessions for food but refused to part with the ammunition. The Manyuema had hoped to starve them into surrendering it, but they had slept with it between them. When they limped, shrivelled and bent, into Fort Bodo, they brought it with them intact save for two boxes of cartridges and a rifle that had been stolen.

On the evening of their return, a meeting was called to discuss the next move. Stanley had suddenly become concerned about Barttelot and Jameson, and he planned now to go in search of them. The others urged him first to contact Emin. They came at last to a compromise. Stairs was to return as far as Ugarrowwa's with two couriers who would continue eastwards from there with letters and a map of the route for Barttelot. The others would wait for Stairs until the end of March; then, if he were not returned, they would attempt to find Emin.

Stanley called the men and described to them the frightful sufferings of poor Barttelot and his disabled carriers, who must, he thought, be by now in the worst depths of the forest. Who would return to put a letter into his hands and earn a reward of £10?

The volatile Zanzibaris were deeply affected. Fifty of them rushed to the front, boasting of their courage and fitness for the expedition. They stood, grinning at the bantering criticism of the others, while Stanley selected twenty of the strongest. Next day Stairs and his party set out.

Stanley, the hardiest although the oldest, having leisure to feel the result of long privation, now collapsed. For a month he lay in his hut suffering from gastritis and an abscess. During his convalescence he sat in a deck-chair in the sunlight and watched the amazing rapidity of the corn's growth and observed with contentment the regulated life of the fort.

By the end of March he was recovered and restless again. Stairs had not returned. Stanley decided to set out again on the fortnight's journey to the lake. Before leaving Fort Bodo he induced the natives, still silent and watchful on the hills, to pay the camp a visit. Explanations resulted. The natives had mistaken them for Kabba Rega's men. Stanley now learnt that Emin, "the bearded one", had visited the southern end of the lake in February. He had enquired for his "white brother" and had left for him a package with the chief of the village called Kavalli's.

The next day Stanley gave audience to all the native princes, chiefs and warriors of the district. Sitting in his chair from morning to night he declared himself "a martyr to the cause of human brotherhood". Jephson was chosen to go through a ceremony of blood-brotherhood.

Although the natives were as eager for peace as anyone, they haggled over the terms for hours. In exchange for a valuable rug, some brass wire and ivory horns, they would agree to give only a calf, fifteen goats, a kid and two hens. Worse than all this was the fact that one chief, who made no gift at all, was swaggering about in the cloth with which Stanley had parted on a memorable occasion four months before. There was, however, one moment during the day that must have been delightful—when a native chief saw what no one else in the district had ever seen before, his own face in a mirror.

One hundred and fifty-seven natives led a party consisting of Stanley, Nelson, Jephson, 126 men and the steel boat, to Kavalli's. There the handsome young chief greeted them with friendship and handed over the package from Emin as though fulfilling a mission of the greatest secrecy and importance.

Stanley read:

DEAR SIR,

Rumours having been afloat of white men having made their apparition somewhere south of this lake, I have come here in quest of news. A start to the furthest end of the lake, which I could reach by steamer, has been without success, the people being greatly afraid of Kabba Rega's people, and their chiefs being under instructions to conceal whatever they know.

To-day, however, has arrived a man from Chief Mpigwa, of Nyamsassi country, who tells me that a wife of the said chief had seen you at Undussuma, her birthplace, and that his chief volunteers to send a letter of mine to you. I send, therefore, one of our allies, Chief Mogo, with the messenger to Chief Mpigwa's, requesting him to send Mogo and this letter, as well as an Arabic one, to you, or to retain Mogo and send the letter ahead.

Be pleased, if this reaches you, to rest where you are, and to inform me by letter, or one of your people, of your wishes. I could easily come to Chief Mpigwa, and my steamer and boats would bring you here. At the arrival of your letter or man, I shall at once start for Nyamsassi, and from there we could concert our further designs.

Beware of Kabba Rega's men! He has expelled Captain Casati.

Believe me, dear Sir, to be

Yours very faithfully,

(Signed) DR. EMIN

Tunguru (Lake Albert)
25.iii.1888

When the letter was translated to the Zanzibaris they went mad with delight. Stanley, who could always face with equanimity occasions for rejoicing, merely smiled at the idea of waiting five or six weeks at a village in Central Africa until news of his whereabouts should somehow get through to Emin.

In a footnote he tells us: "When, after reaching Zanzibar, I read Emin's letter to the Editor of Petermann's *Mitteilungen* (see No. 4 of the *Gotha Geographical Journal*), dated March 25th, 1888 (the same date that the above letter was written), which concluded with the significant words: "If Stanley does not come soon, we are lost," most curious thoughts came into my mind which the intelligent reader will find no difficulty in guessing. Happily, however, the Pasha kept his own secret until I was far away from Bagamoyo, and I was unable to inquire from him personally what were his motives for not coming to Kavalli, December 14th, 1887, the date he expected us; for remaining silent two months and a half in his own stations after that date, and then writing two such letters as the one above and that to Petermann's Magazine on the same date."

Stanley's reply to the letter was business-like. He repeated the instructions that had been in the letter sent from Zanzibar and told Emin to come at once with supplies to the southern end of the lake. Jephson was sent off in the steel boat to deliver this reply.

Jephson took with him a picked crew that carried the boat with some difficulty down the drop to the shore and launched it. A bodyguard of Zanzibaris shoved Jephson and his crew far out into the water, then stood knee-deep waving them good-bye. A breeze blew. The early sun glittered on the ripples. The rowers, pulling with unusual energy, suddenly burst into song. Great herds of hippopotami played in the inlets of the lake. On the shore the natives peered wonderingly from behind bushes.

Jephson, who kept a diary, noted that, dependent on himself for the first time in Africa, he got on very well with the Zanzibaris. He observed the natives, too, and described them—"a villainous-looking old fellow", "a queer-looking, ragged fellow", "a nice-looking young fellow" and so on.

At different villages around the lake he heard that Emin and his steamer had been seen only two months before. Thus encouraged, Jephson hurried on—eating dried fish for breakfast, watching the graceful, white-fringed, black monkeys that swung on the shore-side trees, the red, blue and white kingfishers that skimmed the waters, the icy cascades tumbling into the warm lake and the baboons crooking up their tails to display sky-blue backsides. He was particularly entranced by the lake under moonlight.

News of his approach had preceded him. He arrived at the southern-most station of the province, M'swa, near the shore, a little walled-in collection of huts built on a hill-top. In the valley below, a stream twisted its way gently to the lake. As he landed a guard of honour awaited him, the Khedivial Hymn was played and the station commander, Shukri Aga, dressed in a "long blue uniform tunic with enormous gold naval epaulettes, cherry coloured trousers, high-heeled French boots, large sword and fez" gave him an impressive welcome. A bed, bath, beer and excellent food were ready for him. He felt that here, in the very heart of Africa, he had returned to civilisation.

D*

Emin himself was at Tunguru, a day's journey farther on, and Jephson wanted to go there. Shukri Aga advised that instead news of Jephson's arrival be sent to Emin, who would immediately start for M'swa. Someone said: "The Pasha won't sleep much to-night when he hears you are here."

Two days later the steamer *Khedive* was seen rounding the headland. The soldiers were all turned out, the officers put on their best uniforms and the little cannon waited open-mouthed to fire its salute. Jephson, with his crew and his enormous Egyptian flag, marched down to the shore to await Emin's arrival. Evening fell. It was almost dark before the governor was landed and came running with hands outstretched to welcome this arrival from the outside world.

Of this meeting Emin, on April 27th, wrote in his diary: "It was dark and I could scarcely distinguish a man, still very young, who was waiting for me on the shore. Assembled behind him were his Zanzibaris, keeping up a crackling rifle fire. Going to the station, we remained chatting together till nine. The expedition must have undergone awful sufferings."

Jephson wrote of Emin: "Again and again he repeated words of welcome and cordial greeting as he held both my hands in his. I should not have recognised him from the picture and description Dr. Felkin had given of him. Instead of the "tall man, of a military appearance", I saw a small, wiry, neat, but most unmilitary-looking man, with unmistakable German politeness of manner. . . . When the greetings were over, Emin put his hand on my shoulder in a fatherly manner, and we walked up to the station together, followed by all the officials. We sat outside talking in the bright moonlight, and it was late before Emin retired to read the letter I had brought him from Stanley. He told me we could not start for the south end of the lake for two days, as it would take the whole day to collect wood for the steamer.

Next morning Emin produced a cigar. It had been given him by Junker three years before and treasured for such an occasion as this. He and Jephson smoked half each.

Jephson was delighted by Emin. "Emin then took out his note-book which, like everything he had, was a pattern of neatness, and insisted on my telling him of my wants. With a good deal of hesitation and some shyness at begging in this wholesale manner, I told him some salt, soap, a note-book, and a little oil would be most acceptable, all of which things he wrote down, grumbling all the time at the smallness of my demands. He enumerated several things he could give me, and seemed to take the greatest pleasure in being able to give them. His kindness was overwhelming, and evidently thoroughly genuine. It was such a pleasure to me to get someone quite new to talk to, especially such a clever, intelligent man, whose conversation must at all times be deeply interesting."

When they started off in the steamer they took with them milch cows, goats, sheep and chickens, and a hold full of grain—supplies for Stanley and his men.

Ten days after Jephson's departure, Stanley sighted a steamer with boats in tow. That evening the flotilla anchored opposite Kavalli's. The Pasha had arrived.

The Zanzibaris rushed wildly down to the shore carrying torches of dry grass. They fired their rifles in welcome with such vigour that the Sudanese soldiers on board, mistaking them for Kabba Rega's men, fired back. Fortunately no one was hurt and the spirits of the Zanzibaris remained undamped as Emin, followed by Jephson and Casati, walked into the camp to meet Stanley.

Chapter Nine

STANLEY AND EMIN

"Emin has all the signs of intelligence and ability and yet I suspect that he is not forceful, or to put it otherwise, not strong in character. He speaks well, wisely, with a resonant voice, yet when I turn his attention to business his behaviour betrays an unsettled state of mind."

STANLEY: Letters

STANLEY'S letter describing the condition of the expedition had filled Emin and his followers with some misgiving. They had been waiting for relief, now they realised they were being called upon to give it. Emin, with his usual courtesy, however, greeted Stanley enthusiastically:

"I owe you a thousand thanks, Mr. Stanley; I really do not know how to express my thanks to you."

Stanley, who had been standing rigidly in the midst of his men while Emin's party came up from the boat, now bowed gravely: "Ah, you are Emin Pasha," he said. "Do not mention thanks, but come in and sit down. It is so dark out here we cannot see one another."

In a lecture Stanley later said: "Naturally I searched by the light of the torches for a person of heroic size." He saw instead "a small spare figure in a well kept fez and a clean suit of snowy cotton drilling, well-ironed and of perfect fit. A dark grizzled beard bordered a face of a magyar cast, though a pair of spectacles lent it somewhat an Italian or Spanish appearance. There was not a trace on it of ill-health or anxiety; it rather indicated good condition of body and peace of mind."

If Emin were ever given a chance to explain how he had come by the new clothing worn by himself and his men, Stanley did not think the explanation worth repeating. Indeed, he barely managed to hide his annoyance that Emin looked better fed and better dressed than his rescuer, but produced five half-pint bottles of champagne, in which toasts were drunk.

Stanley admitted that he found it difficult to resist Emin's kindness and gentle attentiveness. The Pasha spoke in exact, effortless English and discoursed charmingly on a number of subjects. His manner brought to their savage surroundings the cultivated atmosphere of a salon. This, thought Stanley, would be all very well if they had time to waste, but he had supposed Emin to be in extreme need. Besides, he had not come all this way to rescue a mere botanist.

Stanley, a short man himself, found it hardest to forgive Emin's undeserved reputation for height. A pair of trousers had been bought in Cairo for a governor said to be six feet tall. Stanley ordered six inches to be cut off the legs.

Next morning Stanley and his officers made a return visit to Emin on board the *Khedive*. A detachment of Emin's Sudanese soldiers —enormous, sleek men in elegant uniforms—paraded on the shore and saluted with music their tattered and crippled rescuers.

The officers breakfasted on millet cake fried in honey and glasses of new milk. Emin, leisurely and untroubled in manner, well-dressed and well-fed, continued to entertain them with pleasant conversation. Stanley became very restless. He felt the situation to be absurd. He had spent fifteen months, suffering hunger and hardship, his men dying, to rescue a man in desperate straits, and now the expedition was being entertained as though it were paying a fashionable visit.

Stanley saw Emin as lacking not only in inches but in most of the qualities with which his imagination had endowed him. He overheard him making a request to one of his officers in a manner that could only be described as courteous, indeed "rather pleasantly, I thought". Stanley commented: "It is certainly not like my governor, vice-king, or leader of men, to talk in that strain to a subordinate."

He broke into all this pleasant talk with a straight question: "Exactly when would Emin and his men be ready to return to the coast with the expedition?"

Emin was stunned. He had been waiting for Stanley to hand over the "ample means" to protect the province which the expedition was said to be bringing. He also expected offers from the British Government or a British company in whose name he would hold and develop the country. He had no intention of leaving it—but how could he say this without upsetting his rescuer? Stanley presented him with thirty-one cases of cartridges. He had asked for a regiment and a thousand cases of cartridges.

Stanley's attitude seemed to imply that, as this ammunition would not enable him to hold the province, he had better prepare himself quickly to abandon it. The question was—how soon would he be ready?

Emin became vague. He had been charmingly informative a short while before, talking of the flora and fauna of Equatoria; of the Albert

Edward Nyanza that received all streams at the extremity of the south-western or left Nile basins, and discharged them as the White Nile into the Albert Nyanza; and of the Albert Nyanza that was rapidly receding, so that Emin, who had seen it first seven or eight years ago, could point out headlands, occupied by his own stations and by native villages, that had earlier been islands. Now, on the much more important question of his own safety, he was dumb.

Stanley became very irritated. After his terrible journey, was he to receive no more appreciation and co-operation than this? Emin found it impossible to explain that the arrival of the long-awaited expedition that was to save them all would probably prove to be for the province a last disaster. He knew how quickly it would get round among his demoralised officials that a handful of tattered, half-starved, exhausted men had brought no more than thirty-one cases of cartridges, two bales of spoilt cloth and a letter from the Khedive. True, other men and ammunition had been left at Yambuya, but it would take Stanley eleven months to get there and back.

Stanley, watching Emin read the letters he had brought, noted in him a growing disappointment. He commented: "Those who are interested in motives will not find it difficult to understand the apparent hesitation and indecision that he seemed to labour under when questioned by me as to his intentions. For nothing could have been more unexpected and unwelcome than the official letters from the Khedive and Nubar Pasha, etc." He did not know that Emin had already received from Nubar Pasha an order to abandon the province, so that disappointment had been suffered long before. He described Emin when pressed for an answer as having an infuriating trick of tapping his knee and looking up at the tent-roof with a "We shall see" air. Stanley explained to him at some length Egypt's reasons for abandoning the province, and reports the following conversation:

EMIN: I can see clearly the difficulty Egypt is in as regards retention of these provinces, but I do not see so clearly my way of returning. The Khedive has written to me that the pay of myself, officers and men will be settled by the Paymaster-General if we return to Egypt, but if we stay here we do so at our own risk and on our own responsibility, and that we cannot expect further aid from Egypt. Nubar Pasha has written to me a longer letter, but to the same effect. Now, I do not call these instructions. They do not tell me I must quit, but they leave me a free agent.

STANLEY: I will supplement these letters with my own positive knowledge, if you will permit me, as the Khedive and Nubar Pasha are not here to answer for themselves. Dr. Junker arrived in Egypt telling the world that you were in great distress for want of ammunition but that you had a sufficient quantity to defend your position for a year or perhaps eighteen months, providing no determined attack was made on you, and you were not called upon to make a prolonged resistance; that you had defended the Equatorial provinces, so far successfully; that you would continue to do so to the uttermost of your ability, until you should receive orders from your government to do otherwise; that you loved the country and people greatly; that the country was in a prosperous state—quiet and contented—possessed of almost everything required to maintain it in this happy condition; that you would not like to see all your work thrown away, but that you would much prefer that Egypt should retain these provinces, or failing Egypt, some European power able and willing to continue your work. Did Dr. Junker report you correctly, Pasha?

EMIN: Yes, he did.

STANLEY: Well, then, the first idea that occurred to the minds of the Egyptian officials upon hearing Dr. Junker's report was, that no matter what instructions you received, you would be disinclined to leave your province, therefore the Khedive says that if you remain here, you do so upon your own responsibility, and at your own risk, and you are not to expect further aid from Egypt. Our instructions are to carry a certain quantity of ammunition to you, and say to you, upon your obtaining it: "Now we are ready to guide and assist you out of Africa, if you are willing to accompany us, and we shall be delighted to have the pleasure of your company; but if you decline going, our mission is ended." Let us suppose the latter, that you prefer remaining in Africa. Well, you are still young, only forty-eight; your constitution is still good. Let us say you will feel the same vigour for five, ten, even fifteen years longer; but the infirmities of age will creep on you, and your strength will fade away. Then you will begin to look doubtingly upon the future prospect, and mayhap suddenly resolve to retire before it is too late. Some route will be chosen—the Mombuttu route, for instance—to the sea. Say that you reach the Congo, and are nearing civilisation; how will you maintain your people, for food must then be bought for money or goods? And supposing you reach the sea, what will you do then? Who will assist you to convey your people to their homes? You rejected Egypt's help when it was offered to you, and, to quote the words of the Khedive: "You are not to expect further aid from Egypt." If you stay here during life, what becomes of the province afterwards? Your men will fight among themselves for supremacy, and involve all in one common ruin. These are grave questions, not to be hastily answered. If your province were situated within reasonable reach of the sea, whence you could be furnished with means to maintain your position, I should be one of the last to advise you to accept the Khedive's offer, and should be most active in assisting you with suggestions as to the means of maintenance; but here, surrounded as this lake is by powerful kings and·war-like people on all sides, by such a vast forest on the west, and by the frantic followers of the Mahdi on the north, were I in your place, I would not hesitate one moment what to do.

According to Casati, Stanley did not mention the fact that the Khedive admitted Emin was at liberty to remain and govern the province alone. Casati said that Stanley, unable to hand over the relief stores and ammunition left with Barttelot, merely insisted that Emin must leave the province. Had Emin been capable of explaining how his hopes had grown during the months of waiting; how Felkin's talk of an offer from a company had led him to see himself an independent governor developing and protecting an important exporting state with a direct, guarded route to the coast; had he explained the reason for his bitter disappointment—these two men, temperamentally so opposed, might have come to an understanding. As it was, Emin, with all his fears of seeming discourteous, ungrateful or critical of Stanley's waste of so much of the ammunition, could say nothing. He knew that his people that had been kept in subjection by the threat of the arrival of a strong, well-armed expedition to support the governor, might react with some violence to the suggestion of evacuation. Yet he knew it must now be considered. He said:

What you say is true, but we have such a large number of women and children, probably 10,000 people altogether! How can they all be brought out of here? We shall want a great many carriers.

STANLEY: Carriers for what?

EMIN: For the women and children. You surely would not leave them, and they cannot travel.

STANLEY: The women must walk; for such children as cannot walk, they will be carried on donkeys, of which you say you have many. Your people cannot travel far during the first month, but little by little they will get accustomed to it. Our women on my second expedition crossed Africa; your women, after a little while, will do quite as well.

EMIN: They will require a vast amount of provisions for the road.

STANLEY: Well, you have a large number of cattle, some hundreds, I believe. Those will furnish beef. The countries through which we pass must furnish grain and vegetable food. And when we come to countries that will accept pay for food, we have means to pay for it, and at Msalala we have another stock of goods ready for the journey to the coast.

EMIN: Well, well. We will defer further talk of it till to-morrow

On May 1st Emin wrote in his diary: "I do not want to come to any conclusion until I have heard what my people have to say."

He brooded on the difficulty of evacuating a whole population, many members of which were unfit to face such a journey. How, he wondered, were the herds of cattle to be got across the lake in his two small steamers? how were they to be fed? Profoundly unwilling to leave the province, he sought delay by dwelling on every obstacle he could imagine.

On May 4th he wrote: "I endeavoured to convince Stanley that if I had found support and encouragement, it would never have entered my mind to go away from here."

Still the evacuation had to be faced. The whole of the Sudan must have heard rumours of the great expedition that was bringing an army and unlimited ammunition to save the Equatorial province. The truth would reach Karamalla's spies within a few days. For how much longer would the attack be postponed? Yet Emin still prevaricated as though hoping for a reprieve. He felt that Stanley must have brought some sort of offer to justify Felkin's enthusiastic promise of one. He still waited for Stanley to mention it.

Stanley would have been glad could he have urged a food shortage to hasten Emin's decision, but there was none. The expedition was being royally provided for.

A further conversation was reported in Stanley's own language:

EMIN: What you told me last night led me to think that it is best we should retire from Africa. The Egyptians are willing to go I know. There are about fifty men of them besides women and children. Of those there is no doubt, and even if I stayed here I should be glad to be rid of them, because they undermine my authority, and nullify all my endeavours for retreat. When I informed them that Khartoum had fallen and Gordon Pasha was slain they always told the Nubians that the story was concocted by me, and that some day we should see the steamers ascend the river for their relief. But of the regulars, who compose two battalions, I am extremely doubtful. They have led such a free and happy life here, that they would demur at leaving a country where they enjoy luxuries such as they cannot hope for in Egypt. They are married, and besides, each soldier has his harem; most of the irregulars would doubtless retire and follow me. Now supposing the regulars refused to leave, you can imagine my position would be a difficult one. Would I be right in leaving them to their fate? Would it not be consigning them all to ruin? I should have to leave them their arms and ammunition, and on my retiring all recognised authority and discipline would be at an end. There would presently rise dispute and factions would be formed. The more ambitious would aspire to be chiefs by force, and from rivalries would spring hate and mutual slaughter, involving all in one common fate.

STANLEY: It is a terrible picture you have drawn, Pasha. Nevertheless, bred as I have been to obey orders, no matter what may happen to others, the line of your duty, as a faithful officer of the Khedive, seems to me to be clear. All you have to do, according to my idea, is to read the Khedive's letter to your troops, and ask those willing to depart with you to stand on one side, and those preparing to remain to stand on the other, and prepare the first for immediate departure, while to the latter you can leave what ammunition and guns you can spare. If those who remain number three-fourths or three-fifths of your force, it does not at all matter to anyone what becomes of them, for it is their own choice, nor does it absolve you personally from the line of conduct duty to the Khedive directs.

EMIN: That is very true, but supposing the men surround me and detain me by force?

STANLEY: That is unlikely, I should think, from the state of discipline I see among your men; but, of course, you know your own men best.

Stanley now suggested that Emin should ask Casati what he wanted to do.

Casati's answer did not advance things much further. He said: "If the governor, Emin, goes, I go; if he stays, I stay."

"Well," said Stanley, "I see, Pasha, that in the event of your staying, your responsibility will be great, for you involve Captain Casati in your own fate."

Emin laughed at this remark but Casati answered it seriously: "Oh, I absolve Emin Pasha from all responsibility connected with me, for I am governed by my own choice entirely."

"May I suggest then, Pasha," said Stanley, "if you elect to remain here, that you make your will?"

"Will! What for?"

"To dispose of your pay, of course, which must by this time be considerable. Eight years I believe you said? Or perhaps you meditate leaving it to Nubar Pasha?"

"I give Nubar Pasha my love," said Emin. "There can be only about two thousand odd pounds due. What is such a sum to a man about to be shelved? I am now forty-eight and one of my eyes is utterly gone. When I get to Egypt I will be received with sugared phrases! and then bowed out and shelved on a small pension. And all I have to do is to seek out some corner of Cairo or Stamboul for a final resting-place. A fine prospect truly!"

Casati, who spoke no English, had been urging Emin to make clear to Stanley that one battalion had revolted and the other might follow suit at any time. Emin could not bring himself to show Stanley of all people how little prestige remained to him. He had hoped the people would gain confidence in the expedition if Stanley visited the nearer stations, but Stanley refused to do so. He said he had no time for a trip of that sort.

Emin at last gave as his decision that if his people were willing to leave the province, he would go with them; if not, he would remain. Stanley agreed to send Jephson back with Emin, and while they were discovering the will of the people, he would return through the forest to find what was delaying the rear column. Emin offered him carriers to replace the Zanzibaris who had died. The steamer went to fetch these men; Stanley resigned himself to taking a rest.

He put up as best he could with Emin's conversation, but his temper was short with the carriers. When three of them, who had disobeyed orders and raided a village, returned to camp with spear wounds, he told them they could cure themselves for he would do nothing for them.

Emin and Stanley visited each other's tents and exchanged gifts. Emin was always interesting. He told how the natives hung baskets in isolated trees where bees would be likely to settle. When the baskets were full of honey the natives smoked out the bees and took the honey-comb. Until now the wax had been wasted, but he had hoped that when a road opened to the coast, it could be sold in large quantities. Then there were the hides of the cattle slaughtered for food—these would be sufficient to fill the Khartoum markets; and furs of all kinds, coffee, nutmegs, gum arabic. . . .

Casati, with Emin as interpreter, told the story of his misadventures in Unyoro. Stanley, who had disliked Casati on sight, was annoyed to hear that among the papers pillaged from Casati's house had been letters addressed to himself which Casati had been keeping for him. He seethed with contempt for such a man. As they had no common language, they could not by conversation bridge their mutual antipathy.

Casati, intimidated by the fierce little Welshman, hid behind Emin but did his best to influence Emin against Stanley so the situation would be as complicated as possible. Emin, generous as ever, appraised the best in Stanley's character—his competence, his courage, his remarkable ability for getting things done, and the fact that when everything was going well he could be very pleasant.

Seven days had passed since their first meeting when Emin said: "I feel convinced that my people will never go to Egypt. But Mr. Jephson and the Sudanese whom you are kind enough to leave with me will have an opportunity to see and hear for themselves. And I would wish you would write out a proclamation or message which may be read to the soldiers, in which you will state what your instructions are, and say that you await their decision. From what I know of them I feel sure they will never go to Egypt. The Egyptians, of course, will go, but they are few in number, and certainly of no use to me or to anyone else."

"This," Stanley noted in his diary, "has been the most definite answer I have received yet. I have been awaiting a positive declaration of this kind before venturing upon any further proposition to him. Now, to fulfil my promise to various parties, though they appear somewhat conflicting, I have two other propositions to make. My first duty is to the Khedive, of course; and I should be glad to find the Pasha conformable, as an obedient officer who kept his post so gallantly until ordered to withdraw. By this course he would realise the ideal governor his letters created in my mind. Nevertheless he has but to speak positively to induce me to assist him in any way to the best of my power."

Poor Emin, who had been waiting seven days on tenter-hooks to hear of such an offer, now had revealed to him:

"In the event of your resolve to stay in Equatoria because of your attachment to your troops and province, I have been requested to offer you the post of governor here, with the rank of general, pay of £1,500 and a subsidy of £12,000 per annum."

Emin, beside himself with relief, still kept his head sufficiently to ask: "Under whom?"

"Under Leopold II, King of the Belgians."

It was against such a proposal as this that Felkin had warned him. After a pause of some moments, he replied: "No, Mr. Stanley. I have served the Crescent flag for thirty years and cannot all at once change it for the blue flag and golden star."

"Well spoken, Pasha. You have quite made up your mind upon the subject?"

"Quite, and we will say no more about it."

"Very good, Pasha. Now listen. I have one more proposition for you. Cast your eyes upon that letter which the Foreign Office handed to me among others before I left, in order that I might thoroughly understand your position. In this letter you offer your province and your services to the British."

Emin gazed with dismay at his own letter written in 1886 to Sir John Kirk offering Equatoria to England. "They had no right to publish my private letters," he said. "What will the Egyptian Government think of my conduct? It is a shame."

"I beg your pardon, Pasha," replied Stanley. "These letters are not public. They are printed for those they were intended for." He added that in any case there was no harm in publishing the letters. The Egyptian Government was unable to hold the province; the British Government did not want it. Until Unyoro and Uganda could be subdued, Equatoria was a useless possession. It was just 500 miles too far inland to be of any use to anyone. Only Leopold, for reasons known only to himself and Stanley, seemed to have any interest in it, but as Emin declined to serve the Congo State—well, there was one more proposition that Stanley could make.

Emin asked hopefully what that might be.

Stanley answered: "That you take service with a British company. I propose that you remove from the province and accompany me to Kavirondo, on the north-east of the Victoria Nyanza. I will undertake that the natives receive you and your troops. We shall assist to build a fort or two, and after seeing you all comfortable and provided for, I shall hasten to the coast, send you a caravan with further supplies, and will then proceed to England to form a company, which shall accept you and your troops with the same pay and rank as you possess now; and I feel sure I shall succeed."

Emin was delighted: "Ah!" he said, "that is something like an offer. Indeed, I am most grateful because it is precisely what I should wish, and meets every objection; for my troops only, so far as I know, dislike going to Egypt, and if they are contented with it, I shall be well pleased. But can you guarantee this?"

"No; I can guarantee nothing. I can only promise that I will do my best to make the project a success, and the conditions mentioned will be included."

Emin's vagueness had gone. He discussed the project excitedly. It was decided that Stanley should conduct Emin and his people to the north-east corner of Lake Victoria, where they would settle in a series of new stations established on the road to Mombasa and be of use to the British East African Company. The company would, Stanley knew, be glad of Emin's service. Emin, flattered, relieved and soaring to the peak of one of his optimistic moods, said again and again how delighted he was with the scheme. He scarcely bothered to consider its problems. Here at last was compromise, the solution of an impossible situation.

A few days later two men arrived from the lake-island station of Tunguru and asked for audience with Stanley. These were Achmet Mahmoud, a one-eyed clerk who had formerly been Emin's secretary, and Captain Abdul Wahab Effendi, formerly Emin's adjutant. Both these men were notorious trouble-makers and had been exiled from Egypt for rebellion. Stanley knew nothing of their history and later described them as Emin's commander of troops and head clerk. He agreed to see them, and the moment they were seated in his tent they began to pour out abuse of Emin. The governor was, they said, a liar and father of lies.

Stanley knew enough of Egyptian veracity to remain unimpressed. He asked them did Emin know their opinion of him. They answered: "Oh no, he would cut our heads off if he knew that we are telling you this; but we all want to leave this accursed country. We are tired of our life here. The Pasha will perhaps tell you differently, but he has the most crooked ways with him, and none of us can believe a word he says.

All he cares for are beetles and butterflies," and so they continued for about an hour.

Stanley decided to tell Emin nothing of this visit, but he began to suspect that all was not well within Equatoria. There was, he said, something about it all he could not fathom. As for the Pasha—the man was incomprehensible.

Chapter Ten

IN SEARCH OF THE REAR COLUMN

"A Sir Perceval in search of the Holy Grail could not have met with hotter opposition."

STANLEY: Letter to his publisher.

THE camp was disturbed by a series of storms. Rain clouds burst over the lake. Lightning dipped from a black sky while the black waters rolled foaming upon the lake-shore. The wind wrecked everything. The rain cut through the thickest canvas and the tents collapsed and floated in water.

When the *Khedive* returned, Emin hurried on board and came back with gifts for everyone. Stanley was given a pair of strong shoes, a pound of "Honeydew" tobacco and a bottle of pickles; Jephson a pair of drawers, a shirt and a singlet; Parke a jersey, singlet and pair of drawers. There were bananas, oranges, water-melons, onions, salt and honey for all.

"These gifts," commented Stanley, "reveal that he was not in the extreme distress we had imagined, and that there was no necessity for the advance to have pressed forward so hurriedly."

But that was not all. The steamers went on a second journey and returned with a ten-gallon demijohn of raki from Emin's distillery, more fruit, six sheep, four goats and a donkey each for Stanley and Parke. The Pasha was so delighted at being able to make these gifts that he failed to notice how coldly Stanley received them.

"We," said Stanley in his diary, "left all our comforts and reserves of clothing behind at Yambuya, that we might press on to the rescue of one whom we imagined was distressed not only for want of means of defence from enemies, but in want of clothing."

The *Khedive* had brought a number of carriers, men from the district of Madi. These were handed over to Stanley and by May 20th all was ready for the return journey. On the night before they left the lakeside, the Zanzibaris entertained the officers to a farewell dance with all their usual warm-hearted excitement. Stanley commented morosely: "It is certain that some of them will take their last look at the Pasha to-morrow."

The march began at dawn. Emin walked some miles along the road

114

with Stanley before they parted, the one to return with Jephson to the province, the other to seek Barttelot. Many months were to pass before they met again.

Almost before the Pasha was out of sight, twenty-four of the Madis broke from the column and disappeared rapidly homewards. Fourteen men were sent back to tell Emin what had happened. A little later eighty-nine Madis deserted in a body, first discharging arrows at the column's rear. Parke fired back, killing one Madi and sending the others off in a wild flight. More men were sent back to tell Emin.

It was to be an eventful day. Before camp was reached Stanley's attention was drawn by his boy Sali to a salt-covered mountain. He looked to the horizon that for months had been lost in mist, and saw an oddly shaped cloud of a pure silver colour, its base of so dark a blue he feared another tornado was coming. As he gazed at it, he realised it was not a cloud but a mountain. It must be the fabled Ruwenzori, "the Cloud King", that the natives said was crowned with metal.

In December Parke and Jephson believed they had glimpsed a snow-topped mountain, but Stanley had told them they must be mistaken. Snow could not lie on these low ranges.

Stanley was very excited. Here, of tremendous size, probably no more than seventy miles distant, was the disappearing mountain that, located since Homer's time, was always lost again because so seldom seen. He determined to locate and map it. He later claimed to have seen it first in December 1887, at the time when it had actually been seen by Parke and Jephson. He noted all those who had had no glimpse of it failed where he had succeeded. Sir Samuel Baker, who had discovered the Albert Nyanza in 1867, admitted that he and his wife had failed to see the mountain during their years in the district. Others who had failed were Gessi Pasha, first circumnavigator of the lake; Mason Bey, who in 1877 closely investigated the lake-shore; Emin and Casati.

Actually Casati, in a book published a year after Stanley's *Darkest Africa*, claimed he had seen the mountain early in 1887 and gives the native description of it as a mountain of measureless height and dreadful cold where certain death awaited an intruder. The highest peaks were said to be inhabited by a powerful, malignant spirit always enveloped in cloud, while on the lower slopes dwelt the Vacongio, a fierce people with white skin and a peculiar language.

As Stanley observed it, the mountain disappeared and did not reappear until April 1st, 1889.

Stanley noted: "It is quite a mysterious fact that from the localities reached by Sir Samuel Baker, Ruwenzori ought to have been as visible as St. Paul's dome from Westminster Bridge. And any person steaming round the Lake Albert, as Gessi Pasha and Mason Bey did, would be within easy view of the snow mountain—provided, of course, that they were not obscured by the dense clouds and depths of mist under which for about 300 days of the year the great mountain range veils its colossal crown." He then wrote to Emin announcing the discovery and Emin replied with all the enthusiasm of his generous heart:

"Allow me to be the first to congratulate you on your most splendid discovery of a snow-clad mountain. We will take it as a good omen for further directions on our road to Victoria. I propose to go out on your track to-day or to-morrow, just to have a look at this giant." And in a further letter: "I shall try hard to get a glimpse of the new snow mountain, as well from here as from some other points I propose to visit. It is wonderful to think how, wherever you go, you distance your predecessors by your discoveries. . . . Let me another time thank you for the kindness and forbearance you have shown me in our mutual relations. If I cannot find adequate word to express what moves me in this instant you will forgive me. I lived too long in Africa for not becoming somewhat negrofied."

Eighty-two fresh Madis were fetched by the *Khedive* and dispatched after Stanley. Each Madi was put in charge of a Zanzibari, so that desertion became difficult.

Stanley, with the aid of Kavalli and his men, had to ward off further attacks by the natives. After a decisive victory Kavalli's warriors celebrated with a phalanx dance, which Stanley—who dismissed most African dances as "rude buffoonery"—found sufficiently to his taste to describe:

"The phalanx stood still with spears grounded until, at a signal from the drums, Katto's deep voice was heard breaking out into a wild triumphant song or chant, and at a particular uplift of note raised his spear, and at once rose a forest of spears high above their heads, and a mighty chorus of voices responded, and the phalanx was seen to move forward, and the earth around my chair, which was at a distance of fifty yards from the foremost line, shook as though there was an earthquake. I looked at the feet of the men and discovered that each man was forcefully stamping the ground, and taking forward steps not more than six inches long, and it was in this manner that the phalanx moved slowly but irresistibly." He went on to describe the flashing spears, "the blades tossed aloft and lowered again to hoarse and exciting thunder of drums", the stamping, the heads rising and falling, the shouts suggesting "quenchless fury, wrath and exterminating war", the low wailing that described war's sorrow, the defiant snorts, the exulting howls, "the proud pulses of triumph". The natives advanced upon his chair and dropped their spears in a thrice-repeated salute, then breaking into a run wheeled round in circles until Stanley was quite bewildered with excitement.

Following this appreciation of the entertainment, he was embarrassed to discover that the victors had taken possession of some fine herds, the property of the defeated. The chief explained that these herds had been brought to him by another tribe that had asked for his protection. He had not had the heart to turn men or beasts away.

Next day the expedition continued to Fort Bodo. In all other districts news passed more rapidly than any runner could carry it. Here an area devastated by the Manyuema drew a belt of silence between north and south. During the sixty-seven days of separation, Stanley had had no news of the camp and no rumours had warned the camp of his coming. But it was still standing. When the expedition fired its rifles, the rifles of Fort Bodo responded at once. The travellers marched in with six head of cattle, a flock of sheep and goats, some loads of native tobacco and four gallons of Emin's home-made whisky. They were very welcome.

Stairs was awaiting Stanley. That evening he gave an account of his journey to Ugarrowwa's with the couriers. He had lost his way on the outward road and wandered for a month in the forest before finding the slavers' settlement. From there the couriers went on in search of Barttelot. Of the men who had been left at Ugarrowwa's, twenty-six had died and the rest were skin and bone, disfigured by sores and grey with disease. Seven were too weak to face the march back to Fort Bodo, but Ugarrowwa refused to keep them any longer and Stairs had to force them to follow him. This seven and seven other carriers died before the fort was reached. Stairs himself, sick with fever and having no one to carry him, marched day after day in a delirium. He struggled on with the rain falling continually, the road a swamp, the sick dying one by one, the stronger ones becoming low-spirited and despairing, and at last, after an absence of seventy-one days, arrived to the bitter disappointment of learning Stanley had left for the lake without him.

So few of the carriers had recovered from their months in the forest that Stanley realised there could be no question of taking the whole expedition back in search of Barttelot. He would have to form a column of Zanzibari volunteers. He mustered the men and delivered to them one of those long speeches he enjoyed so much. Who would return to find the rear column now labouring "under God alone knew what difficulties"? They all knew what treasures of cloth and beads had been left at Yambuya—how could these be better bestowed than upon the tireless, faithful fellows who had taken their master twice to the Nyanza and then back to Barttelot! "I pray you, then, come to my side ye that are willing, and ye that prefer to stay in the fort remain in the ranks!"

The appeal was too much for the Zanzibaris. They leapt to their feet with cries of "To the Major! To the Major!" Even the sick staggered forward to offer themselves for the journey back through the forest to Yambuya. Only six men, hopelessly crippled by ulcers, remained in their places.

"Those who understand men," commented Stanley, "will recognise some human merits exhibited on this occasion, though others may be as blind in perceiving the finer traits in human nature, as there are many utterly unable to perceive in a picture the touches which betray the masterful hand of a great painter, or in a poem the grace and smoothness, combined with vigour and truth, of the true poet."

The chosen men started at once to prepare bags of plantain and cornflour to see them through the famine area. Stanley "had many personal details to attend to, such as repairs of pantaloons, shoes, chair, umbrella, rain-coat, etc."

The fort had been strengthened and made safe from attack. Nelson was still very weak, and he, Stairs and Parke were to be left behind with the sick. Emin had promised to visit the camp within two months and the three officers would then return with him to the lake.

Stanley estimated that his new journey would take about a hundred days each way.

On the evening before his departure, as the officers were gathered in his tent, there was discussed the possible reason for Barttelot's long delay. Stairs ill-advisedly suggested that perhaps he had been held up by the non-arrival of the steamer *Stanley* at Yambuya.

Stanley, very annoyed, replied: "That is rather a cruel suggestion, my dear sir; that is the least I fear, for as well as I was able I provided against that accident. You must know that when the *Stanley* departed from the Yambuya on June 28th, I delivered several letters to the captain of the steamer. One was to my good friend Lieutenant Liebrichts, Governor of Stanley Pool district, charging him, for old friendship's sake, to dispatch the steamer back as soon as possible with our goods and reserve ammunition.

"Another was to Mr. Swinburn, my former secretary, who was the soul of fidelity, to the effect that in case the *Stanley* met with an accident as to prevent her return to Yambuya, he would be pleased to substitute the steamer *Florida* for her, as the owners were business men, and full compensation in cash, which I guaranteed, would find as ready an acceptance with them as profits from the ivory trade. . . ." He continued at length to describe how other letters had been sent and promises made to guard against such a possibility, and "besides, you must remember that both captain and engineer of the *Stanley* were each promised a reward of £50 sterling if they would arrive within reasonable time. Such amounts to poor men are not trifles, and I feel assured that if they have not been prevented by their superiors from fulfilling their promise, all goods and men arrived safely at Yambuya."

"You still think, then," suggested Stairs, "that in some way Major Barttelot is the cause of this delay?"

"Yes," replied Stanley, "he and Tippu-Tib. The latter of course has broken his contract. There is no doubt of that. For if he had joined his 600 carriers, or half that number, with our Zanzibaris, we should have heard of them long ago, either at Ipoto, when you returned there for the boat, or later, when you reached Ugarrowwa's, March 16th this year. The letter of September 18th, 1887, when only eighty-one days absent from Yambuya, and which the Arab promised without delay, would certainly have produced an answer by this if the Major departed from Yambuya. Those carriers, all choice men, well armed, acquainted with the road, dispatched with you to Ugarrowwa's on February 16th, and seen by you safely across the river opposite his station on the 16th of the following month, would surely by this have returned if the rear column was only a few weeks' march from Yambuya; therefore I am positive in my mind that Major Barttelot is in some way or other the cause of the delay."

Stairs, made bold perhaps by Emin's whisky, now began: "Well, I am sure, however you may think the Major is disloyal, I . . ."

"Disloyal!" interrupted Stanley in shocked tones. "Why, whatever put you in mind of that word? Such a word has no connection with any man on this expedition, I hope. Disloyal! Why should anyone be disloyal? And disloyal to whom?"

Stairs, crushed at last, attempted to explain: "Well, not disloyal, but negligent, or backward in pressing on; I feel sure he has done his best."

"No doubt he has done his level best, but as I wrote to him on September 18th, in my letter to be given to him by Ugarrowwa's carriers, it is his 'rashness and inexperience I dread', not his disloyalty or negligence. I fear the effect of indiscriminate punishments on his people has been such that the vicinity of Stanley Falls and the Arabs have proved an irresistible temptation to desert. If our letters miscarry in any way, our long absence—twelve months nearly to this day, and by the time we reach Yambuya fourteen months at least!—will be a theme for all kinds of reports. When the Zanzibaris from Bolobo reached him he ought to have had over 200 carriers. In twelve months—assuming that the goods and men arrived in due date, and that, finding Tippu-Tib had broken faith, he began the move as he promised—he would be at Panga Falls; but if the severe work has demoralised him, and he has demoralised his carriers, well, then, he is stranded far below Panga Falls— probably at Wasp Rapids, probably at Mupé or at Banalya, or at Gwengweré Rapids—with but 100 despairing carriers and his Sudanese, and he is perforce compelled by the magnitude of his task to halt and wait. I have tried every possible solution, and this is the one on which my opinion becomes fixed."

"Do you allow only 100 left?" asked Stairs. "Surely that is very low."

"Why? I estimate his loss at what we have lost—about 50%. We have lost slightly less; for from our original force of 289 souls there are 203 still alive; four at Nyanza, sixty in the fort, 119 going with me, and twenty couriers."

"Yes; but the rear column has not endured a famine such as we have had."

"Nor have they enjoyed the abundance that we have fed upon for the last seven months, therefore we are perhaps equal. But it is useless to speculate further upon these points. The success which was expected from my plans has eluded me. The Pasha never visited the south end of the lake, as I suggested to him in my letter from Zanzibar. This has cost us four months, and of Barttelot there is not a word. Our men have fallen by scores, and wherever I turn there is no comfort to be derived from the prospect. Evil hangs over this forest as a pall over the dead; it is like a region accursed for crimes, whoever enters within its circle becomes subject to Divine wrath. All we can say to extenuate any error that we have fallen into is, that our motives are pure, and that our purposes are neither mercenary nor selfish. Our atonement shall be a sweet offering, the performance of our duties. Let us bear all that may be put upon us like men bound to the sacrifice, without one thought of the results. Each day has its weight of troubles. Why should we think of the distresses of to-morrow? Let me depart from you with the conviction that in my absence you will not swerve from your duty here, and I need not be anxious for you. If the Pasha and Jephson arrive with carriers, it is better for you, for them, and for me that you go; if they do not come, stay here until my return. Give me a reasonable time, over and above the date—December 22nd; then if I return not, consult with your friends, and afterwards with your men, and do what is best and wisest. As for us, we shall march back to the place where Barttelot may be found, even as far as Yambuya, but to no place beyond, though he may have taken everything away with him down the Congo. If he has left Yambuya and wandered far away south-east instead of east, I will follow him up and overtake him, and will cut through the forest in the *most* direct way to Fort Bodo. You must imagine all this to have taken place if I do not arrive in December, and consider that many other things may have occured to detain us before you yield to the belief that we have parted for ever.

The next morning Stanley started off. To save him another long journey, Randy, the terrier, was left in charge of Stairs. The poor dog, supposing himself deserted by his master, refused to eat and on the third day after Stanley's departure died of a broken heart.

In 1888 so great was the interest in England in the expedition that Emin's note-books were published with great success under the title of *Emin Pasha in Central Africa*.

In June of the same year the Press was agitated by reports of a mysterious white Pasha who had appeared in Bahr-el-Ghazal and was advancing victoriously against the Mahdist forces. Deserters from Osman Digna's army in the east said that Khartoum was in a state of alarm. The Press decided that this must be Stanley, or possibly Emin. In August pilgrims from Bahr-el-Ghazal, crossing from Suakin to Jeddah, said they had stayed in a camp where there were many white men armed with Remington rifles. The mystery of this white Pasha was never solved, but after every other possible explanation had been abandoned, it was supposed that he must have been a Captain von Gèle of the Congo Free State, who, like so many before him, was exploring the Welle basin.

Certainly it was not Stanley, who, far from advancing victoriously into Bahr-el-Ghazal, was at that time retracing his steps through the forest. He had entered into it on an early June morning. Once again the cries of the column leaders were passed down the line: "Red ants afoot! Look out for a stump, ho! A pitfall to right! a burrow to left! Thorns, thorns, 'ware thorns! Those ants; lo! a tripping creeper! Nettles, 'ware nettles! A hole! Slippery beneath, beneath! Look out for mud! a root! Red ants! red ants amarch! Look sharp for ants! A log! Skewers below!" Each minute the men were leaving farther behind them the comforts of Fort Bodo. Ahead lay only the terrible forest.

The villages, long deserted, were falling into decay. The damp had covered the huts with a green mould and sprouting fungi. Creepers, nettles and gourd vines were thick on the roofs. Although the desolate huts were sources of malaria, fever and rheumatism, the men were glad to crawl into them away from the iron blows of the rain. But they could this time avoid the worst hardships of the journey. The path was known; they had learnt to conserve their food; they were travelling light.

When the carriers reached Kilonga-Longa's settlement, they were still strong and glossy. They met the Manyuema glances with such scornful and hating eyes that Kilonga-Longa, now present, hastened to apologise for the behaviour of his men during his absence. He, of course, would not have permitted such discourtesy. In atonement he produced nineteen of the thirty Remingtons the starving carriers had traded for food.

Most of the Manyuema were absent on a slaving expedition and those that remained were obviously terrified of the armed and healthy Zanzibaris. Stanley knew, however, that any attack would probably be revenged by the absent ones on Fort Bodo. Apologies, rifles and gifts of goat and rice were thrust upon the column that accepted them coldly. An unnecessary escort of fifteen Manyuema was ordered to lead Stanley through the forest. The escort did not go far. In fear of the Zanzibaris it next day fled. Four Madis deserted, each taking with him the kit of a Zanzibari, but reappeared sheepishly at sunset. Kilonga-Longa, to whom they had gone, had sternly ordered them back to their jobs.

The journey continued now through the wilderness where the men had suffered so much nine months before. The bones of their dead friends lay on their path. They passed the camp where Nelson's hope and men had died daily. All the time watch was being kept for the couriers dispatched with a letter to Barttelot.

They found Ugarrowwa's station deserted. He had exhausted the neighbourhood and gone off in search of another. He had unfortunately taken the road to Yambuya and his thousands of followers, like locusts, had cleared every edible scrap on the way. The Zanzibaris following after had to go farther and farther afield in search of food. They now knew their way about. This time it was the wretched Madis who did everything wrong. They scattered their corn to lighten their loads, then found themselves without food. When they found plantains they ate wildly and were sick. When they felt the rain through their clothes, they collapsed. In despair, they refused to live longer and one by one distributed their jewellery among their friends and sat down to await death. Soon only thirty remained alive and those hideous with tumours and running sores, wretched with dysentery and exuding a horrible stench. Stanley, ill himself, was heartily sick of them.

He was no longer young and the long strain of the journey had affected his system. His muscles shrank and an ague shook his limbs. His nerves were on edge and his anxiety about the rear column became neurotic. At last he gave in and lay for some days motionless in his tent. As he lay he overheard Sari saying that the Master could not live much longer; he needed meat.

"If the Zanzibaris were men instead of being brutes," said the boy, "they would surely share with the Master what meat they get while foraging."

"There are few here so wicked as not to do it," replied the man to whom he spoke, "if they get anything worth sharing."

"But I know better," said Sali. "Some of the Zanzibaris find a fowl or a goat almost every day, but I do not see any of them bringing anything to the Master."

Stanley was roused at once. He called the boy, questioned him and realised he spoke the truth. Next day the Zanzibaris presented him with three fowls and he began to make a recovery.

When the column continued it came upon a little girl who spoke the Zanzibari language. She, with five sick women, had been abandoned by Ugarrowwa's caravan. The women had been killed by natives and

E

she, who had hidden herself, managed to keep alive on wild fruits. When she heard gun-fire she ran out gladly, telling herself these must be her own people because "the Pagans have no guns".

On August 10th they caught up with Ugarrowwa and heard that the missing couriers were in his camp. Ugarrowwa himself brought them to Stanley. Their headman told this story:

"Master, when you called for volunteers to bear your letter to the Major, there was not a man of us but intended to do his very best, knowing that we were all to receive a high reward and great honour if we succeeded. We have done our best, and we have failed. We have, therefore, lost both reward and honour. It is the men who have gone with you to the Nyanza and found the Pasha, and can boast of having seen him face to face, who deserve best at your hands. But if we have not succeeded in finding the Major and gladdening his heart with the good news we had to tell, God he knows it had not been through any fault of our number, and I am the only one who cannot show a wound received during the journey. We have two, who though alive, seem to be incurable from the poison in their blood. Some of our men have as many as five arrow wounds to show you. As far as Avisibba we came down the river smoothly enough, but then the sharp work soon commenced. At Engweddé two were wounded. At Panga Falls three men were most seriously hurt by arrows. Between Panga and here was a continued fight day after day, night after night; the natives seemed to know long before we reached them our full strength, and set on us either in full daylight or in the darkness, as though resolved to exterminate us. Why they should show so much courage with us when they had shown themselves so cowardly when we went up with you, I cannot say, unless our deserters, coming down river by half-dozens, have enabled the Pagans to taste the flavour of Zanzibari blood, and they having succeeded so well with them, imagined they could succeed with us. However, when we reached this village wherein you are now encamped, there were only eleven of us fit for anything; all the rest were sore from their wounds and one was helpless; and soon after our coming the fight began in real earnest. Those from that great river opposite us joined with the natives of Bandeya; the river seemed to swarm with canoes, and the bush around this village was alive with natives. After an hour's trial, during which time many of them must have been killed, for they were so crowded, especially on the river, we were left in peace. We availed ourselves in fortifying, as well as we could, the few huts we had selected for our quarters during the night.

"When night fell we placed sentries as usual, as you and Lieutenant Stairs and Ugarrowwa, all of you, enjoined on us; but, wearied with work and harassed by care, our sentries must have slept, for the first thing we knew was that the natives had pulled down our zeriba and entered into the camp, and a wild cry from a man who received a fatal thrust with a spear woke us up to find them amongst us. We each grasped our rifles and fired at the nearest men, and six of them fell dead at our feet. This for a moment paralysed them; but we heard a chief's voice say: 'These men have run away from Bula Matari.* Not one of them must live.' Then from the river and the bush they came on in dense crowds, which the flashes of our rifles' fire lit up, and their great numbers seemed for a short time to frighten the best of us. Lakkin, however, who is never so funny as when in trouble, shouted out: 'These fellows have come for meat—give it them, but let it be of their own people,' and wounded men and all took their rifles and took aim as though at a target. How many of them fell I cannot say; but when our cartridges were beginning to run low they ran away, and we were left to count the dead around us. Two of our men never answered to their names, a third called Jumah, the son of Nassib, called out to me, and when I went to him I found him bleeding to death. He had just strength enough to charge me to give the journey up. 'Go back,' said he, 'I give you my last words. Go back. You cannot reach the Major; therefore whatever you do, go back to Ugarrowwa's.' Having said this, he gave up his last breath, and rolled over, dead.

"Next morning we buried our own people, and around our zeriba there were nine natives dead, while within there were six. We beheaded the bodies, and after collecting their heads in a heap, held council together as to the best course to follow. There were seventeen of us alive, but there were now only four of us untouched by a wound. Jumah's last words rang in our ears like a warning also, and we decided to return to Ugarrowwa's. It was easier said than done. I will not weary you with details—we met trouble after trouble. Those who were wounded before were again wounded with arrows; those who were unwounded did not escape—not one excepting myself, who am by God's mercy still whole. A canoe was capsized and we lost five rifles. Ismailia was shot dead at Panga Falls. But why need we say over again what I have already said? We reached Ugarrowwa's after an absence of forty-three

* Native name for Stanley.

days. There were only sixteen of us alive, and fifteen of us were wounded. Let the scars of those wounds tell the rest of the story. We are all in God's hands and in yours. Do with us as you see fit. I have ended my words."

Everyone was affected by this story. The Zanzibaris, weeping copiously, rushed upon the couriers and caressed them with praises and compliments. Despite their failure, they were honoured as though they had succeeded. The letter for Barttelot was returned to Stanley. Still nothing was known of the fate of the rear column.

Sixty days after leaving Fort Bodo, 560 miles of the journey had been completed and only ninety remained to Yambuya. Half the Madis had died; of the hardened Zanzibaris only three had been lost, two drowned and one "missing through a fit of spleen". The rear column should have set out exactly a year before, yet there was no rumour of it.

Two days later, on a bleak morning of grey skies and black, shivering tree tops, a stockaded village at a river bend came into view. Men in white dresses were moving through it. A red flag flew above it. As the flag unrolled in the wind, the star and crescent could be seen. Stanley sprang to his feet and cried out: "The Major, boys! Pull away bravely." The Zanzibaris, in canoes, shrieked in wild excitement and raced one another down the river.

Some yards from the village stood a group of carriers. Stanley called to them: "Whose men are you?"

"We are Stanley's men," came the reply in mainland Swahili.

The canoes sped on. Now a European could be seen standing at the gate to the village. Stanley watched him through his binoculars until he was recognisable as William Bonny, the medical assistant. They met and shook hands.

"Well, Bonny, how are you? Where is the Major? Sick, I suppose?"

"The Major is dead, sir."

"Dead? Good God! How dead? Fever?"

"No, sir, he was shot."

"By whom?"

"By the Manyuema—Tippu-Tib's people."

"Good heavens! Well, where is Jameson?"

"At Stanley Falls."

"What is he doing there, in the name of goodness?"

"He went to obtain more carriers."

"Well, then, where is Mr. Ward, or Mr. Troup?"

"Mr. Ward is at Bangala."

"Bangala! Bangala! What can he be doing there?"

"Yes, sir, he is at Bangala, and Mr. Troup has been invalided home some months ago."

And where, asked Stanley, was his Madeira? That, with most of the tinned food and Stanley's personal belongings, had been sent down the river to Bangala. Why? That was not easy to say. Not without justice, Stanley wondered if everyone in the rear column had gone insane. He prepared to hear "as deplorable a story as could be rendered of one of the most remarkable series of derangements that an organised body of men could possibly be plunged into".

Chapter Eleven

THE STORY OF THE REAR COLUMN

"The only quality perhaps in which he was deficient was that of forbearance."

STANLEY on Barttelot

STANLEY'S parting shout to Barttelot had been: "Good-bye, Major. Shall find you here in October when I return." As the last of the advance guard disappeared into the forest, the Major contemplated his position with misgiving.

He was stranded in this desolate place with 600 loads of goods and 200 sick carriers. Only a few of the men were fit to move at all, much less to attempt a journey into the unknown. He was dependent for the power to move upon Tippu-Tib, a man he distrusted utterly.

On the night before they parted, Barttelot had asked Stanley: "Do you think Tippu-Tib will keep his contract, and bring his 600 people?"

Stanley replied: "You ought to know that as well as I myself. What did he say to you before you left him?"

"He said he would be here in nine days, as he told you at Bangala. Inshallah!"

"If Tippu-Tib is here in nine days, it will be the biggest wonder I have met."

"Why?" asked the unhappy Major.

"Because to provide 600 carriers is a large order. He will not be here in fifteen days or even twenty days. We must be reasonable with the man. He is not a European—taught to be rigidly faithful to his promise. Inshallah! was it he said? To-morrow—Inshallah means the day after—or five days hence, or ten days. But what does it matter to you if he does not come within twenty days? The *Stanley* will not be here until the 10th, or perhaps the middle of August; that will be about seven weeks—forty-two days—hence. He has abundance of time. What do you want to look after 600 men in your camp doing nothing, waiting for the steamer? Idle men are mischievous. No; wait for him patiently until the *Stanley* comes, and if he has not appeared by that time he will not come at all."

"But it will be a severe job for us if he does not appear at all, to carry 500 or 600 loads with 200 carriers, to and fro, backwards and forwards, day after day!"

"Undoubtedly, my dear Major, it is not a light task by any means. But which would you prefer; stay here, waiting for us to return from the Albert, or to proceed little by little—gaining something each day—and be absorbed in your work?"

"My God! I think staying here for months would be a deuced sight the worse."

"Exactly what I think, and, therefore, I made these calculations for you. I assure you, Major, if I were sure that you could find your way to the Albert, I would not mind doing this work of yours myself, and appoint you commander of the advance column, rather than have any anxiety about you."

"But tell me, Mr. Stanley, how long do you suppose it will be before we meet?"

"God knows," replied Stanley.

From the first Barttelot was filled with a foreboding that was almost neurotic. He suspected that Stanley, whose dislike he felt keenly, had left him to get rid of him; that Stanley knew how hopeless his position was and was not merely joking when he said farewell with the words: "Shall find you here in October when I return." He felt that he, who had come so eagerly on this adventure, was to miss all the excitement and spend his time in dreary inactivity.

In order to have something to do while awaiting the *Stanley*, Barttelot and Jameson set themselves to collecting firewood. The steamer arrived on August 14th with Troup, Ward, Bonny and the stores and men who had been left at Bolobo.

As Tippu-Tib had sent no word, now was the time for the rear column to march without his aid. To do so was little short of impossible. One third of its force was now dead, the rest scarcely able to crawl. Ward wrote in a report to Stanley: "Tippu-Tib continued to procrastinate, and in the meantime a large number of our Zanzibaris, many of whom, however, from the first were organically diseased and poorly, sickened and died. They were always employed, and the cause of their death cannot be attributed to inaction. Being fatalists, they resigned themselves without an effort, for the Bwana Makubwa,* with their comrades, had gone into the dark forest, and they all verily believed had perished. They themselves, when they found that upon no consideration would there ever be a chance of returning to their own country except by the deadly forest route, looked upon the situation as

* Zanzibari name for Stanley.

hopeless, gave way, and died. We expected you to return to Yambuya about the end of November; but time passed away and we received no news from you. We were unable to make triple marches owing to the sad condition of our people. Every means was tried to urge Tippu-Tib to produce the men, but without avail."

Jameson wrote home to his wife that he doubted whether they now had eighty sound carriers. These eighty were in poor enough state and to move the loads would mean having to do each stage of the journey eight times. Who was to guard the loads at either end of the stage? And who was fit to hack a road through the forest undergrowth that had by now almost obliterated Stanley's tracks?

There was no doubt that without Tippu-Tib's men they were now helpless. Barttelot began to be filled with a frenzied longing to move. His natural reaction to the situation was a desire to force Tippu-Tib to supply the carriers, but he was in no position to force anyone to do anything. He dare not even offend the man by seeming to doubt his integrity. He had to hide his revulsion and, more difficult still, keep his temper. To one of Barttelot's temperament, the strain of the position was scarcely bearable.

Why, he asked himself, should Tippu-Tib fulfil the contract? Like all the Manyuema, the slaver was cunning and dishonest, and now, back among his own followers in an almost inviolable stronghold, he could laugh even at the combined forces of the Congo State. It looked as though the wretched rear guard would indeed have to wait for Stanley's return.

Apart from the nervous exhaustion of waiting, the rear column had to face the problem of obtaining food. This was difficult enough. In the 600 loads were quantities of tinned foods and cereals, but these were reserved for use by the lakeside. They must not be touched at Yambuya or on the journey through the forest. The waiting column had to buy its food from the natives whom Stanley had turned out of their village. Here, in the midst of a famine area, they had nothing to sell. The carriers did not so much bargain as plead for food, and their pleadings were treated as a joke. Even a salary of one brass rod and six cowrie shells a week could not buy when there was nothing for sale. The men, having exhausted the rations left with Barttelot, began to dig up for themselves the bitter manioc growing in the fields round the village. On this diet one after another began to sicken and die of a mysterious ailment. The men from Bolobo, who arrived plump and well, soon began to sicken, too. Both officers and men were sure the fault must lie in the manioc, yet they knew that half the native population of the Congo existed on it. They decided that a curse was upon them and on this dreary place where they were imprisoned from sheer lack of physical strength to move.

The five white officers remained well. When their rations ran out, they tried to eat the manioc but were nauseated by it. They took to seizing native women and children, whom they ransomed for food. This naturally increased the enmity of the natives, who harassed the camp by firing arrows, shouting threats and stealing everything they could lay hands on. The officers at last tried to win the friendship of the natives by protecting them from the Manyuema. They sheltered refugee natives and exacted from the slavers promises, readily given and never kept, to leave the villagers alone. There was little else they could do. They did not feel free to use the ammunition intended for Emin, but had they done so, they would have been no match for the marauders from Stanley Falls. There was also the need to maintain a semblance of friendship with Tippu-Tib until the carriers arrived.

The months passed; no carriers arrived. Barttelot's appeals became more frequent and frantic. Tippu-Tib, polite as ever, repeated his promises and did nothing.

At last one day firing was heard on the opposite bank of the river where the dispossessed natives had built a temporary village. Looking through binoculars the officers could see the villagers fleeing before men in white robes. Bonny and Ward were sent across to plead with the slavers and they brought back with them a Manyuema chief, Abdallah. Abdallah assured Barttelot that Tippu-Tib had sent 500 men in canoes to join the rear guard. They had suffered from the hostility of the natives and in the end had completely lost themselves. Their leader, Salim bin Mohammed, had at last divided them into small groups and sent them in different directions to find the camp. Abdallah was at the head of one group. Other Arabs, when questioned, told the story differently and Barttelot said he did not believe any of them. Abdallah indignantly offered to guide any white man who cared to go to Stanley Falls and question Tippu-Tib himself.

Jameson and Ward undertook the journey. They were met by a smiling Tippu-Tib who confirmed Abdallah's story. He said that of course he intended supplying the carriers, but now they had become disbanded it would take a few days to collect them again.

E*

Jameson offered to wait and return with them. Tippu-Tib courteously agreed.

Ward hurried back to the camp with the good news that the carriers would arrive within ten days. When the time was up Jameson appeared, bringing with him Salim bin Mohammed, a nephew of Tippu-Tib, and a small party of Manyuema. The rest Tippu-Tib would bring himself after he had settled some trouble that had broken out in a distant trading-station. A month passed and no Tippu-Tib arrived. The officers began to suspect that he had no intention of coming.

On October 1st Barttelot set out with Salim bin Mohammed to find him. They met him on the road to Yambuya. He had with him no carriers, but six of Stanley's deserters, each of whom was carrying a stolen ivory tusk. Barttelot thought it was best to present the tusks to Tippu-Tib and the two went to Stanley Falls to talk.

Tippu-Tib, charming as ever, explained that he could not muster all the 600 in his own district and he would now have to go to Kasongo—a forty-two days' journey—to find the remainder. Barttelot could do no more than thank him for the trouble.

Back at Yambuya the Manyuema were making mischief. Their headman, Majato, in the hope either of starving the rear column into moving without the promised carriers or of profiting as middle-man between natives and Zanzibaris, had been intimidating the few natives who would trade with the camp so that they dared not sell anything. Ward now set out for Stanley Falls to complain of Majato and get him withdrawn.

Meanwhile time passed; more of the Zanzibaris sickened, more died. Any ghost of a hope that the column might move without Tippu-Tib's men had now completely faded. Ward wrote home: "This eternal waiting is awful. Day after day passes; we see no strange faces, we hear no news; our men are growing daily thinner and weaker, except in a few cases. It was a truly pitiable sight, a few days ago, to see an emaciated skeleton crawl, with the aid of a stick, after a corpse that was being carried on a pole for interment. He staggered along, poor chap, and squatted down alongside the newly made grave watching the proceedings with large, round, sunken eyes, knowing it was only a matter of a few days and he himself would be laid in the sod. He told me in a husky, hollow voice: 'He was my friend.' " But this sympathy, depleted by overmuch demand, turned gradually to indifference and irritability. Why did the men get weaker instead of stronger, ill instead of well? It was difficult not to blame them for it; to put it all down to a lack of will and spirit.

The officers themselves were worn down by frustration and boredom. Jameson wrote to his wife: "This hope deferred and weary waiting, month after month, with no brighter outlook, is horrible work—far, far worse than any amount of hardship and fighting."

Barttelot suffered most. He was a man who, prevented from expressing himself through action, had no reserves of imagination or creative thought to which to retire. His helpless position brought him to the verge of a nervous breakdown. His health failed and he suffered one tropical fever after another with the mental disorders that followed them.

It was unfortunate, also, that he could feel no sympathy with the Zanzibaris. He could not, as Stanley could, adopt their outlook, or excuse their foibles and appreciate their good nature. He had over them none of the personal influence necessary to keep them in control.

They were gregarious creatures, deeply attached to one another, and, cut off from the main body of their brothers who had disappeared into the forest, they felt deserted and doomed. Rumours were continually being passed round that Stanley had died with all his men. When Barttelot sternly refused to consider returning to the coast, they felt that all hope was lost to them. They might just as well die now as later. And die they did. The mysterious sickness seized them all. They grew weak, tremulous and filled with aches and pains. Fits of nausea and fainting caused them to fall at their work. They became convinced that this evil was caused by the white men. Why, otherwise, should the whites thrive and the blacks, born to the tropics, wither and die? They became sullen, disorderly and disobedient. Barttelot expected from them immediate and unquestioning obedience, and would not realise that whatever he might get from a Zanzibari, it would not be that.

He began to hate Africa. He hated the deceits and trickeries of the blacks, whether Manyuemas, Zanzibaris or natives. Suffering physically and mentally, depressed by inactivity, suspense and the arid, dust-ridden, tropical heat, he saw Africa as contemptible and hideous. If he could not act in any other way, at least his spirit could combat the enmity of this place and its people. His every word and action began to have in it a neurotic aggression.

Every day he ordered men to be flogged for some such crime as thieving or lying or cheating or plotting with the Manyuema. The other officers hated these continual punishments, but the camp was by now so demoralised that they could think of no other means by which to control the men.

The Manyuema from Stanley Falls seemed deliberately to be making things more difficult for the rear column by constantly choosing this area for their activities. Barttelot tried to persuade the native chief to bring the villagers within the protection of the camp, but these white men who had stolen their village, kidnapped their women and children, and forced them to hand over their miserable scraps of food had roused in the natives no more confidence than had the slavers.

At the beginning of the New Year Salim bin Mohammed paid a visit to the camp. This young man, described as "of medium height and slender build, with good and regular Arab features, much marred by the smallpox, and a face that reflected courage and audacity", had taken a dislike to Barttelot. He realised the Major feared to offend Tippu-Tib and he began to behave as though he were in command at Yambuya. He frightened off the native so that the meagre food supplies were cut off from the camp and never renewed, and he began constructing a mud village so fortified that it was "as though he were preparing for a siege of the place".

Barttelot bore as well as he could with the young Arab's swaggering and bullying, but at times he was driven to making a mild complaint, at which Salim bin Mohammed put up a show of being very offended. In a panic Barttelot would then search through his boxes to find a uniform jacket, a bale of cloth, a forty-five-guinea rifle or a pair of ivory-handled revolvers for a gift to placate his tormentor. Salim bin Mohammed was obviously enjoying himself and he decided to settle for a while at Yambuya.

For some reason Barttelot and Jameson now offered Salim a fee of £1,000 if he would lead a Manyuema contingent in Stanley's tracks. The young man neither accepted nor refused, but spent a long time arguing over the offer. It was soon clear that he had no intention of accepting and hoped to make as much by merely lounging at Yambuya. At last Barttelot and Jameson set out again for Stanley Falls to interview Tippu-Tib.

Afraid he had gone too far and they intended complaining of him, Salim insisted on going with them. The three went together—but Tippu-Tib was not at the Falls. Salim remained there, but in March turned up again at Yambuya with the news that Tippu-Tib would soon supply 250 carriers. These, however, he could not permit to follow Stanley's dangerous forest route. The rear guard must journey across Manyuema territory to the great slaving station of Ujiji on Lake Tanganyika and then through Unyoro to Equatoria. This route was a feasible one, and Barttelot, who was by now convinced that Stanley must have perished in the forest, would have considered it had the promised number of carriers been bigger.

Jameson, later called ironically by Stanley "the indefatigable Jameson", worried and unhappy for his friend more than for himself, set out for Kasongo in the hope of finding Tippu-Tib and persuading him to supply the whole 600. By now it was understood that another £1,000 would be paid for the carriers, this sum to be provided by Jameson and Barttelot.

Hopeful that they might at last be able to make a move, Barttelot sent Ward to the coast with a telegram for the London committee:

"No news of Stanley since writing last October. Tippu-Tib went to Kasongo, November 16th, but up to March has only got us 250 men. More coming, but uncertain in number, and as precaution, presuming Stanley in trouble, be absurd in me to start with less than he did, while carrying more loads—minus Maxim gun. Therefore I have sent Jameson to Kasongo to hasten Tippu-Tib in regard to originally proposed number of 600 men, and to obtain as many fighting men as possible up to 400, also to make as advantageous terms as he can regarding service, and payment of men, he and I guaranteeing money in name of expedition. Jameson will return about the 14th (May), but earliest day to start will be June 1st, when I propose leaving an officer with all loads not absolutely wanted at Stanley Falls. Ward carries this message; please obtain wire from the King of the Belgians to the Administrator of the Free State to place carriers at his disposal, and have steamers in readiness to convey him to Yambuya. If men come before his arrival I shall start without him. He should return about July 1st. Wire advice and opinion. Officers all well. Ward awaits reply.

BARTTELOT"

To this frenzied enthusiasm a reply eventually came and Ward returned with it. It ran:

"Committee refer you to Stanley's orders of the 24th June, 1887. If you still cannot march in accordance with these orders, then stay where you are, awaiting his arrival or until you receive fresh instructions from Stanley. Committee do not authorise the engagement of fighting men. News has been received from Emin Pasha via Zanzibar, dated Wadelai, November 2nd. Stanley was not then heard of: Emin Pasha is well and in no immediate want of supplies, and goes to south-west of lake to watch for Stanley. Letters have been posted regularly via east coast.

CHAIRMAN OF COMMITTEE"

Barttelot did not see this reply. When Ward arrived at Bangala he found awaiting him an order to stay there and receive the superfluous goods that would be sent down to him. He had been chosen to remain with them at Stanley Falls.

It was now the end of March and the 250 carriers had not arrived, but Salim's behaviour had become so overbearing that Barttelot begged for him to be withdrawn and he was ordered back to Stanley Falls. Instead of going, however, he conducted a raid on a riverside village and a few days later returned to Yambuya with the news that Stanley's column was coming down the Aruwimi.

This rumour, like many similar, proved false.

April came. Ward was at Bangala. Jameson was seeking Tippu-Tib. Troup was seriously ill. Only Bonny, who seems to have treasured, behind his negative manner, the ambition to "prove himself" one day, was assisting at the camp. There is no knowing what understanding was reached by Bonny and Barttelot, but for no deducible reason Barttelot wrote and presented to Bonny the following letter:

"Yambuya Camp,
April 22nd, 1888.

SIR,—In event of my death, detention by Arabs, absence from any cause from Yambuya camp, you will assume charge of the Sudanese company, the Zanzibar company, and take charge of the stores, sleeping in the house where they are placed. All orders to Zanzibaris, Somalis, and Sudanese will be issued by you and to them only. All issues of cloth, matako (brass rods), etc., will be at your discretion, but expenditure of all kinds must as much as possible be kept under. Relief to Mr. Stanley, care of the loads and men, good understanding between yourself and the Arabs must be your earnest care; anything or anybody attempting to interfere between you and these matters must be instantly removed.

I have the honour to be, Sir, etc.,

EDMUND M. BARTTELOT, MAJOR"

What had happened to cause Barttelot to overlook in this way his friend Jameson, "whose alacrity, capacity and willingness to work" he declared "unbounded", was never disclosed. If Bonny knew, he kept it to himself. Ward, too, might reasonably have claimed to be a man superior to Bonny in resource and intelligence.

Neither Barttelot, who was by now in a state scarcely normal, nor Bonny spoke of this letter to Jameson when he returned.

Jameson's journey appears to have been effective, for on May 9th Barttelot made a sixth trip to Stanley Falls and this time returned with 400 Manyuema carriers.

At last, at last, the rear guard could move! Barttelot's activity became feverish and wild. Although it was believed that the illness of the Zanzibaris resulted from their manioc diet, he packed loads of the tinned foods and sent them down the river to Ward. He opened Stanley's boxes and threw out his clothing, medicine, provisions and Madeira. He considered these personal goods as of less importance than the ammunition they had been sent to convey, but to Stanley his action seemed merely reckless lack of discrimination.

Troup was now wretchedly thin and weak and seemed, indeed, on the verge of death. Barttelot ordered him to return to England and put him in charge of the loads being sent to Ward.

On May 25th Tippu-Tib himself arrived. He asked to see the loads his Manyuema porters were to carry, and Barttelot, showing them, explained they were made up to the regulation sixty-pound weight. At first the slaver appeared to approve, but when all the loads had been completed he suddenly objected to the weight. His men, he said, could not carry more than forty pounds and some not more than twenty pounds.

The officers dared make no complaint. They undid the loads and spent three days repacking them to Tippu-Tib's orders. A lot more things had to be sent down the river.

The slaver now demanded, in part payment of the £1,000, forty-seven bales of cloth and a large quantity of ammunition and powder. He made Barttelot and Jameson sign an agreement that he would still receive the sum promised by Stanley. The Manyuema headman, Muini Sumai, also received an advance payment of £128 worth of goods.

The Manyuema carriers promised nothing but trouble. They were cannibals and their headman admitted that they were thinking only of "what a lot of natives they will eat farther on" and "when their stomachs were full they will catch others to carry their loads". They defied orders and terrified the remaining sick and dying Zanzibaris. No one in the rear guard was permitted to give them orders save Muini Sumai whose control of them seemed very uncertain.

But move they must. None of the officers could face a further stay at Yambuya. It was now June 1888—and Stanley had expected to return in September or October of 1887. If he were dead, then the rear guard must find Emin and deliver the ammunition. Neither for Barttelot nor for Jameson was there any question of returning with the steamer to safety.

The Manyuema, however, were worried by no sense of duty. Some of them deserted daily, always taking any revolvers, ammunition and food they could find. The Zanzibaris would have done the same had they been strong enough. As it was, fearful and wretched, they could only complain. Barttelot was maddened by them. He thrashed his boy servant for some trifling offence. When the servant deserted next day taking a revolver, belt and ninety-five rounds of ammunition, Barttelot disarmed all the Zanzibaris and threatened to put them in chains.

Men and goods were dwindling noticeably. Barttelot asked Tippu-Tib to replace the Manyuema who had disappeared. Tippu-Tib did not think it possible. Barttelot asked where were the 250 men collected at Kasongo. Tippu-Tib told him that, owing to reports brought to Stanley Falls by Stanley's deserters, they had refused to start the journey. They were free men, not slaves, and who could force them to come?

This remark put into Barttelot's head an idea that would have horrified the London committee. Why should he not buy from Tippu-Tib slaves who would have no choice but to follow the rear guard?

While he was considering the possibility of this, he ordered the column to start for Banalya. It was June 11th—exactly a year after Stanley's own departure. Only 139 of the 271 Zanzibaris left at Yambuya were still alive, and of these only 101 made an attempt to follow Barttelot. The main body of the column consisted of Manyuema with their crowds of women and children.

As the desertions increased in frequency, Barttelot became convinced that the only hope of completing the journey lay in getting slaves. When they reached Banalya—a village that had lately become one of Tippu-Tib's stations—he decided to make one more journey to Stanley Falls and offer to purchase a column of natives. Jameson was left in charge during his absence.

While Barttelot was away, smallpox broke out among the Manyuema. Muini Sumai told Jameson that he had received a letter ordering them all back to Stanley Falls, and when the Englishman refused to believe this, the Manyuema protested by firing their guns wildly throughout the night. The uproar was horrible and only a threat to execute the next man who fired kept them quiet. It had by now become evident that Muini Sumai had almost no control over the other headmen. The camp was in confusion.

Bonny, who was at the head of the column, was first led astray then deserted by his guides. Jameson remained in the rear to try and get the stragglers to Banalya. When Barttelot returned he had not got the slaves but had brought a letter ordering the Banalya headman, Karoni, to supply them. Karoni refused to part with his men and Barttelot threatened to take him to Stanley Falls.

According to Bonny's long report on the events of this time, Barttelot asked him: "Don't you think I am doing the correct thing by going to Stanley Falls?"

Bonny answered: "No, I don't see why you want sixty more men; you have men enough and to spare! You had better issue the rifles and ammunition to the men, and that will reduce the number of our burdens by fifteen, and trust the men. Mr. Stanley is obliged to trust the men. If they run away from you, they run away from him, but if you leave them in my hands I don't think they will run."

The Major answered: "I intend that you shall have command of the Zanzibaris and Sudanese from here, and you shall precede the Manyuema a day's march. Mr. Jameson and I will march with the Manyuema and get them into some order, and see they do not mix up with your people. I don't want to go to the Falls, but I want you to try to get some few men. If you only get me twenty I shall be satisfied."

Barttelot had by now reached that state of extreme febrile anxiety when any noise is torment. At night he was kept awake by the Manyuema, who fired their guns for the fun of it. One night, having been deprived of sleep by this uproar, he fell into a doze just as dawn was breaking. He was suddenly awakened by a wild beating of drums and the howls of a woman said to be possessed of devils. He sent his thirteen-year-old servant to silence this uproar. The boy was greeted by loud and angry threats, and two defiant shots were fired into the air. Barttelot now ordered some Sudanese soldiers to find the men who had fired them. As they went, he got out of bed himself, saying: "I will shoot the first man I catch firing."

Bonny, who was in the house, advised him not to interfere. This noise was a daily custom of the Manyuema and, if left alone, they would become quiet. Barttelot did not listen. Revolver in hand, he went out to the Sudanese, who said they could not find the men who had fired. Barttelot then pushed his way through the Manyuema and came to the woman, who was still beating the drum and howling. He ordered her to be quiet. At that moment a shot was fired from an opposite hut. It hit him below the heart and passed out through his body. He fell dead.

The camp broke at once into tumultuous confusion. The Sudanese ran away and would not return when Bonny called them. He went with one Somali and one Sudanese and carried the body into the house. From the screams that resounded everywhere he thought the Zanzibaris were being massacred, but actually they were hiding in their huts. Bonny reported: "I now turned and saw one of the headmen of the Manyuema, who with rifle and revolver in hand was leading a body of sixty of his people to attack me. I had no arms. I walked up to him and asked him if he was leading his men to fight me. He replied 'No'. I said: 'Then take your men quietly to their houses and bring all the headmen to me, for I wish to speak to them.'"

The camp was in chaos. About 1,000 people—nearly 900 of them cannibals—had been crowded into the little village. When Barttelot fell they stampeded into the forest and rice fields, screaming hysterically, shouting, firing guns, and looting and scattering their loads as they went. Not only the Manyuema, but the Zanzibaris and Sudanese joined the pillage. For hours no headmen could be found. When at last a few were collected and brought to Barttelot's house, Bonny told them:

"The trouble is not mine, but Tippu-Tib's. I want you to bring me all the loads, and tell all your fellows to do the same. Tippu-Tib knows what each of you has in charge and is responsible for this. This is Tippu-Tib's trouble. Tippu-Tib will have to pay up if the goods are lost, and will punish the headman who causes him a loss. I shall write to him, and he will come here, and he shall know the name of him who refuses to do what I now wish."

Loads were gradually collected in from the fields and forest. Some were discovered in native huts. Forty-eight were lost altogether. Bonny searched the quarters of the Zanzibaris and Sudanese and recovered cloth, beads and tinned food. These were the only culprits who remained on the spot to be punished and they suffered for the rest.

Practically all the Manyuema had disappeared by now. Muini Sumai had been the first to take to his heels. The murderer, Sanga, husband of the mad woman, had gone with him.

Barttelot's body was sewn up in a blanket and buried at the edge of the forest. Bonny wrote to Jameson: "Major Barttelot shot dead early this morning; Manyuema, Muini Sumai and Abdullah Kihamira (Karoni) all gone." He wrote to Baert, a Congo State official and secretary to Tippu-Tib, requiring him to tell his employer that if he did not now assist the rear guard all Europe would blame him—a consideration that must have weighed with Tippu-Tib very lightly indeed.

Bonny added to his report: "The Major wrote and handed me the official order appointing me in command of the Zanzibaris and Sudanese when the camp at Yambuya was in great danger, and his own life especially. I therefore take command of this second column of the Emin Pasha Relief Expedition until I see Mr. Stanley or return to the coast. It shall be my constant care under God's help to make it more successful than heretofore. Mr. Jameson will occupy the same position as shown in Mr. Stanley's instructions to Major Barttelot on his going to Stanley Falls to settle with Tippu-Tib for another headman of the Manyuema. He has free hands, believing himself to be in command. I did not undeceive him. On his return here I will show him the document, a copy of which I have given above."

Yet Jameson was never shown the letter. Perhaps Bonny was waiting until the Irishman recovered from his grief for Barttelot; perhaps he realised that at the moment command of the rear column was no enviable position. When Jameson reached Banalya he took command without question.

Ten days later he set out for Stanley Falls. He found Sanga there in hiding. The murderer's defence was that he thought "the Major was going to beat the woman as he had beaten the men the day before, and so fired at him". At a trial before Jameson, Tippu-Tib and Baert, Sanga was found guilty. He was shot and his body thrown into the Congo.

Jameson tried now to find a new headman to take the place of Muini Sumai. He could find no one willing to take charge of Manyuema. Tippu-Tib offered to go himself in return for £20,000 paid unconditionally, but said if he met with any superior force or saw his men threatened, he would return. Also he insisted they must take the route via Ujiji, but if there was war between Unyoro and Uganda (as there very likely would be) he could not guarantee delivery of the loads.

Only Tippu-Tib's refusal to follow Stanley's path prevented Jameson from accepting this fantastic offer. He said he would go without a headman. Tippu-Tib roared with laughter. Unless there was a headman to control them, the Manyuema would merely throw away their loads and scatter to hunt for ivory.

At last Tippu-Tib agreed to follow Stanley's track and Jameson said he would give half the £20,000 himself as a subscription to the expedition. All seemed settled, but at the last moment he realised how hopeless it would be to depend on Tippu-Tib and he decided to take Ward as a headman instead.

Bewildered by worry and still grieving over Barttelot's death, Jameson set out for Bangala, where Ward was still waiting with the committee's reply to the Major's cable. He travelled in a canoe with ten Zanzibari paddlers.

In his last letter to Bonny beginning: "The expedition is at a very low ebb at present, as I think you will acknowledge," he repeated in a muddled way his conversations with Tippu-Tib, and Tippu-Tib's demands and conditions. He ended with a friendly pat for the good Bonny, who was still waiting to spring on him the unaccountable letter: "You remember that in camp I had serious thought for reasons you know of not bringing Ward; but if we do start this time without any headmen, it is most necessary that there should be three of us. I assure you that his coming will not in the least interfere with your command of the Zanzibaris. And now, old man, good-bye, and God bless you. . . ."

Jameson's canoe travelled day and night. At Lumanii he was seized with an attack of bilious fever. His constitution weakened by months of underfeeding, his resistance weakened by grief and the strain of a responsibility for which he was unfitted, he collapsed completely but he would not let the Zanzibaris pause in the journey. While he lay delirious at the bottom of the canoe, they sped on downstream. When they arrived at their destination, Jameson was beyond hope. He died a few hours later.

On the day of Jameson's death at Bangala, Stanley arrived at Banalya. He was revolted by the conditions he found existing among the wretched remnant of the Zanzibaris at the camp. "Pen cannot picture nor tongue relate the full horrors witnessed within that dreadful pest-hold," he tells us, but goes on to describe the hideous appearance of the carriers with their dysentery, anæmia, ulcers and their unknown sickness. Weary and ill himself, he said he scarcely knew how he endured the first hours with their repellent sights and the trusting, pleading gaze of the dying men. A hundred graves at Yambuya, thirty-three more at this camp, ten dead on the road, twenty deserted—possibly sixty that might, with care, survive! And what had happened to the gallant band of Englishmen?

Bonny said: "Barttelot's grave is but a few yards off, Troup went home a skeleton, Ward is somewhere a wanderer, Jameson has gone to the Falls, I don't know why."

"And you—you are the only one left?"

"The only one, sir."

But why had this happened? "Were you not all anxious to be at work?" asked Stanley.

"Yes, sir."

"Were you not burning to be off from Yambuya?"

"Yes, sir."

"Were you not all equally desirous to be on the road?"

"I believe so. Yes, sir."

"Well, Mr. Bonny, tell me—if it be true that you were all burning, eager, and anxious to be off—why you did not devise some plan better than travelling backwards and forwards between Yambuya and Stanley Falls?"

"I am sure I don't know, sir. I was not the chief, and if you will observe, in the Letter of Instructions you did not even mention my name."

"That is very true; I ask your pardon; but you surely did not remain silent because I omitted to mention your name, did you—you a salaried official of the expedition?"

"No, sir. I did speak often."

"Did the others?"

"I don't know, sir."

That and his written reports were all that was to be got from Bonny.

The more Stanley thought about it all, the more angry he became. If only Barttelot had followed the "suggestions" made to him in Stanley's letter of instructions, all would have been well. The letter had said: "It may happen that though Tippu-Tib has sent some men, he has not sent enough to carry the goods with your own force. In that case you will of course use your discretion as to what goods you can dispense with, to enable you to march. . . . If you still cannot march, then it would be better to make marches of six miles twice over, if you prefer marching to staying for our arrival, than throw too many things away."

Stanley said his first fear was that he himself had become insane. It was beyond comprehension that something that would have been so simple and straightforward to him had been made so difficult by these foolish young men! He could only conclude, on going through the reports, that the officers had "manifestly been indifferent to the letter of instructions, and had forgotten their promises". He added: "When Mr. Bonny told me that one of them had risen at a mass meeting to propose that my instructions should be cancelled, and that the ideas of Major Barttelot should be carried out in future—it did appear to me that the most charitable construction that could be placed upon such conduct was that they were indifferent to any suggestions which had been drawn out purposely to satisfy their own oft-repeated desire of 'moving on'."

He wished he could have been with them for only an hour at that meeting to remind them: "Joy's soul lies in the doing, and the rapture of pursuing is the prize," and also "The path of duty is the way to glory".

The solution of their problem was simple enough. They had, say, 200 sound carriers and, say, 500 loads. The first stage would be about ten miles. By doing repeated journeys, the carriers would do the first stage and bring up the loads in six days. In four months, at this rate, they would have covered 150 miles; in eight months, 300 miles, and so on.

Neither Barttelot nor Jameson was alive to protest that they never had 200 sound carriers, nor any number of carriers capable of taking on a journey of which every stage had to be covered six times.

"The bigger the work," continued Stanley, "the greater the joy in doing it. The whole-hearted striving and wrestling with difficulty; the laying hold with firm grip and level head and calm resolution of the monster, and tugging, and toiling, and wrestling at it, to-day, to-morrow, and the next until it is done; it is the soldier's creed of forward, ever forward—it is the man's faith that for this task was he born. Don't think of the morrow's task, but what you have to do to-day, and go at it. When it is over, rest tranquilly, and sleep well."

As it was, after a year of folly, wasted ammunition and fantastic expenditure, they had got as far as Banalya. What was more, they had sent Stanley's clothing down the river so that he was reduced "to absolute nakedness. I am so poor as to be compelled to beg a pair of pants from Mr. Bonny, cut another pair from an old white blanket in the possession of a deserter, and another from a curtain in my tent."

Bonny appears to have kept silent through all Stanley's rages. He made no attempt to explain the impossibility of moving with their handful of sick carriers, the impossibility, had they moved, of guarding the loads from the natives or the Manyuema at Ugarrowwa's and Kilonga-Longa's. He let Stanley, who had become by now elated by a sense of his own superiority and confidence, sweep over the difficulties he had left these inexperienced men to face, and write to Jameson who was now dead and buried:

"Bonny showed me your letter of the 12th inst. wherein you stated it your purpose to go to Bangala. I cannot make out why the Major, you, Troup, and Ward, have been so *demented*—demented is the word. You understand English; an English letter of instructions was given you. You said it was intelligible—yet for some reason or another you have not followed one paragraph. You paid £1,000 to go on this expedition; you have voluntarily thrown away your money by leaving the expedition. Ward is not a whit better; he has acted all through, as I hear, more like an idiot than a sane being. You have left me naked. I have no clothes, no medicine; I will say nothing of my soap and candles, photograph apparatus and chemicals, two silver watches, a cap and a score of other trifles. You believed I was dead, yet you brought along my boots and two hats and a flannel jacket. Though, as reported to me, you and all of you, seem to have acted like madmen, your version may modify my opinion."

By the time he came to write *Darkest Africa*, his anger had settled down to a bleak resentment:

"Implicitly believing as we did in the *élan* of Barttelot, in the fidelity of Jameson, in the vigorous youth and manly promise of Ward, in the prudence and trustworthiness of Troup, and the self-command and steadiness of Bonny, all those revelations came to me with a severe shock." Take Barttelot—"I would have wagered he would have seized that flowing grey beard of Tippu-Tib and pounded the face to pulp, even in the midst of his power, rather than allow himself to be thus cajoled time and time again." Take Jameson, who was "such a still, and patient, and withal determined man that we all conceded a certain greatness to him"! As for Troup and Bonny—"the two last-named receive salaries, and both present their accounts and are paid, not a penny deducted, and a liberal largess besides in first-class passages home is granted to them." Ward, one may add here, got his money only after his claim had come into court.

Well—"though they all are undoubtedly animated by the purest motives, and remain to the end unquestionably loyal—throughout every act they are doing themselves irreparable injury, and unconsciously weighing their friends of the advance column down to the verge of despair with anxieties."

This chapter of *Darkest Africa* ends with a poignant cry: "Mr. Ward informed me that he had discovered my eight boxes of reserve clothing and expedition necessaries at Bangala; that he took them with him to Stanley Falls—500 miles above Bangala—and then brought them down to Banana Point on the sea-coast, where he left them. No person knows—though diligent enquiry has been made—what has become of them."

Chapter Twelve

WHAT'S BECOME OF JEPHSON?

"To have friends, one must be friends, and men, especially savage men, are moved mostly by what relates to man. If Emin had shown less attention to bugs and beetles, more sympathy would have existed between him and the people placed under his charge by Gordon."

STANLEY: Lectures

STANLEY wrote to Tippu-Tib: "And now, my friend, what are you going to do? I am waiting to hear your words. If you go with me, it is well. If you do not go with me, it is well also. I leave it to you—whatever you have to say to me, my ears will be open with a good heart, as it has always been towards you."

While awaiting a reply he refused to stay at Banalya. The expedition must push on. Jameson had erred and Jameson must be punished. Whatever happened, when he returned he would not find the expedition awaiting him. Stanley wrote: "When he descended from Stanley Falls he deliberately severed himself from the expedition, and no inducement would tempt me to remain in the neighbourhood of Banalya. I had given my word to the officers at Fort Bodo and to Emin Pasha and the Egyptians that on December 22nd, or thereabouts, I should be in the neighbourhood of Fort Bodo, and by January 16th, or near that date, on the Nyanza. It was natural that we should grieve and deplore the loss of Mr. Jameson to the expedition, for the log-book entries pleaded powerfully for him, but the fatality that attached itself to the rear column was not to deplete our numbers also, nor should the garrison at Fort Bodo wonder and bewail our long absence, and lose their wits in consequence of our breach of promise."

So it was determined that Stanley's men, with the few Zanzibaris who had been with Bonny and those of the Manyuema who had wandered back to camp, should start out next day. Before the move, the Yambuya contingent of Sudanese and Zanzibaris mustered to lay complaints before Stanley.

Bonny's reports of his own courage, his intention "under God's help, to make the expedition more successful than it had been hitherto", the letter written by Barttelot giving him command, had impressed Stanley.

He began to wonder if Bonny had remarkable qualities he had over-looked. His satisfaction was considerable when he was proved to have been right after all.

The first thing the Zanzibaris in the fullness of their hearts were persuaded to confess was that at the beginning of their march eastwards with Bonny they had planned to abandon him, Zanzibaris and Manyuema alike. The expedition under Bonny would have been no more successful than under Barttelot or Jameson.

"Well," said Stanley to the Zanzibaris, "sit down, children, and let us talk this matter over quietly."

The carriers sat in a circle before him. Some appeared heart-broken, others had a look of hatred and spite, all were so wretchedly ill that it would be remarkable if they survived a few days' journey into the forest.

Stanley addressed them: "Ah, my poor men, the days of weeping and grieving are over. Dry your tears and be glad. See these stout fellows behind you. They have seen the white Pasha, they have shared his bounties of meat, and milk and millet, and have heard him praise their manliness. They are the people who should weep, but weep for glad-ness, for every step hence is one step nearer to Zanzibar. We came back from the Nyanza to seek you who were so long lost to us. We have found you, thanks be to God! Now, let bygones be bygones. I cannot restore the dead, but I can rejoice the hearts of the living. Think no more of your sufferings, but live in hope of a brighter future. It was necessary for us to go before you, to clear the road and assist the white man before he perished. We told you all this before we departed from you. You should have remembered our promise that as soon as we had found him whom we sought we should come back with the good news to you. We have kept our word—have you kept yours?

"No, you lost faith in us. When the runaways from our party returned to you, and they, with gaping mouths, told you what was false to hide their crime of desertion, you listened with wide-open ears, and accepted their tales as truths. Did they bring a letter from any of us? No! But you found silver watches, and Arab cloaks striped with gold in their baggage. Do common carriers find such things in the forest? If they do, then you should have said to them: 'Come, turn back with us, and show us the place where we may also find such wealth.' Those carriers had stolen those things from us, and had run away with their booty. You saw these things, and yet you believed that we were all destroyed, that I was shot in seventeen places, and all the white men except one had been killed, and the one remaining had gone to Ujiji! Oh, men of little wit!

"What, nearly 400 Zanzibaris, and six white men, all lost except a few, and those few gone to Ujiji instead of coming to you, their brothers and friends! That is too much for belief. I thought Zanzibaris were wiser men, for truly I have seen wise ones in my time.

"And, if I were not dead, how came you to believe that I would forget you, and my white sons whom I left with you? Whither could I go, except to my own children, if I were distressed or unable to go on? Was not the fact of our long absence a proof that we were still going on doing our work, since even deserters and thieves had nowhere to flee except back to you?

"Aye, I see well how it has happened unto you. You lay on your backs rotting in camp, and have been brooding and thinking until the jiggers have burrowed into your brains, and Shaitan has caused you to dream of evil and death. You became hardened in mind, and cruel to your own bodies. Instead of going to the little masters, and telling them of your griefs and fears, you have said Mambu Kwa Mungu—it is God's trouble. Our masters don't care for us, and we don't care for them.

"Now, Ferajji, you are a headman, tell me what cause of complaint in particular you have. Did the white men ill-treat you?"

"No, they treated me well; but they were hard on some of the men."

"How hard, and on whom?"

"On the Zanzibaris, and if they were not chap-a-chap (active)."

"But what did they wish to be chap-a-chap for? Had you important work to do?"

"No, for when the steamer went away there was little to do. Only fixing the earth work, sweep camp, cut fuel, and stand guard at night. But the goee-goees (lazy or useless) would not come when called. Then the white men got impatient, and would call again louder. Then the goee-goees would come slowly—lazily—little by little, and say they had pains in the head, or in the body, back, chest, or feet. Then the masters would get angry, and say it was shamming. Every day it was the same thing."

"But how could sweeping camp, getting fuel, and standing guard be hard work for 250 people?"

"It was no work at all."

"Was anybody punished except the goee-goees?"

"No one except the thieves."

"Did you have many of them?"

"I think all the thieves of Zanzibar joined the 'journey-makers' this time."

"That cannot be, Ferajji, because we had some thieves with us, and there must have been a few left on the coast."

This raised a laugh. Ferajji replied: "That is indeed truth, but we had a great many. Brass rods, cowries, and garments were lost daily. Zanzibaris accused Sudanese, Sudanese accused Somalis, Somalis accused Zanzibaris, and so it went round. Nothing was safe. Put anything under your pillow, roll it under the sleeping-mat, bind it tight, and make it into a head-rest, and lo! in the morning it was gone! Indeed, I became afraid my teeth would be stolen next."

"But those white teeth of yours are not purchased, are they, Ferajji?"

"No, thank Allah, they were born with me, but those who thrive on thieving may well be feared."

"That is true, Ferajji; but why should they have stolen all the time?"

"Hunger made them steal. Hunger killed the strong lion in the fable, and hunger will kill the best man."

"Hunger! What are you talking of? Hunger, with all those fields of manioc near here?"

"Manioc, master! Manioc will do for a time, but manioc with sauce is better."

"Sauce? I don't understand you, Ferajji!"

"Why, dry manioc—that is manioc with nothing but itself—manioc in the morning, and at noon, and at the sunset meal, and nothing but eternal manioc, with neither salt, nor fish, nor meat, nor oil, nor butter, nor fat of any kind to assist its passage down the gullet, is apt to cloy. Give the appetite something now and then new to smell or see with the manioc, and the Zanzibari is satisfied. Without that the stomach by and by shuts the door, and won't take anything, and men die."

"I see, but I left salt in the store-room. It was to purchase fish, bananas and palm oil that the brass rods, cowries and beads were for."

"Ah, now you are drawing near the point, master. Sometimes—nay, we were a long time without either."

"But if they were in the store, surely there must be some reason why they were not given out?"

"We come to the thieves again, who became so active that they sold our axes and bill-hooks, and sold them to the natives for fish. Those who shared in the fish refused to tell who the thieves were, and our rations of cowries and brass rods were stopped."

"After all, Ferajji, though manioc by itself is very dry eating, it is very good food. Think of it, all the blacks from Banana to Stanley Falls live on it; why should not Zanzibaris of this expedition live on it as they lived during six years on the Congo with me? I cannot see any reason for manioc to kill 100 men in eleven months. Tell me, when did the people begin to sicken?"

Ferajji replied: "There were about a dozen sick when you left, sick of ulcers, bowel and chest complaints. A few recovered; then, in about four weeks, many got very feeble, and some sank lower and thinner until they died, and we buried them. When our friends came up from Bolobo, we thought they looked very different from us at Yambuya. They were stout and strong—we were thin and dying. Then, in another month, the men from Bolobo began to sicken and die, and every few days we buried one, or two, or even three at a time. There was no difference after a while between the Yambuya and Bolobo men."

"Had you any cholera, smallpox, fever, or dysentery among you?"

"No, the men did not die of any of those things. Perhaps the Somalis and Sudanese did not take kindly to the climate, but it was not the climate that killed the Zanzibaris."

"And you say it was not by the stick, or hard work, or cholera, smallpox, fever, dysentery or climate?"

"Nothing of any of those things killed the Zanzibaris."

"Were they shot, or hanged, poisoned, or drowned?"

"Neither was any of those things done unto them, and a proper and good man was never punished, and we had one day out of seven in the week to ourselves."

"Now in the name of the Prophet Mohammed—throw your eyesight on these forty men here who sit apart. Look at those big eyes, hollow cheeks, thin necks, and every rib bare to the view. You see them? What has caused those men to be thus?"

"God knows!"

"Yet they are wasting away, man, and they will die."

" It is true."

"Well, then, give me some idea—of what is killing them?"

"I cannot tell you, master; maybe it is their fate to be thus."

"Bah! God has done His best for you. He has given you eyes, hands to feel, feet to walk, a good stomach to digest your food, and a sense to

pilot your path through the world. Don't say that God made strong
men to wither them away in this manner. I must and will find the reason
of this out. Now, you Salim, the son of Rashid, speak to me. The son
of a wise father should know a few wise things. There is Death among
you, and I want to find out why. Say, how you and your comrades
living in camp for a year can lose more lives than we did during all our
journey through this big forest, despite all the hunger and hard work
we met?"

Salim became suddenly modest and hung his head: "I am not wise,
and all the world knows it. I am but a youth, and a porter, who for a
little wage has come to gather a little money by carrying my load
through Pagan lands. What strength I have I give freely to the owner
of the caravan. Bitter things have happened to us while you were away.
I have lost a brother since I came here. You must know, sir, that dry
manioc and water is not good for a son of Adam. If our friends and
relatives have sickened and died—it must surely be that the manioc
has had something to do with it. Thank God, I am well, and still
strong, but I have seen the days when I would willingly have sold my
freedom for a full meal. Whatsoever tended to fill the void of the
stomach I have sought out and have continued to live on day after day,
until, praise be to God and the Prophet—you have come back to us. But,
sir, all men are not the same—the sense of all men is not equal,
and it may be that white men differ one from the other as much
as we blacks; for I see that some of them are rich, and some are poor,
some attend the engines down in the belly of the ship, and some walk
the quarter-deck and command."

When he paused to breathe, his friends murmured admiringly: "Aye,
Salim has the gift of speech."

Encouraged by this, Salim cleared his throat and continued with
increased confidence: "There is no doubt that the main fault lies in the
manioc. It is a most bitter kind, and the effects of eating it we all know.
We know the sickness, the retching, the quaking of the legs, the softening
of the muscles, the pain in the head as if it were bound with iron and the
earth swimming round the place whereon we stand, and the fall into a
deadly faint. I say we have felt all this, and have seen it in others. Some
of us have picked up the knack of making it eatable; but there are others
who are already too feeble or too lazy to try, or try to care how to live.

For some time we have been thinking that in every camp of ours
there is nothing but graves, and dying and burying. There has been no

meat, nor salt, nor dripping, nor gravy. There has been manioc, always manioc, and no more. But if the gullet be dry, what will drive the food down the passage? If the stomach is filled with loathing it requires a little gravy or dripping to make the food palatable.

We know that in a few weeks we were to leave here for Stanley Falls, or for up the river, and we had made up our minds to leave the white men's service—every one of us. There has been death among us, it is here still, and no one knows what is the cause of it. I myself don't quite believe that it is because we are working for white men, but there are some of us who do. But we were all agreed until you came that we had seen enough of it. There is another thing I wished to say, and that is—we have wondered why we who belong to the continent should die, and white men who are strangers to it should live. When we were on the Congo and on other journeys it was the white men who died, and not we. Now it is we who die, 100 blacks for one white. No, master, the cause of death is in the food. The white men had meat of goat, and fowls, and fish; we have had nothing but manioc and therefore died. I have spoken my say."

"You say that manioc was your food at Yambuya, and that it made you sick and your men died?" said Stanley.

"Yes," replied the Zanzibaris' spokesman.

"And you say that the men of Bolobo when they came to Yambuya were in good condition?"

"Yes."

"But that afterwards they became sick and died also?"

"Yes."

"What did the men of Bolobo eat when there?"

"Chikwanga."

"Well, what is chikwanga but bread made out of manioc?"

"That is true."

"Did you make it into bread?"

"Some of us."

"And some of you have lived. Now the truth of the matter is this. You went into the fields, and gathered the manioc tubers, the finest and best. And you cut some leaves of manioc and brought them in, to bruise them and make greens. This manioc is of the bitter kind. This bitterness which you taste in it is poison. It would not only kill a few hundreds. It would kill a whole race.

"As you peeled the tubers, you cut raw slices and ate them, you pounded your greens, and as 'kitowêo' you ate them also. These are two instances in which you took poison.

"Now the men from Bolobo had bought the manioc bread from the native women. They had steeped the tubers in the river for four or five or six days until the poison had all been washed away, they had then picked the fibres out, dried the mush, and when dry they had made it into good bread. That was what fed the Bolobo men, and fattened them. But the men of Yambuya had scraped their manioc, and cut the roots for drying in the sun, and as they did so they ate many a piece raw, and before the slices were well dried they had eaten some, because they had no reserve of food, and hunger forced them. Even those of you who put your roots to soak in the water ate many a nice-looking bit, and you bruised and cooked your greens to serve with your badly-prepared bread, and men naturally sickened and died of the poison; and the men of Bolobo, when they came up, did like the men of Yambuya, and by and by they fell ill and died also. That is the reason why there are a hundred graves at Yambuya, and that is what ails these sick men here. Not one of the white men died, because they had rice, beans, biscuits and meat of fowl and goat. If it were the climate that had killed your friends, the white men less adapted for it would have died first, as they have done on the lower Congo; but neither the climate nor the camp had anything to do with your mortal sickness—the retching and quaking of limbs, the vertigo and pain in the head, the weakening of the knees, and the softening of the muscles, the final loathing, and indifference to life— nothing else than the poison of the bitter manioc.

"What you should have done was to have sent two or three daily out of each mess to gather in the manioc in sufficient quantities and steep it in the river, and have always plenty of prepared flour on hand to make porridge or dumplings when hungry. Had you done so, I should have about 200 sleek and strong men ready for travel with me to Zanzibar."

The Zanzibaris merely shook their heads in wonder at Stanley's wisdom.

"Now follow what I say to you now," said Stanley more gently. "Eat as little of this manioc as you can. Go, gather plenty of it, put it in the river to soak, and while it is soaking eat your fill of bananas and plantains. In a day or two I will move away from here. The sick shall be carried to a big island a few hours' distant, and there you will prepare twenty days' provisions of flour. Those who cannot get sufficient bananas, make gratings over the fire, slice your manioc thin, and let them dry till morning; then pound, and make it into flour, and eat what is good for white man as well as black. To-morrow, all of you come back again to me, and you will throw away those filthy rags of clothing into the river, and I shall clothe you anew. Meantime, rejoice, and thank God that we have come to save you from the grave."

Probably more effective than Stanley's reassurances were the descriptions that his Zanzibaris gave of the beautiful grass-land that lay beyond the forest, of the grain and vegetables and stores of food they had found there after their days of starvation. They scarcely bothered to mention the long forest journey that lay between them and this glorious, abundant land.

"Inshallah!" they said. "We shall feast on beef once again, then you will laugh at the days you fed on manioc roots and greens."

The wretched Yambuya Zanzibaris listened with wide eyes. Thoughts of deserting to a slave life on dried fish at Stanley Falls faded before this glowing vision. Even the weakest of them stumbled to his feet and asked only to be led eastwards with the rest.

The column left Banalya. A halt of ten days was made on the island of Bungangeta to get the baggage into order. The cloth, beads and brass rods that could not be carried were distributed among the men. With these they bought from Ugarrowwa's people well-prepared food on which the sickly Zanzibaris began to revive.

Now the Manyuema, recovered from the arrival of the famous Stanley, began to be troublesome again. One day their headmen would vow eternal fidelity and the next would come to Stanley full of complaints and threats. Moody and unscrupulous, they stole, menaced the other carriers, and deserted. The Zanzibaris, who had been vaccinated, were not affected by the epidemic of smallpox that had broken out, but the Manyuema were dying daily. They were obviously going to be perpetual trouble-makers on this journey.

Stanley did not publish his letter to Tippu-Tib, but he tells us: "My answer to them all (the Manyuema) was almost similar in terms to that used in my note to Tippu-Tib on the 17th: 'If you decline the journey it is well, if you proceed with me it is well also. Exercise your own free will. I do not need you, but if you like to follow me I can make use of you, and will pay according to the number of loads you carry.' Some of them understood this as implying leave to proceed upon their own business—that of ravaging and marauding—but three headmen volunteered to accompany me. I engaged them on the condition that if they followed me of their own will for thirty days I would after that time trust them with loads."

Thirteen days had passed on the island and no reply had been received from Tippu-Tib. Stanley, who would not wait a week at Banalya for Jameson, now began to feel he had waited long enough on the Arab.

At last a move was made with sixty-one Manyuema carriers to supplement the Zanzibaris. A few days later Ugarrowwa, who was wandering up and down the river in search of ivory, paid Stanley a visit and brought with him Tippu-Tib's nephew Salim bin Mohammed.

At an earlier meeting Stanley had found the young Arab a sympathetic character, but Bonny's accounts of Salim's behaviour towards Barttelot had made him wonder if he could have been mistaken. This second meeting confirmed his faith in his own instinct. Salim like Tippu-Tib was of Arab blood and must be judged accordingly. When the Arabs had made the ridiculous excuse that the carriers could not find the camp, the white men should have realised that no carriers were coming, and continued without them. Instead they had stupidly pleaded and offered bribes, so Tippu-Tib began to raise his price "not out of ill-will, but out of an uncontrollable desire to make more profit".

Salim said he had come in person from his uncle in reply to Stanley's six letters, in English, Arabic and Swahili, sent seventeen days before.

Stanley said: "Now, Salim, listen. If I thought you or Tippu-Tib were in any way implicated in the murder of my friend, you would never leave this camp alive. You have only seen hitherto one side of me. But I know and believe from my soul that it was neither you nor Tippu-Tib who caused the death of the Major. Therefore we can speak together as formerly without anger. Tippu-Tib has not injured me beyond what the consul and the Seyyid of Zanzibar can settle easily between them. Into their hands I will commit the case. Tell your uncle that the passage of himself and his ninety-six followers from Zanzibar to Stanley Falls must be paid, that the loss of goods, rifles, powder, and ammunition, the loss of time of this entire expedition will have to be made good. Tell him to do what he likes, but in the end I shall win. He cannot hurt me, but I can hurt him. Tell him to consider these things, and then say whether it would not be better to prove at the last that he was sorry, and that in future he would try to do better. If he would like to try, say that if he gathers his men, and overtakes me before I cross the expedition over the Ituri in about fifty days hence, he shall have a chance of retrieving my good opinion, and quashing all legal proceedings."

"Very well, I hear all you say. I shall return to-night to Banalya; Ugarrowwa will lend me canoes. I shall be with Tippu-Tib in eight days, and on the seventeenth day I shall be back here, on your track. I shall overhaul you before forty days."

"Good, then," said Stanley, "we had better utter our last farewells, for we shall not meet again unless we meet at Zanzibar, about eighteen months hence."

"Why?"

"Because neither you nor Tippu-Tib have the least intention of keeping your word. Your business here has been to order the Manyuema who are with me back to Stanley Falls. But it is perfectly immaterial. Take them back, for once more I say, it is not in your power to hurt me."

"Inshallah, Inshallah, let your heart rest in peace, we meet in less than forty days, I swear to you."

After that Salim went straight to the three Manyuema headmen in Stanley's train and tempted them to return with him. Strangely enough they gave a decided refusal and, when Salim threatened them, went to Stanley for protection.

Smiling, Stanley said to Salim: "What you promised me just now is true; you have seen me in less than forty days! But what is the meaning of this? These are independent Manyuema chiefs, who were sent by Tippu-Tib to follow us. They are obeying Tippu-Tib in doing so. Let them alone, Salim, there will be less people for you to look after on the road, you know, because you also will follow us. Don't you see? There, that will do. Come and get into your canoe, otherwise we shall make two marches before you leave here—and you have promised to catch me, you know, in forty days."

Smallpox was spreading rapidly among the men. Emin's Madis suffered worse than the Manyuema. This epidemic, and the fact that two insane women kept the camp awake nightly with their howling, made the return journey a depressing one. The Zanzibaris, to whom meat was irresistible, were continually raiding the native stockyards, but instead of feeding themselves often ended as food for the natives.

Stanley lectured them angrily. He had given them cattle, sheep, goats, handfuls of silver and a thousand pound's worth of clothing—and not one of them had offered his throat to him to cut. Yet for the sake of a goat they would risk becoming meat for cannibals! What monstrous ingratitude! The Zanzibaris hung their heads in shame and promised never to go out goat-stealing again.

Within five days of his address twelve men had been killed on raids—nine of them eaten as well—and one seriously wounded, causing him to brood on the infidelity of mankind. "Any person who has travelled with the writer thus far will have observed that almost every fatal accident hitherto in this expedition has been the consequence of a breach of promise. How to adhere to a promise seems to me to be the most difficult of all tasks for every 999,999 men out of every million whom I meet."

The journey was varied by little incidents—the pathetic death from arrow wounds of a beautiful young Manyuema wife; the devotion of a husband to his wife made hideous by smallpox; the sight of a cloud of lavender-coloured moths so dense that it looked like a fog or a snow-storm; the death of a little girl seized and stabbed from breast to back by a native who cried: "Death to the invader."

Deaths from poisoned arrow wounds and from smallpox continued daily. The sick moved freely amongst the well and no effort was made to isolate them. One Zanzibari who had refused to be vaccinated caught the disease and, in delirium, flung himself into the rapids and was drowned.

Jameson's box, for some reason, had been taken along by the expedition. A month after leaving Bungangeta, it was opened and most of the things in it thrown away.

So, passing from incident to incident, the expedition reached Ugarrowwa's old station, where the great house stood deserted. A rice crop had grown within the courtyard, but the birds had picked every grain. Here was comfortable shelter but no food. The column hurried on.

The Zanzibaris had gained a little wisdom from their past experiences in the forest, but the wretched Madis and Manyuema had none. The column struggled still against the old enemies, hunger and disease. Men died as before, yet again Stanley reached the verge of the forest, again grass-land was sighted and again the rejoicings were great.

In a skirmish with the natives some Remington cartridges were captured. These were of the type left at Fort Bodo and Stanley began to fear that the officers left there might have suffered a misfortune.

Having ordered Nelson and Stairs to evacuate men and loads to the lakeside as soon as Jephson arrived with fresh carriers to conduct them to the new camp, Stanley had had no intention of visiting the old camp. Now he decided to alter his course and see what had happened there. He found Fort Bodo flourishing. The corn stood high. The granary was full. There were crops of plantains, sweet potatoes and beans. All the Zanzibaris were well except a few unfortunates who would never be well again. Nelson was completely recovered. Stairs "the officer *par excellence*, was precisely what he ought to have been—the one who always obeyed and meant to obey". No word had come from Jephson.

Stanley could find no cause for complaint against Nelson and Stairs. They had obeyed orders but "we were now left to conjecture what had become of the energetic Jephson, the man of action, who had been nicknamed *Buburika*, or the Cheetah, because he was so quick and eager, and strained at the leash." It looked as though Jephson was not "precisely what he ought to have been".

Stanley was very much annoyed. Here he was, returned from an expedition in which 106 lives had been lost, faced with the miserable problem of how to transport fifty-five extra loads. But, as he frequently said, the cure for all grief, misery and doubt is action. He could not remain passive at the fort. He must press on to the lake no matter under what difficulties. The problem of the extra loads was easily solved. When offered payment of cloth for extra work, fifty-five men volunteered to do double-shifts.

A few days later the fort was evacuated. The buildings and palisades were fired, and the united expedition marched on to the grass-land. When it reached a crossing point of the Ituri river, ground was cleared and a new camp built. There the officers were to stay with the sick while Stanley went on to the lake.

Before parting from them Stanley addressed them suitably:

"Gentlemen, I have called you to give you a few parting words. You know as well as I do that there is a constant unseen influence at work creating an anxiety which has sometimes tempted us to despair. No plan, however clear and intelligible it may be, but is thwarted and reversed. No promises are fulfilled, instructions are disregarded, suggestions are unavailing, and so we are constantly labouring to correct and make amends for this general waywardness which pursues us. We are no sooner out of one difficulty than we are face to face with another, and we are subjected to everlasting stress and strains of appalling physical miseries, and absolute decimation. It is as clear to you as to me why these things are so. They will go on and continue so, unless I can gather the fragments of this expedition together once and for all, and keep it together never to be separated again. But each time I have wished to so do, the inability of the men to march, the necessity of hurrying to one place and then to another, keep us eternally detached. After bringing the rear column, and uniting it with the advance, and collecting your garrison at Fort Bodo, we are astonished at this total absence of news from Jephson and the Pasha. Now I cannot manœuvre with a hospital in tow, such as we have with us. At the muster of to-day, after inspection, there were 124 men suffering from ulcers, debility, weakness, dysentery, and much else. They cannot march, they cannot carry. Jephson and the Pasha are perhaps waiting for me. It is now January 10th, I promised to be on the Nyanza again, even if I went as far as Yambuya, by the 16th, I have six days before me. You see how I am pulled this way and that way. If I could trust you to obey me, obey every word literally, that you would not swerve one iota from the path laid down, I could depart from you with confidence, and find out what is the matter with Jephson and the Pasha."

"I don't see why you should doubt us," said Stairs, "I am sure we have always tried to do our very best to please and satisfy you."

"That is strictly true, and I am most grateful to you for it. The case of Yambuya seems to be repeated. Our friend Jephson is absent, perhaps dead from fever or from some accident; but why do we not hear from the Pasha? Therefore we surmise that some other trouble has overtaken both. Well, I set out for the Nyanza, and either send or cause to hear the news, or cut my way through Melindwa to behind M'swa Station to discover the cause of this strange silence. Have the Mahdists come up river, and annihilated everybody, or has another expedition reached them from the east, and they are all too busy attending to them to think of their promise to us? Which is it? No one can answer, but because of this mystery we cannot sit down to let the mystery unfold itself, and I can do nothing towards penetrating it with 124 men, who require a long rest to recover from their fatigues and sicknesses. Therefore I am compelled to trust to you and the doctor, that you will stay here until I know what has happened, whether for one month or two months. I want you to stay here and look after the camp alertly, and I want the doctor to attend to these sick men and cure them, not to stint medicines, but nurse them with good food from morning until night. Do you promise this faithfully, on your words as gentlemen?"

"We do," replied Stairs and Nelson.

"Now Doctor, I particularly address myself to you. Stairs will perform all that is required as superintendent and governor of the camp, but I look to you mostly. These 124 men are on the sick list, some are but slightly indisposed, and some are in a dreadful state. But they all require attention, and you must give it devotedly. You must see that your worst cases are fed regularly. Three times a day see that their food is prepared, and that it is given to them; trust no man's word, see to it yourself in person; we want these men to reach home. I warn you solemnly that your 'flood-tide of opportunity' has come. Are you ambitious of distinction? Here is your chance; seize it. Your task is clear before you, and you are required to save these men, who will be the means of taking you home, and of your receiving the esteem of all who shall hear of your deeds.

"Gentlemen, the causes of failure in this world are that men are unable to see the thing that lies ready at their hands. They look over their work and forget their tasks, in attempting to do what is not wanted. Before I left England I received some hundreds of volunteers to serve with me on this expedition. They at least believed that they could win what men vulgarly call 'kudos', though I do not believe that one in a thousand of them know what is the true way to glory. For instance, there are only six whites here in this camp, yet one of the six sought me the other night to request permission to explore the Welle-Mubangi River—of all places in Africa! His duty was clearly before him, and yet he did not see it. His opportunities were unheeded. He cast yearning looks over and above what was right at his feet. He seemed as if wakened out of a dream when I told him that to escort refugees to their homes was a far nobler task than any number of discoveries. On this expedition there was a man who received a salary for being loyal and devoted to me, yet when there were opportunities for distinguishing himself, he allowed his employer's baggage to be sent away before his very eyes, and his own rations to be boxed up, and sent out of camp, and he never knew until told that he had lost his opportunities to gain credit, increase of salary, and promotion. I point out your opportunities, therefore hold fast to them with a firm grip; do all you can with might and main to make the most of them. Don't think of 'kudos', or 'glory', but of your work. All your capital is in that; it will give you great or little profit, as you perform it. Good night.

To-morrow I go to do something, I know not what, and do not care until I hear what it is I have to do. As I will do mine, do yours."

The next morning Stanley continued with the carriers and goods and crossed the grass-land. Among the villages he heard rumours that the Pasha was building big houses near the lake and intended crossing the country with his followers. That was reassuring. They were also told that Emin had sent ten men to Kavalli's in search of news of them, and that he had caused some fields to be cultivated near the lake and corn planted. Stanley tells us there passed through his mind the reflection: "What a good, thoughtful, kind man he must be!"

Stanley remained in unusually good spirits all afternoon, but "at 5.0 p.m. two Wahuma messengers came with letters from Kavalli's, and as I read them a creeping feeling came over me which was a complete mental paralysis for the time, and deadened all the sensations except that of unmitigated surprise. When I recovered myself the ears of Jephson and the Pasha must certainly have tingled. I need not criminate myself, however, and any person of any imagination may conceive what I must have felt after he had read the following letters":

Dufilé,
November 7th, 1888

DEAR SIR,

I am writing to tell you of the position of affairs in this country, and I trust Shukri Aga will be able by some means to deliver this letter to Kavalli in time to warn you to be careful.

On August 18th a rebellion broke out here, and the Pasha and I were made prisoners. The Pasha is a complete prisoner, but I am allowed to go about the station, though my movements are watched. The rebellion has been got up by some half-dozen officers and clerks, chiefly Egyptians, and gradually others have joined; some through inclination, but most through fear; the soldiers, with the exception of those at Laboré, have never taken part in it, but have quietly given in to their officers. The two prime promoters of the rebellion were two Egyptians, who we heard afterwards had gone and complained to you at Nsabé. One was the Pasha's adjutant, Abdul Vaal Effendi, who was formerly concerned in Arabi's rebellion; the other was Achmet Affendi Mahmoud, a one-eyed clerk. These two and some others, when the Pasha and I were on our way to Rejaf, went about and told the people they had seen you, and that you were only an adventurer, and had not come from Egypt; that the letters you had brought from the Khedive and Nubar Pasha were forgeries; that it was untrue that Khartoum had fallen, and that the Pasha and you had made a plot to take them, their wives and children out of the country, and hand them over to become slaves to the English. Such words, in an ignorant and fanatical country like this, acted like fire amongst the people, and the result was a general rebellion, and we were made prisoners.

The rebels then collected officers from the different stations, and held a large meeting here to determine what measures they should take, and all those who did not join in the movement were so insulted and abused that they were obliged for their own safety to acquiesce in what was done. The Pasha was deposed, and those officers who were suspected of being friendly to him were removed from their posts, and those friendly to the rebels were put in their places. It was decided to take the Pasha away as a prisoner to Rejaf, and some of the worst rebels were even for putting him in irons, but the officers were afraid to put these plans into execution, as the soldiers said they would never permit anyone to lay a hand on him. Plans were also made to entrap you when you returned, and strip you of all you had.

Things were in this condition when we were startled by the news that the Mahdi's people had arrived at Lado with three steamers and nine sandals and nuggars, and had established themselves on the site of the old station. Omar Sale, their general, sent down three peacock dervishes with a letter to the Pasha demanding an instant surrender of the country. The rebel officers seized them and put them in prison, and decided on war. After a few days the Donagla* attacked and captured Rejaf, killing five officers and numbers of soldiers, and taking many women and children prisoners, and all the stores and ammunition in the station were lost. The result of this was a general stampede of people from the stations of Bidden, Kirri, and Muggi, who fled with their women and children to Laboré, abandoning almost everything. At Kirri the ammunition was abandoned, and was at once seized by the natives. The Pasha reckons that the Donagla numbers about 1,500.

The officers and a large number of soldiers have returned to Muggi, and intend to make a stand against the Donagla. Our position here is extremely unpleasant, for since this rebellion all is chaos and confusion; there is no head, and half a dozen conflicting orders are given every day, and no one obeys; the rebel officers are wholly unable to control the

* Name applied to Mahdist forces.

F*

soldiers. We are daily expecting some catastrophe to happen, for the
Baris have joined the Donagla, and if they come down here with a rush
nothing can save us. After the fall of Rejaf, the soldiers cursed their
officers and said: "If we had obeyed our governor, and had done what
he told us, we should now be safe; he has been a father and a mother
to us all these years; but instead of listening to him we listened to you,
and now we are lost."

The officers are all very much frightened at what has happened, and
are now anxiously awaiting your arrival, and desire to leave the country
with you, for they are now really persuaded that Khartoum has fallen,
and that you have come from the Khedive. The greater part of the
officers and all the soldiers wish to reinstate the Pasha in his place, but
the Egyptians are afraid that if he is reinstated vengeance will fall on
their heads, so they have persuaded the Sudanese officers not to do so.
The soldiers refuse to act with their officers, so everything is at a standstill, and nothing is being done for the safety of the station, either in
the way of fortifying or provisioning it. We are like rats in a trap; they
will neither let us act or retire, and I fear unless you come very soon you
will be too late, and our fate will be like that of the rest of the garrisons of
the Sudan. Had this rebellion not happened, the Pasha could have
kept the Donagla in check for some time, but as it is he is powerless
to act.

I would make the following suggestions concerning your movements
when you arrive at Kavalli's, which, of course, you will only adopt if
you think fit.

On your arrival at Kavalli's if you have a sufficient force with you,
leave all unnecessary loads in charge of some officers and men there,
and you yourself come to Nsabé, bringing with you as many men as
you can; bring the Sudanese officers, but not the soldiers, with you.

Dispatch natives in a canoe to M'swa with a letter in Arabic to
Shukri Aga, telling him of your arrival, and telling him you wish to see
the Pasha and myself, and write also to the Pasha and myself telling us
the number of men you have with you; it would, perhaps, be better to
write to me, as a letter to him might be confiscated.

On no account have anything to do with people who come to you
unaccompanied by either the Pasha or myself, whoever they are, or
however fair their words may be. Neither the Pasha nor I think there
is the slightest danger now of any attempt to capture you being made,
for the people are now fully persuaded you come from Egypt, and they

look to you to get them out of their difficulties; still it would be well for you to make your camp strong.

If we are not able to get out of the country, please remember me to my friends. With kindest wishes to yourself and all with you.

I am,

Yours faithfully,

(Signed) A. J. MOUNTENEY JEPHSON

To H. M. STANLEY, Esq.,
Commander of the Relief Expedition.

Wadelai,

November 24th, 1888

My messenger having not yet left Wadelai, I add this postscript, as the Pasha wishes me to send my former letter to you in its entirety, as it gives a fair description of our position at the time I wrote, when we hardly expected to be ever able to get out of the country. Shortly after I had written to you, the soldiers were led by their officers to attempt to retake Rejaf, but the Donagla defeated them, and killed six officers and a large number of soldiers; amongst the officers killed were some of the Pasha's worst enemies. The soldiers in all the stations were so panic-stricken and angry at what had happened that they declared they would not attempt to fight unless the Pasha was set at liberty; so the rebel officers were obliged to free him and sent us to Wadelai, where he is free to do as he pleases, but at present he has not resumed his authority in the country; he is, I believe, by no means anxious to do so. We hope in a few days to be at Tunguru, a station on the lake two days by steamer from Nsabé, and I trust when we hear of your arrival that the Pasha himself will be able to come down with me to see you.

Shukri Aga tells us he has everything ready against your arrival, in the shape of cattle, goats, chickens, corn, etc.; he has behaved capitally throughout this rebellion, and is the only chief of station who has been able to stand against the rebels.

Our danger, as far as the Donagla are concerned, is, of course, increased by this last defeat, but our position is in one way better now, for we are further removed from them, and we have now the option of retiring if we please, which we had not before when we were prisoners. We hear that the Donagla have sent steamers down to Khartoum for reinforcements; if so, they cannot be up for another six weeks; meantime I hope that until the reinforcements arrive they will not care to come so far from their base as Wadelai or Tunguru. If they do, it will be all up with us, for the soldiers will never stand against them, and it will be a mere walk-over.

These people are not the same sort that the soldiers fought three years ago, but are regular fanatics, and come on with a rush, cutting down men with their long sharp swords and broad spears. Everyone is anxiously looking for your arrival, the coming of the Donagla has completely cowed them. Everything now rests on what the Donagla decide on doing. If they follow up their victories and come after us, we are lost, as I said before, for I do not think the people will allow us to retire from the country; but if the Donagla have sent down to Khartoum for reinforcements, and have decided to wait for the arrival of their reinforcements, then we may just manage to get out if you do not come later than the end of December, but it is utterly impossible to foresee what will happen.

A. J. M. J.

Tunguru,
December 18th, 1888

DEAR SIR,

Mogo not having yet started I send a second postscript in order to give you the latest news I can. We are now at Tunguru. On November 25th the Donagla surrounded Dufilé and besieged it for four days, but the soldiers, of whom there were some 500 in the station, managed at last to repulse them, and they retired to Rejaf which is their head-quarters. They have sent down to Khartoum for reinforcements, and doubtless will again attack and take the country when they are strengthened. In our flight from Wadelai I was asked by the officers to destroy our boat lest it should fall into the hands of the Donagla; I therefore broke it up, as we were unable to save it.

Dufilé is being evacuated as fast as possible, and it is the intention of the officers to collect at Wadelai, and to decide on what steps they shall next take. The Pasha is unable to move hand or foot, as there is still a very strong party against him, and the officers are no longer in immediate fear of the Mahdi's people.

Do not on any account come down to Nsabé, but make your camp at Kavalli's; send a letter directly you arrive, and as soon as we hear of your arrival I will come down to you. I will not disguise the fact from you that you will have a difficult and dangerous task before you in dealing with the Pasha's people. I trust you will arrive before the Donagla return, or our case will be desperate.

I am,

Yours faithfully,

(Signed) A. J. MOUNTENEY JEPHSON

The Pasha's letters were short and filled with the consciousness of having failed. He commended his little daughter to Stanley's care, and wrote as though neither hoping nor caring for rescue: "Mr. Jephson will tell you what has happened and is able to give you the benefit of his experience, and to make some suggestions, should you decide to come here as people wish. Should you, however, decide not to come, I can only wish you a good and safe return to your own country."

Neither Emin's pathetic resignation nor Jephson's common-sense explanations and suggestions could temper Stanley's wrath as he read these letters. He had expected to find Emin and Jephson awaiting him on the lakeside. Instead, like a couple of fools, they had somehow got themselves imprisoned. Neither could be trusted. There was no excuse for either of them.

He believed the first instalment of the ammunition, brought with such difficulty through the forest, was lost. Completely lost. And what else might have resulted from the idiocy of Jephson and Emin? When the letters had been written, a month before, the Mahdi's fanatics had been expected to descend any day. Perhaps the Pasha was already dead. If so, the whole journey had been undertaken for nothing.

Brooding over the situation, Stanley believed he now understood the dreamy uncertainty of Emin's manner. The Pasha must have known all the time of the unreliability of his own people. Indeed he had no people to command.

Stanley wrote to Jephson:

January 17th, 1889

MY DEAR JEPHSON,

Your letter of November 7th, 1888, with two postscripts, one dated November 24th, and the other dated December 18th, is to hand and contents noted.

I will not criticise your letter nor discuss any of its contents. I wish to be brief, and promptly act; with that view I present you with a précis of events connected with our journey.

We separated from the Pasha on May 23rd last, with the understanding that in about two months you, with or without the Pasha, would start for Fort Bodo with sufficient porters to take the goods at the fort and convey them to the Nyanza, the Pasha expressing himself anxious to see Mount Pisgah and our fort, and, if words may be relied on, he was anxious to assist us in his own relief. We somewhat doubted whether his affairs would permit the Pasha's absence, but we were assured you would not remain inactive.

It was also understood that the Pasha would erect a small station on Nyamsassi Island as a provision depot, in order that our expedition might find means of subsistence on arrival at the lake.

Eight months have elapsed, and no one single promise has been performed.

On the other hand, we, faithful to our promise, departed from the Nyanza Plain May 25th, arrived at Fort Bodo June 8th—fifteen days from the Nyanza. Conveying to Lieutenant Stairs and Captain Nelson your comforting assurances that you would be there in two months, and giving written permission to Stairs and Nelson to evacuate the fort and accompany you to the Nyanza with the garrison, which, with the Pasha's soldiers, would have made a strong depot of Nyamsassi Island, I set out from Fort Bodo on June 16th to hunt up the Major and his column.

On the morning of August 17th, at 10.0 a.m., we sighted the rear column at Banalya, ninety miles (English) from Yambuya—592 miles from the Nyanza on the sixty-third day from Fort Bodo, and the eighty-fifth from the Nyanza shore.

I sent my dispatches to Stanley Falls and thence to Europe, and on August 31st commenced my return towards the Nyanza. Two days before the date stated I was at Fort Bodo—December 20th. On December 24th we moved from Fort Bodo towards the Ituri Ferry. But as your non-arrival at Fort Bodo had left us with a larger number of goods than our force could carry at one time, we had to make double journeys to Fort Bodo and back to the Ituri Ferry, but by January 10th all that remained of the expedition, with all its effects, were on this side of the Ituri River, encamped half a mile from the ferry, with abundance of food assured for months. On January 12th I left Stairs; your absence from the fort, and the absolute silence respecting you all, made us suspect that serious trouble had broken out. Yesterday your letter, as above stated, came to hand, and its contents explained the trouble.

The difficulties I met at Banalya, are repeated to-day, near the Albert Lake, and nothing can save us now from being overwhelmed by them but a calm and clear decision. If I hesitated at Banalya very likely I should still be there waiting for Jameson and Ward, with my own men dying by dozens.

Are the Pasha, Casati and yourself to share the same fate? If you are still victims of indecision, then a long good-night to you all. But, while I retain my senses, I must save my expedition; you may be saved also if you are wise.

In the "High Order" of the Khedive, dated February 1st, 1887, No. 3, to Emin Pasha, a translation of which was handed to me, I find the following words:

"And since it is our sincerest desire to relieve you with your officers and soldiers from the difficult position you are in, our government have made up their minds about the manner by which relief from these troubles may be obtained. A mission for the relief has been found, and the command of it given to Mr. Stanley, the famous, etc., etc., etc., and he intends to set out on it with all the necessary provisions for you, so that he may bring you, with your officers and men, to Cairo by the route he may think proper to take. Consequently we have issued this 'High Order' to you, and it is sent to you by the hand of Mr. Stanley, to let you know what was being done. As soon as it reaches you convey my best wishes to the officers and men, and you are at full liberty with regard to your leaving for Cairo or your stay there with officers and men.

"Our government has given a decision for paying your salaries, with that of the officers and men.

"Those who wish to stay there of the officers and men may do so on their own responsibility, and they may not expect any assistance from the government.

"Try to understand the contents well, and make them well known to all the officers and men, that they may be fully aware of what they are going to do."

It is precisely what the Khedive says that I wish to say to you. Try and understand all this thoroughly that you may be saved from the effect of indecision, which will be fatal to you all if unheeded.

The first instalment of relief was handed to Emin Pasha on or about May 1st, 1888. The second and final instalment of relief is at this camp with us, ready for delivery at any place the Pasha designates, or to any person charged by the Pasha to receive it. If the Pasha fails to receive it, or to decide what shall be done with it I must then decide briefly what I must do.

Our second object in coming here was to receive such at our camp as were disposed to leave Africa, and conduct them home by the nearest and safest route. If there are none disposed to leave Africa our expedition has no further business in these regions, and will at once retire. Try and understand what all this means. Try and see the utter and final abandonment of all further relief, and the bitter end and fate of those obstinate and misguided people who decline assistance when tendered to them. From May 1st, 1888, to January, 1889, are nine months—so long a time to consider a simple proposition of leaving Africa or staying here!

Therefore, in this official and formal letter accompanying this explanatory note to you, I designate Kavalli's village as the rendezvous where I am willing to receive those who are desirous of leaving Africa, subject, of course, to any new light thrown upon the complication by a personal interview or a second letter from you.

And now I address myself to you personally. If you consider yourself still a member of the expedition subject to my orders, then, upon receipt of this letter, you will at once leave for Kavalli's with such of my men—Binza and Sudanese—as are willing to obey you, and bring to me the final decision of Emin Pasha and Signor Casati respecting their personal intentions. If I am not at Kavalli's then, stay there, and send word by letter by means of Kavalli's messengers to Mpinga, Chief of Gavira, who will transmit the same to Mazamboni's, when probably I shall receive it. You will understand that it will be a severe strain on Kavalli's resources to maintain us with provisions longer than six days, and if you are longer than this period we must retire to Mazamboni's, and finally to our camp on the Ituri Ferry. Otherwise we must seize provisions by force, and any act of violence would cut off and close native communication. This difficulty might have been avoided had the Pasha followed my suggestion of making a depot at Nyamsassi. The fact that there are provisions at M'swa does not help us at all. There are provisions in Europe also. But unfortunately they are as inaccessible as those of M'swa. We have no boat now to communicate by lake, and you do not mention what has become of the steamers, the *Khedive* and *Nyanza*.

I understand that the Pasha has been deposed and is a prisoner. Who, then, is to communicate with me respecting what is to be done? I have no authority to receive communications from the officers—mutineers. It was Emin Pasha and his people I was supposed to relieve. If Emin Pasha was dead, then to his lawful successor in authority. Emin Pasha being alive prevents my receiving a communication from any other person, unless he be designated by the Pasha. Therefore the Pasha, if he be unable to come in person to me at Kavalli's with a sufficient escort of faithful men, or be unable to appoint some person authorised to receive this relief, it will remain for me to destroy the ammunition so laboriously brought here, and return home.

Finally, if the Pasha's people are desirous of leaving this part of Africa, and settle in some country not far remote from here, or anywhere bordering the Victoria Nyanza, or along the route to Zanzibar, I am perfectly ready to assist, besides escorting those willing to go home to Cairo safely; but I must have clear and definite assertions, followed by prompt action, according to such orders as I shall give for effecting this purpose, or a clear and definite refusal, as we cannot stay here all our lives awaiting people who seem to be not very clear as to what they wish.

Give my best wishes to the Pasha and Signor Casati, and I hope and pray that wisdom may guide them both before it is too late. I long to see you, my dear fellow, and hear from your own lips your story.

Yours very sincerely,

(Signed) HENRY M. STANLEY

To A. J. MOUNTENEY JEPHSON, Esq.

A private postscript was added to this:

Kavalli,
January 18th, 1889. 3.0 p.m.

MY DEAR JEPHSON,

I now send thirty rifles and three of Kavalli's men down to the lake with my letters, with urgent instructions that a canoe should set off and the bearers be rewarded.

I may be able to stay longer than six days here, perhaps for ten days, I will do my best to prolong my stay until you arrive, without rupturing the peace. Our people have a good store of beads, cowries, and cloth, and I notice that the natives trade very readily, which will assist Kavalli's resources should he get uneasy under our prolonged visit.

Be wise, be quick, and waste no hour of time, and bring Binza and your own Sudanese with you. I have read your letters half a dozen times over, but I fail to grasp the situation thoroughly, because in some important details one letter seems to contradict another. In one you say the Pasha is a close prisoner, while you are allowed a certain amount of liberty; in the other you say that you will come to me as soon as you hear of our arrival here, and "I trust", you say, "the Pasha will be able to accompany me". Being prisoners, I fail to see how you could leave Tunguru at all. All this is not very clear to us who are fresh from the bush.

If the Pasha can come, send a courier on your arrival at our old camp on the lake below here to announce the fact, and I will send a strong detachment to escort him up to the plateau, even to carry him, if he needs it. I feel too exhausted, after my 1,300 miles of travel since I parted from you last May, to go down to the lake again. The Pasha must have some pity on me.

Don't be alarmed or uneasy on our account; nothing hostile can approach us within twelve miles without my knowing it. I am in the midst of a friendly population, and if I sound the war-note, within four hours I can have 2,000 warriors to assist to repel any force disposed to violence. And if it is to be a war of wits, why then I am ready for the cunningest Arab alive.

I wrote above that I read your letters half a dozen times, and my opinion of you varies with each reading. Sometimes I fancy you are half Mahdist or Arabist, and then Eminist. I shall be wiser when I see you.

Now don't be perverse, but obey; and let my order to you be as a frontlet between the eyes, and all, with God's gracious help, will end well.

I want to help the Pasha somehow, but he must also help me and credit me. If he wishes to get out of this trouble, I am his most devoted servant and friend; but if he hesitates again, I shall be plunged in wonder and perplexity. I could save a dozen Pashas if they were willing to be saved. I would go on my knees to implore the Pasha to be sensible in his own case. He is wise enough in all things else, except in his own interest. Be kind and good to him for many virtues, but do not you be drawn into that fatal fascination which Sudan territory seems to have for all Europeans of late years. As soon as they touch its ground, they seem to be drawn into a whirlpool, which sucks them in and covers them with its waves. The only way to avoid it is to obey blindly, devotedly, and unquestioningly, all orders from the outside.

The committee said: "Relieve Emin Pasha with this ammunition. If he wishes to come out, the ammunition will enable him to do so; if he elects to stay, it will be of service to him." The Khedive said the same thing, and added: "But if the Pasha and his officers wish to stay, they do so on their own responsibility." Sir Evelyn Baring said the same thing, in clear and decided words; and here I am, after 4,100 miles of travel, with the last instalment of relief. Let him who is authorised to take it, take it. Come; I am ready to lend him all my strength and wit to assist him. But this time there must be no hesitation, but positive yea or nay, and home we go.

Yours very sincerely,
HENRY M. STANLEY

A. J. MOUNTENEY JEPHSON, Esq.

To Emin he wrote:

Camp at Mpinga's, one long march from the Nyanza, and ten miles east of Mazamboni's.

January 17th, 1889

To HIS EXCELLENCY EMIN PASHA,
    Governor of the Equatorial Province.

SIR,

I have the honour to inform you that the second instalment of relief which this expedition was ordered to convey to you is now in this camp, ready for delivery to any person charged to receive it by you. If you prefer that we should deposit it at Kavalli or at Kyya Nkondo's, on the lake, we shall be ready to do so on the receipt of your instructions.

This second instalment of relief consists of sixty-three cases of Remington cartridges, twenty-six cases of gunpowder, each forty-five pounds in weight; four cases of percussion caps, four bales of goods, one bale of goods for Signor Casati—a gift from myself; two pieces of blue serge, writing-paper, envelopes, blank books, etc.

Having after great difficulty—greater than was anticipated—brought relief to you, I am constrained to officially demand from you receipts for the above goods and relief brought to you, and also a definite answer to the question if you propose to accept our escort and assistance to reach Zanzibar, or if Signor Casati proposes to do so, or whether there are any officers or men disposed to accept our safe conduct to the sea. In the latter event, I would be obliged to you if you would kindly state how these persons desirous of leaving Africa can be communicated with. I would respectfully suggest that all persons desirous of leaving with me should proceed to and form camp either at Nsabé or at Kyya Nkondo's on the lake, with sufficient stores of grain, etc., to support them one month, and that a note should be sent to me informing me of the same via Kavalli, whence I soon may receive it. The person in charge of the people at this camp will inform me definitely whether the people are ready to accept of our safe conduct, and, upon being thus informed, I shall be pleased to assume all further charge of them.

If, at the end of twenty days, no news has been heard from you or Mr. Jephson, I cannot hold myself responsible for what may happen. We should be glad to stay at Kavalli's if we were assured of food, but a large following cannot be maintained there except by exacting contributions by force, which would entirely close our intercourse with the natives, and prevent us from being able to communicate with you.

If grain could be landed at Kyya Nkondo's by steamer, and left in charge of six or seven of your men, I could, upon being informed of the fact, send a detachment of men to convey it to the plateau. It is only the question of food that creates anxiety.

I am, your obedient servant,

(Signed) HENRY M. STANLEY,

Commanding Relief Expedition.

When these were sent off, Stanley settled down to a period of righteous disgruntlement. In his book he tells us he realised that Emin and Jephson had been taken prisoner on August 18th—on the very day he had arrived to hear Bonny's depressing story at Banalya and Jameson had been buried at Bangala. He could no longer doubt that some force had militated against the expedition from the first. Were it not for the fact that he had had all the worry, he might almost suppose that Higher Powers disapproved of the Pasha.

As for Jephson's letter—that might bewilder anyone! How Emin, whom Stanley believed to be absolute governor of an adoring people, came to be deposed and made prisoner by those people—and a prisoner who, in some mysterious way, was free to walk out of prison—might easily be a matter beyond the comprehension of anyone outside the province. Even Jephson, when he later came to write of it, found it no easy matter to clarify his adventure. We may now try to follow it for ourselves.

Chapter Thirteen

REBELLION AT THE EQUATOR

"I learned then for the first time that the Pasha had had no Province, government nor soldiers for nearly five years; that he was living undisturbed, and that some yielded sometimes to his wishes, apparently through mere sufferance and lack of legitimate excuse to cast him off utterly. But when he permitted himself by a gust of awakened optimism to venture into the presence of his soldiers, he was at once arrested, insulted, menaced and imprisoned."

STANLEY: Letter to the Relief Committee.

JEPHSON had gone willingly enough with Emin to read Stanley's letter to the soldiers, but he thought it all an odd business. "If by going round and addressing the people, I can induce them to come out with us, I shall do good work. At the same time it seems so strange to us who have come out to help these people, that it is necessary to explain who we are. I think there must be a screw loose somewhere." He was soon to discover where.

The first station he reached with Emin was M'swa, where they had met a few weeks before. Shukri Aga, the commander, appeared to be very attached to the Pasha and here all seemed well.

For some reason Emin chose this occasion to send his men across the lake to Kabba Rega's country, where great salt stores stood on the shore. The men were under orders to avenge Casati's undignified expulsion. They set the salt on fire but unfortunately burnt down the village of the one chief who had shown Casati kindness. The watchers at M'swa saw the black demon figures of the Sudanese outlined against the flames. Casati tells us: "Everywhere were heard cries, imprecations and the despairing anguish of the dying; the miserable fugitives were shot down; the country became a scene of extermination; women, children and infants were seized, stabbed and cast into the flames by the frenzied assailants." Emin was horrified by the cruelty he had let loose. To the commander and his men, returning triumphantly with goats, sheep and chickens, he said: "I do not thank you for the zeal you have displayed and the cruelty you have committed."

The Sudanese must have been bewildered by this condemnation of their zeal. According to Casati they were: ". . . never trained for

176

military work in the real sense of the word, and still less for attaining
the virtues of their calling such as obedience, self-abnegation, temper-
ance and respect to everyone." Nothing of which is surprising in face
of the facts that the Egyptians in the province, all ex-convicts, were
noted as thieves, bullies, hypocrites and slave-makers, and the
Sudanese, like all primitive peoples, tended to emulate their masters.

The steamer now continued to Tunguru. Here the one-eyed clerk
and the ex-adjutant who had visited Stanley had started to make
mischief. They had, they said, seen for themselves the famous expedition and it was nothing but a little band of sickly and tattered men.
They described it with indignation and contempt. For two years the
province had been awaiting arms and a force of soldiers that would
enable it to drive off the enemy upon the frontier. Instead there had
arrived this doubtful crew with a mere thirty-one cases of ammunition
and they expected a whole province full of men to follow them meekly
back to the coast. Did Stanley think they were all fools? Did he
think they could not realise the true purpose of the expedition—which
was, of course, to lead them to some British colony where they would
all, men, women and children, be sold into slavery?

When Emin and Jephson arrived at the island, the two trouble-
makers, like the rest of the officials, met them with hand-kissing and
assurances of loyalty and devotion, but next day one of their friends
told the Pasha of their visit and complaints to Stanley. Emin was
deeply hurt by their behaviour; his pride was wounded by the knowledge that Stanley should, in this manner, have discovered something
of the state of things inside the province. He ordered Achmet to be
conveyed under arrest to Dufilé and Abdul, with two officers who
supported him, to be confined to his house.

To Jephson's amazement uproar resulted. The whole station argued
and protested wildly before anyone attempted to carry out Emin's
commands.

Casati advised the Pasha to adopt a conciliatory attitude towards the
troops, but Emin, hurt, angry and encouraged by Jephson's indignant
misunderstanding of the situation, decided on a policy of repression
that might possibly have succeeded some five years before. Jephson
urged Emin to execute the clerk and captain, but Emin knew better
than to do that. The clerk was put in irons and the three officers
reduced to the ranks.

Casati protested that this was unwise, at which Emin turned on him furiously, accusing him of trying to rule him and usurp his privileges. Casati retired wounded to his quarters, where he was visited by Jephson. The young Englishman, still shining with public-school ideals, hoped to make peace. He gently reproached Casati for lack of respect towards the head of the government. Casati, feeling that this was too much, gave Jephson a frank description of a state of affairs inside the province for which he largely blamed Emin's weak policy. Jephson, shocked to hear such an opinion of a governor well known to be a brilliant administrator, leader of men and intellectual, could only shake his head in pained disbelief.

Next morning, June 23rd, the Tunguru garrison was assembled to hear read the letter from the Khedive. Soldiers, clerks and other employees, dressed in their best, stood in rows with five Turkish flags flying over their heads. As Emin and Jephson approached, the flags were dipped and trumpeters played the Khedivial Hymn. Jephson took his place and read the letter through an interpreter:

To His EXCELLENCY MEHMED EMIN,
Mudir of Hatalastiva.*

Some time ago I commended you for your bravery and for the stand you and your officers and soldiers made, and for your victory over the adversities which beset you I have rewarded you by conferring upon you the exalted rank of a general, and I have confirmed every promotion you have conferred on your officers, and have informed you of all this by my sovereign letter of November 29th, 1886, No. 31. And most certainly this letter reached you, together with the post forwarded by our Prime Minister, His Excellency Nubar Pasha. I am very pleased with your good behaviour and with whatever you have done, you, your officers and soldiers, and therefore my government has busied itself with the means to extricate you, and save you if possible from the straits in which you find yourself. And now there has been constituted a force, under the direction of Mr. Stanley, the famous savant, who is known in all parts of the world for his great qualities and pre-eminence as a traveller. This expedition is now ready to start for you, and with it whatever you are in need of in the way of provisions of every description, to bring you, your officers and soldiers, to Egypt, by the road Mr. Stanley considers is most preferable and easiest to march on. Therefore I command you, by this my order, sent by the hands of Mr. Stanley,

* Egyptian name for Equatoria.

to make known to you all these things, that after the arrival of this you will communicate them to your officers and soldiers, and read before them my Sovereign greetings with the intention to inform them of this. At the same time I give to you, to your officers and soldiers, full liberty to rest where you are, or to do your best to come out with the expedition which is now sent to you. Our government has decided to pay you and all the employés, officers and soldiers, all the appointments and allowances due to you. If, however, anyone, officer or soldier, wishes to rest in the country, he is free to do so, but he does so on his own responsibility, and must not in future expect any assistance from this government. And now make them understand all this distinctly, and communicate it word for word to all your officers and soldiers, in order that every one may make up his mind. This is our Sovereign Order.

(Signed) MOHAMMED TEWFIK

After this, Jephson read a letter from Stanley describing the hardship through which the expedition had come to rescue them and his willingness to do all in his power for them.

The two letters seemed to impress the excitable Egyptians. They said they would do just what the Pasha did. If he stayed, they would stay. If he went, they would go. The Pasha sighed deeply.

When interviewed apart in Emin's house, the officers and officials emphasised their devotion and respect for their governor, but behind his back they discussed angrily and with growing suspicion what might lie behind these plans. Even if the expedition were genuine and would take them to safety, what had they to gain? The letter only promised them pay until they reached Egypt and there was no mention of future employment. Then supposing they left the province—how could young children, without proper food, stand such a journey? How, indeed, could any of them stand it? But, supposing they arrived safely! What then? Most of them were ruffians who would have descended to thieving and beggary in Egypt and they knew that never again would they be so well off as they were here. An Egyptian's wealth was indicated by the number of his dependents. These officials had crowded their homes with wives, concubines, servants and slaves at very little cost. They took whom and what they wanted from the native villages. The danger that threatened here might not come; their degeneration in Cairo was a certainty. How to choose whether to stay or go? They preferred to let the responsibility lie with Emin.

As for the soldiers—the majority of them, although called Sudanese, were members of surrounding tribes. Here they were in their native land. If they went to this northern, alien land of Egypt, their religions and customs would be laughed at as barbarities. They had set up households in the Egyptian manner, had become sophisticated and felt superior to their fellows. In Egypt they would be at best mere poverty-stricken privates. Yet if the officers went and they remained, what could they hope for? A Mahdist invasion, when they would be taken into slavery, or, if left free, suffer a gradual return to savagery. Savagery, being the thing they had just cast off, they despised more than anything.

Suliman Aga, commander of the Tunguru garrison, tried to take a more hopeful view. He was a Nubian of narrow but quick intelligence. He had heard, either from Emin or Casati, of the suggestion that they should evacuate to Lake Victoria. He now approached the white men and said he thought it would be a good thing were the governor and his people conducted to a country near the sea and left to settle there. Jephson made no comment. He had been "strictly enjoined to understand that the expedition's first duty was to the Khedive".

As soon as Emin and Jephson, on donkey-back, had departed for Wadelai, Suliman Aga adopted a different tone. He advised his men to resist the Christians to the end, and showered on the departing backs of his beloved governor and the courteous young visitor the grossest insults. Casati, who had been left at Tunguru, was ordered to remain in his house. "If he will not obey," swore Suliman Aga, drunk with rebellion, "I will have him thrashed."

Casati wrote to warn Emin of this disloyalty but Emin replied: "I have no cause to be afraid now; I hold the knife by the handle and am accompanied by an Englishman."

On the journey to Wadelai Emin took observations every few minutes with a prismatic compass. It had been his intention to survey all the roads round his station. Although he might soon be in flight never to return, he saw in this possibility no hindrance to his life's routine. Having no will to leave, he behaved as though there was no question of his doing so.

They spent the night at the village of a chief named Boki. This Boki, who a few months before had accepted a fine gift of ivory while failing to deliver in return a letter to Kabba Rega, was now in prison. As the white men sat beneath the trees in the evening, Boki's favourite wife threw herself at Emin's feet and begged her husband's release. The Pasha, melted at once, promised her all she asked.

Next morning the little procession reached Wadelai. It was met by a parade of soldiers, picked men in smart uniforms, and a number of clerks in full robes of white cotton. It was as well Stanley was not present to note this finery.

Here, in the largest, most strongly fortified station in the province, fine bamboo huts stood on either side of wide streets. Emin's hut was the biggest in the province. Inside the domed main room were European chairs and tables, the two divans that custom required as seats of honour, and the supreme luxury of two large bookcases filled with books. Jephson, sitting on a divan, was presented to the officers and officials and had his hand covered with smacking kisses.

When this ordeal was over, Emin carried in his adored child, Farida, a pretty, delicate, light-skinned little creature dressed in Arab costume. Jephson found her delightful. He realised that Emin, living in this pleasant place with his daughter, had created for himself a life that justified his hesitation to leave it. Here, where he had laboured and created, he had provision and occupation for his old age. What comparable future could there be for him outside? He saw himself in Egypt, half-blind and ailing, merely a shelved official in exile with about £2,000 on which to eke out his days.

Jephson was shown to his own hut, which stood in a garden of fruit-hung lime, orange and pomegranate trees. He soon settled down to the life of the station and, living agreeably, eating well, suffering no more than a few bouts of fever that were cured by Emin's pills, be began to feel troubled that things should be so easy for him while his comrades trudged back through the forest. Events were soon to put his conscience at rest.

First came a letter from Hamad Aga, Major of the 1st Battalion, a man loyal to Emin but forced by weight of opinion to join the rebellion. He said they had heard of the expedition's arrival, realised the governor had been right all the time and now wished to apologise. They asked to be taken back into favour and would accept whatever terms the Pasha might dictate.

Emin was jubilant. Everything sounded fine. Jephson saw himself returning triumphantly from the province with every inhabitant behind him. But time was getting short. He had promised to join Nelson at

Fort Bodo within a few weeks and he thought the citizens of Wadelai should begin their packing. When urged, however, the citizens made no move. They wanted first to hear what their brethren in the northern stations intended to do. Also, it was harvest time and they could not leave their crops standing in the fields. They would need the grain for the journey.

Jephson, who would require a good many soldiers and carriers, if he were first to evacuate Fort Bodo then build a new fort for Stanley by the lakeside, began to feel worried and frustrated. The people were polite. They spoke of their loyalty to Emin but refused with bland obstinacy to do anything they did not want to do. Jephson realised that the governor by now had resigned himself to this standstill condition but he could not help blaming Emin for submitting to the character of these people. He became very restless.

There was little he could do. An envoy was expected from the 1st Battalion; no one would consider moving before it arrived. He would have to wait like the rest. Unfortunately at this time Emin had a severe heart attack and, while he lay in bed, Jephson wandered about the station alone, quite exhausted by inactivity.

The envoy arrived at last. Emin asked Jephson to interview the men and to give them the impression that the governor's pardon would not be too easy to obtain.

The leader of the envoy, Hamad Aga, admitted that the rebels were bored by rebellion. Their grain crop had failed. The soldiers had got out of hand. They had robbed the natives until the natives had fled and no one remained to be robbed. Hamad Aga felt that the primary trouble had been Emin's self-sacrifice and indulgent attitude towards them. His people did not appreciate kindness. To them it seemed merely weakness.

But, commented Hamad: "All will come right, now that you have arrived."

This Jephson very much doubted. He was, he said, "getting terribly sceptical about these people". He saw on one side the Pasha, with his vast experience, assuring him that the people were good and faithful— and the fact they had repulsed the Mahdi and, in spite of lack of supplies, held the country, seemed to prove this. There was also to be considered the Pasha's European reputation for wisdom and firmness that could not be without basis! Yet on the other side was Jephson's own instinct which, he says, whispered "Beware". He asked himself who was he, with his small experience, to set up his opinion against that of a world-famous man like Emin? He decided he must be mistaken.

Next day he brought the envoy to Emin and interceded for the rebels. Emin, delighted by this little play, received them coldly and upbraided them for three years of disobedience. To their surprise he ended by saying he would have nothing to do with them, and they became more humble than before. When they left Emin's presence they crowded round Jephson and begged him to intercede for them again. For a few days the Pasha refused to appear moved, then he decided the time had come for forgiveness. The members of the envoy wept with gratitude when they heard that their governor and Jephson would return with them to Rejaf.

On July 16th they all set out by steamer for Dufilé, beyond which the cataracts made river travel impossible. Dufilé was *en fête* for Jephson's visit. The soldiers paraded and the trumpeters played the Khedivial Hymn. On the quayside a bullock's throat was slit and to the reluctant young Englishman was accorded the special privilege of wading through the beast's blood. The guests were led by a guard of honour to a tree-shaded square, where they held court and drank sherbet. They were accommodated in brick houses that kept out the heat.

This reception had been arranged by Major Hawashi, whose past treachery was now forgiven and forgotten. In the evening Jephson was shown over the station. Dufilé had been established by Gordon and rebuilt by Emin on a healthier site. With its moat and earthworks, its cannon raised over the countryside, and its heavy, iron-studded gates, it resembled a little fortress. The oldest station of the province, with the air of a city in the making, Dufilé had the beginnings of a history. The central square of the old town remained part of the new and beneath its fig-trees was the spot where Gordon often sat with map and compasses and expounded schemes that widened for his audience the bounds of possibility. The great Sir Samuel Baker, the first governor, and his Hungarian wife whose mercy and long, brilliant hair had become a legend, Gessi Pasha, Prout and Mason Bey, had all talked and drunk their coffee there.

On one side of the square was Emin's compound. On the others the brick-built quarters of officers and civil servants. The clerks and soldiers lived in huts. There was a mosque in traditional style and a school that was presided over by a man banished from Egypt for assisting in a murder. Now as teacher, lawyer, priest and conductor, five times a day, of prayer-meetings, his social position was impeccable.

The government gardens faced the river and were bordered by an esplanade. Here boats were built and launched. Inside the fortifications were orchards and vegetable gardens; outside a two mile wide belt of grain fields, a market and native villages. The streets of the town were swept twice a day. The whole place presented an appearance of pleasant order and to it Emin had given much care and thought.

Living there in luxury, the Mahdi forgotten, what Egyptian would wish to abandon all and trek across unknown country to the doubtful welcome of a city from which he had been expelled in disgrace? Not Major Hawashi.

That evening he joined Emin and Jephson beneath the trees for coffee. Jephson took against him at once. He realised that here was a man who was quite frankly a scoundrel, bumptious, grasping and generally hated. Hawashi held his place by his energy, education and ability—extremely rare among Egyptians—to obey orders scrupulously and make others obey them. Jephson appreciated his value, but did not find his cynical shamelessness amusing. He seemed to enjoy telling the visitor what a bad lot the Egyptians were.

"And you?" smiled Emin.

"Oh," replied the Major, "you know, your Excellency, I am just as bad as the rest." Turning to Jephson, he said: "You are quite a stranger in this country, so bear in mind what I am going to tell you, and be warned by what I say. In this country there are only Sudanese and Egyptians. If a Sudanese comes at you with scowls on his face and a loaded gun, whilst on the other hand an Egyptian comes to you with a carpet and a friendly salutation, turn to the Sudanese; he with his loaded gun will do you less harm than the Egyptian with his smiles and carpet."

That evening a dinner party was given at which poor Jephson, surfeited with oily foods, had to listen to Hawashi's reasons for disliking and distrusting everyone in the province. The Pasha was prudently praised but even this praise was qualified. Emin, he said, was weak and easily imposed upon by politeness and protestations of loyalty made by anyone intriguing against him. (A fact Hawashi very well knew.) He warned Jephson not to venture too confidently among the rebel 1st Battalion—indeed he would be wise not to go near them.

Jephson began to feel **very** discomforted: "This conversation had a great effect on me, for it strengthened the doubt, which was daily growing stronger in my mind, that Emin had not grasped the situation, and did not really know his people. Stray words which had been let drop by different people—words which at the time had not conveyed much meaning to my mind, kept rising before me, as I lay awake all night, thinking, thinking, thinking. Ah! for five minutes only, now, with Stanley, to listen to his clear shrewd advice.''

But Stanley was deep in the forest and Jephson had to face this alone. Depressed and worried, he persuaded Emin that when they reached the next station, Kirri, they would be wise to wait while the envoy proceeded to try the mood of Rejaf.

Between rows of soldiers, to the sound of trumpets and the fluttering of innumerable flags, the governor marched out of Dufilé next morning. His eyes grew moist at this display of loyalty and Jephson's heart was so lightened he could turn his attention to the beauty of the mountain scenery and make nature notes all the way to Kirri.

Huts were prepared for them at the little station. They settled in and Hamad Aga continued to Rejaf. Emin promised forgiveness on condition that the ringleaders of the rebellion were handed over to him. He was very optimistic and told Jephson he was sure that if the officers did not agree, most of the men would desert and join him at Kirri.

"This," commented Jephson, "I very much doubted."

A few days later Hamad wrote to say that the two chief trouble-makers were absent from Rejaf and no decision could be reached until they returned. It was evident the officers were terrified of these two, who during the rebellion had lived like robber chiefs, making raids on the natives, seizing their women and cattle, and hanging, shooting and mutilating the men.

Emin hoped that, were the two sent to him, he would reform them. Jephson was doubtful and very uneasy. His uneasiness was increased by the fact that the one-eyed clerk of Tunguru, supposed to be in prison, was busily writing round to the stations to cause trouble. To the chief at Kirri he wrote that Jephson was only a tool put up by Emin and Stanley to deceive the province. He had really come only from Uganda, his Sudanese orderlies were a blind, and the expedition was merely an expedition of travellers. They could not possibly have come from Egypt, for had they been sent by the Khedive he would surely have sent 300 soldiers, not three.

"But," Jephson asked the Kirri chief when shown this letter, "what can it matter whether we come from Egypt or not, so that we are willing to help you?"

The chief told him that if the people could not be convinced the expedition came from Egypt, they would never move.

Jephson was tired of these people. When he next read the Khedive's letter, he did so in a disinterested fashion. He told his listeners they could stay if they wished. They would be the losers by so doing. Their ammunition would soon run out, then the natives from outlying parts would fall on them and the few that survived would have no choice but to lapse into savagery.

It was soon evident Jephson had struck the right note. The people of Kirri were disturbed. Like spoilt children who would make things difficult for anyone silly enough to worry about them, they would if they felt neglected worry about themselves. They all now declared they wished to follow Emin. They wanted nothing better than to be removed from the influence of the Rejaf rebels. One non-commissioned officer, stepping from the ranks, said: "What a pity it is you do not go down to Rejaf, and speak these words to the soldiers, for if they heard the words you have spoken to-day, they would see their position clearly, and there would be no more trouble."

Everyone seemed pleased by the decision to go. Kirri, a bleak, outlying station in a district denuded by the rebels, had none of the attractions of Dufilé. No one would be sorry to leave it and a triumphal dance was hastily organised to celebrate departure.

Just as the dance began a disturbing letter arrived from Hamad Ago:

To His Excellency the Governor of Hatalastiva.

After having kissed your hands with all veneration, I ask God the Highest not to keep me long from your Excellency's presence. I beg to report I am still in Rejaf, and look anxiously for an opportunity to leave here, where I am detained, and rejoin your Excellency. I now report for your favour, that I have heard that the officers here have conspired to retain your Excellency here, should you honour this place with your presence. They do not intend to permit you to return, but propose to start by way of Gondokoro, to rejoin their government, which they are convinced still exists at Khartoum.

Your Excellency is not aware of what these people are capable, and as I consider it my duty through my devotion to you to inform your

Excellency of this, I venture to expose this plot. As for myself, since my arrival here, I have not entered in any way into affairs, and whatever has been done, has been done without consulting me. It is my utmost wish now to find a way to escape from here. If our Lord gives me His hands and saves me, praises be to Him; but if not, His will be done. This is all I am able to tell your Excellency.

(Signed) HAMAD MAHOMET,

Major, 1st Battalion.

July 28th, 1888

This news brought the dance to an abrupt stop. Emin and Jephson hurriedly started packing their bags. The man who brought the letter whispered to Emin that were his Excellency to go to Rejaf most of the soldiers would help him arrest the rebel officers. Emin became filled with doubts and worries. He would willingly take the risk of going to Rejaf, but would it be the right thing to do? If the officers proved the stronger and arrested him, he would be letting down his loyal people in the south. Then there was Jephson to be considered, and the expedition. . . . No. No, he could not take such a risk.

Soon the governor's party was ready for the road. Before leaving the station Emin, with the idea of starting its evacuation, ordered the ammunition in the store house to be sent after them. They had gone about a mile when a messenger caught up with them. He brought the news that the Kirri garrison had closed round the ammunition and refused to permit its removal.

Jephson was outraged to hear of such behaviour. He urged Emin to return, as Stanley would have done, and enforce obedience. Emin listened to this advice without enthusiasm. The news had troubled rather than surprised or angered him. He could not now summon the spirit necessary to make such action effective. He refused to return. He sent the messenger back to say that he insisted on the ammunition being sent at once.

Jephson showed frank disapproval of such leniency. This he knew was not the way to rule such a province. He realised how well Hawashi had summed Emin up.

But this disapproval had no effect on Emin. He was weary of trouble and merely wanted to get away from it. Unfortunately the importunate messenger caught him up again. The soldiers, he said, had refused to listen to the repeated order. They were convinced that the

G

governor was taking the ammunition for his own purposes and intended to abandon them. They threatened to join the Rejaf rebels.

Jephson was young in years, considerate and well bred. It was not in his nature to attempt to override an older man whose experience and authoritative position should denote a wisdom greater than his own. He had been the first among the officers to place an admiring confidence in Stanley and would as willingly have placed it in Emin, but he felt forced to write: "From that day I lost faith in Emin's advice and assurances with regard to his people; I felt that a heavy cloud was gathering over us, and that serious trouble was impending." He believed that had Emin returned the short distance to Kirri, explained his order and seen it carried out, all might have been well. Now what might result? He himself had no choice but to follow Emin.

The next pause was at Muggi, a station on the river a few miles south of Kirri. In the middle of the night Emin wakened Jephson to show him a letter that said the Rejaf rebels had descended on Kirri, seized the ammunition and taken the Kirri chief prisoner. Pathetically, Emin asked the young man's advice. Jephson was only too willing to give it. He suggested that a letter be sent to Kirri to say that those of the inhabitants who wished to follow Emin should come to Muggi, the rest might stay with the rebels. The letter was sent.

Jephson was touched by the governor's confidence in him. He wrote: "I pitied Emin terribly, he was worn out by years of residence in the Equatorial province, with all its unceasing anxiety. He had stuck to his people, and had repulsed the Mahdi's attacks unaided by the outside world, and now for the last three years the trouble of rebellion had been added to his other anxieties. He told me he was perfectly worn out by it all, and would gladly lay down his burden: 'But,' he said, 'who will take it up?'

"I had a long talk with him that night, and I felt ashamed, as I listened to his story, that I had been so irritated by his want of promptness two days ago. It is difficult for a young man, full of vigorous life, to understand how hard it must sometimes be for an elderly man, worn out in body and mind by long years of hard work and anxiety, to act with energy and promptness."

Jephson's sympathy had overcome Emin's pride and the older man now confided in the younger that the situation was almost beyond him. During the five years he was cut off from supplies, assistance and advice, the innumerable problems of the state and the ingratitude of the people had utterly exhausted him. He suffered from heart disease and insomnia, and from fits of despairing melancholy that he could overcome only by a tremendous effort of will.

The two men, both sensitive, kindly natures, the one prematurely aged in a destructive climate, the other a mere youth, sat talking in complete sympathy until daybreak. It was, Jephson said, a night he would never forget: "He told me of his life, of his hopes and fears, his struggles and disappointments, and all with a simple earnestness which touched me with remorse when I thought how often I had allowed myself to be irritated by his want of energy and decision."

Next day a crowd of the Kirri soldiers, converted by the eloquence of Emin's messenger, and fifteen of the Rejaf men arrived at Muggi. They all expressed themselves penitent and willing to follow Emin to death if need be. Emin put up a show of sternness but was easily overcome by their plea that they had rebelled under orders from their officers. The Rejaf men asked him why he had not come to Rejaf and were very indignant when he told them their officers had plotted to seize him.

Emin at once became wildly hopeful that these men, when they returned among their fellows, would persuade all the rebels of their error. Jephson thought it wonderful "that Emin should, after long years of experience among them, place such confidence in people who had already deceived him half a hundred times".

The next stage of the journey took Emin and Jephson twenty miles south to Laboré. There the chief, Surore Aga, told them he had already spoken to the soldiers, who said they were willing to begin evacuating the station at any time. Possibly Surore Aga hoped that the governor would accept this assurance and ask for no other. But Jephson had to read the letters, and as he did so was surprised to notice that the soldiers, far from greeting him as a deliverer, seemed inattentive and whispered among themselves. The crowd of civilians behind kept stirring uneasily as though waiting for something to happen.

When the letters were finished, no comment was made. Emin stepped forward to speak, and as he did so the ranks were broken by a big, sullen-faced, bull-headed Sudanese, who declared they were willing to depart but the date should not be fixed until after the harvest. Jephson sharply replied that he must know their intention by the next morning. At this the soldier shouted arrogantly: "All you have been telling us is a lie, and the letter you have read out is a forgery, for if it had come from Effendina he would have commanded us to come, and not have told us we might do as we please. You do not come from Egypt, we know of only one road to Egypt, and that is by Khartoum, we will either go by that road, or will live and die in this country."

Emin sprang forward at once, seized the man and, trying to snatch away the gun pointed at him, called to his four orderlies to arrest and imprison this mutineer. The mutineer himself shouted to his companions for help. All was confusion in a moment. The soldiers, levelling their guns, surrounded the two white men and shouted threats. Emin drew his sword and dared anyone to touch him.

Emin's secretary ran and hid behind a tree; his hunter sank to the ground and begged Allah for mercy; a clerk ran screaming into Surore Aga's house where, hiding beneath a bed, he cried forth that the governor was murdered and so set the servants howling with terror; an orderly, a notable drunkard much given to prayer, staggered off, fell and was trampled underfoot.

Then someone shouted that Emin's orderlies were about to seize the powder-magazine. At once the mutineers, forgetting their prisoners, dashed off in a body to defend the ammunition. The Pasha and Jephson found themselves alone with an apologetic Surore Aga.

Emin was persuaded to stay where he was while Jephson followed the soldiers and tried to calm them. He found them gathered excitedly round the powder-magazine and they broke into screams as he approached. They told him to go back. He said he had come only as a friend.

"You see," he said, "I am unarmed and alone. I have no fear of you, because you are soldiers and not savages."

After some moments of similar flattery had persuaded them to listen, Jephson told them they had been wrong in suspecting any evil intention on his part. If they did not wish to leave the province, no one would force them to go.

They were soon calmed and convinced, but, like children who must retain some excuse for their folly, they insisted that Emin had caused all the trouble by seizing the Sudanese.

When Jephson returned to Surore Aga's house he found Emin in a very excitable state. He was certain the soldiers would attack them that night. Jephson was equally certain they would not. Surore Aga kept expressing his regrets that such an incident had occurred at his station, but it was later discovered that the mutineer, who was his orderly, had acted under his orders.

Next morning the soldiers asked Jephson to address them again. They kept insisting that Emin was to blame for the outbreak and said they disliked and distrusted him because he intended deserting their brothers at Rejaf. Nothing Jephson could say could convince them of anything else. For all that, they were now ashamed that they had behaved so rudely towards a guest and were as apologetic as Surore Aga.

No decision to go or stay had been made at Laboré when the governor took to the road again. He had decided to stop at the little station of Khor Ayu between Laboré and Dufilé. The three-day Mohammedan festival of Idel Keber was due to start and Emin was in no mood for the noisy rejoicings that would be taking place at Dufilé. While resting at Khor Aju he received a letter from Hamad Aga which said the two notorious rebel leaders had now returned from their hunt. If Emin wished to see them he could come and do so.

Jephson was indignant at this impertinence. He wrote that if the officers wished to see him they could come to Dufilé. He enclosed a copy of the Khedive's letter that later fell into Mahdist hands and was sent to Egypt as a proof that the Equatorial province had fallen.

Emin, deeply depressed, told Jephson that had Stanley arrived six months later he would have been too late to save him. His prestige, he said, had suffered a heavy blow in the Rejaf rebellion. Jephson said that had Emin sent news of the rebellion to Europe, a more suitable expedition would have set forth.

Later in the day another letter arrived, more disturbing than the first. It was from Hawashi Effendi and his news was grave. Dufilé was in rebellion and he a prisoner. Three officers had seized the store-houses and powder-magazines and had, without much difficulty, convinced the men that the Khedive's letter was a forgery and Emin plotting with Stanley to lead them all into slavery. An officer named Fadl-el-Mulla had been elected in Hawashi's place.

The fear of slavery was an old one. The natives had lived with it for generations; the Egyptians had a natural dread of suffering the ill-treatment they had inflicted on others.

Achmed Effendi, the one-eyed mischief-maker of M'swa, far from being imprisoned, had followed Emin to Dufilé. Trouble-making increased his self-importance but this time he started more than he would have imagined possible. After listening to his malicious description of the state of the expedition and his talk of slavery, the town panicked. In this country every official, every new arrival, was a potential slaver. No one was above suspicion and no one out of danger. It was easy to believe the expedition might be a hoax. It had come, not from the direction of Egypt, but from the very forest where the Manyuema had their headquarters.

As for the Pasha—with his peculiarly Christian virtues and his out-rageously democratic ideals, he had always been incomprehensible and half-suspect. Now it could be seen that he had been a deceiver all the time. He knew Khartoum had not fallen. He was plotting with these criminal English to enslave the whole province.

No one had wished to leave Dufilé, but everyone had been worried by the need to make a decision. Here was the solution of the situation—rebellion. In a few hours the whole station was in an uproar.

The officers at once saw the chance to get rid of Hawashi. Fadl-el-Mulla, the captain of a garrison at Fabo, acted with remarkable promptness. He marched to Dufilé, arrested Hawashi, and declared himself the saviour of the province. Being a popular character, he was acclaimed at once. When the garrison and townspeople gathered round him, he told them there was no question of evacuating the province. No one was in any danger. He was the hero of the hour. Nothing remained but to depose and arrest the governor. Crowds gathered on the ramparts to await his arrival.

The two Europeans were trapped. Behind them waited the Rejaf rebels; before them the rebels of Dufilé. They knew that even if they tried to evade capture, somewhere in this disturbed country they would be caught and sent ignominiously to one of the centres of rebellion. They realised there was nothing to be done but proceed to Dufilé.

Jephson said he "pitied poor Emin intensely". The Pasha was, he knew, in no fear, for he was "plucky from head to foot", but he was cut to the heart that his people, for whom he had done everything and given up everything, should so turn against him.

The journey to Dufilé was made in silence. When they reached the crest of the hill overlooking the city they saw the people, white-clad for the feast, awaiting them in excited groups. As they descended the hill, all chatter ceased. Expectant faces crowded the ramparts. From within came an uproar that was gradually stilled as Emin advanced. The waiting people parted silently to let pass the desolate figure of the governor who had given ten years of his life to their welfare.

No salutes were fired. There was no guard of honour. The flags were not for Emin.

When the two white men reached the gates, sentries stepped before and behind them, cutting them off from their few followers. They continued under arrest. The people, seeing this, now crowded forward to stare and point derisively at them. The clerks and officers remained in the background as though ashamed of humiliating their governor in this way, but the soldiers, most of them drunk, shouted insults and roared insulting songs. Only one man—a little Circassian tinker, a Christian, a man from another world—showed compassion. In spite of the threats of the crowds, he pushed his way forward, seized and kissed Emin's hand and gazed at him with tear-filled eyes.

Emin and the doctor, Vita Hassan, were informed they were prisoners and put into a compound surrounded by a fence. Jephson was not actually a prisoner but he chose to go into the compound with the others. Within was bare ground and two miserable, unfurnished huts. The crowd, made confident by drink, jeered over the fence top and spat at the orderlies as they brought in the luggage.

All the blame was put on to Emin. The people, most of whom treasured minor grievances of one sort or another, at once saw their governor, whom a month before they had acclaimed and honoured, as an arch-enemy.

Emin, making no protest and no attempt to defend his dignity, accepted arrest as though he could fight no more. He sat within the compound in a state of deep depression. Jephson, against whom no definite charge could be made, was free to wander round the station in the company of his guard. Neither had any idea what was going to happen to them.

The officers of the rebel 1st Battalion were now invited to attend a council meeting at which Emin's fate would be decided. While awaiting the guests, Fadl-el-Mulla and his officers compiled a list of his crimes. The list grew daily longer and longer.

Life in the compound was not pleasant. The square outside was always crowded and people enjoyed speculating loudly on what sort of unpleasant death Emin might soon expect. On one side of the compound was the incessant noise of a school. On another lived a sadist whose day was spent in flogging his wives and slaves. To the tender Emin and chivalrous young Jephson, the cries of these women formed the least supportable part of their captivity.

Emin's orderlies and boys brought in what news they could. Apparently the chief difficulty the rebels faced was merely to decide what form Emin's execution should take. All agreed it should be spectacular and painful.

Parts of the steamers' engines had been locked away, so no one could attempt to rescue the prisoners. Jephson was particularly upset to learn that a plot was afoot to fall on Stanley's camp when he returned, seize his weapons and supplies, then turn him adrift. He wrote Stanley a warning letter which he managed to send secretly to the chief of M'swa, a man he trusted. This was the first of many letters which he sent out whenever possible. One only reached Stanley.

Days passed without event. Then the orderlies told the prisoners that some letters had arrived which had caused Fadl-el-Mulla to call a special council meeting. Emin and Jephson sat up late speculating what the news could be. Next morning they were delighted to hear that Stanley, with many fresh men and loads, a large boat and three elephants, had arrived at the lake. Jephson had some doubts about the elephants.

After the first excitement of this news, they suffered a period of anxiety. They could discover nothing more. Jephson continued to write warning letters to Stanley and was in a constant state of anxiety lest the whole expedition should walk into a trap. He had been told he would have to appear before a meeting of the rebels. He could only hope that then he might be able to influence them.

At last the officers of the 1st Battalion arrived from Rejaf. They were accorded a triumphal entry into Dufilé. Soldiers were lined up to salute them, flags were flown, trumpets sounded, and they passed, amid acclamations, to the central square. They halted opposite Emin's prison yard. Speeches were made and the two groups of rebels exchanged congratulations on their rebellions.

That evening a great carousal was held on the beer and millet whisky Emin had taught his people to make. The square resounded with fine speeches, congratulations and playful suggestions of ways in which Jephson, Emin, Vita Hassan and, of course, Hawashi, might be exterminated.

On the next day the council met. Jephson was brought out of the compound to give an account of himself and his expedition. In the divan the officers sat in a semicircle. The majority were Sudanese with heavy-witted and sullen faces, but there were a number of delicate-featured, degenerate Egyptians. Fadl-el-Mulla himself was Sudanese, tall, enormously fat, with a facial expression that was neither unintelligent nor unpleasant.

Jephson's Sudanese orderlies were called first. Jephson impressed on them the need to tell the truth so that their evidence might not conflict. In the divan they were questioned roughly as to their origin. If they were soldiers of the Effendina, where were their uniforms? They answered that their uniforms had been worn to shreds in the forest.

"Liars," shouted the officers. "These men are no soldiers. They have been picked up by Stanley, who is a common adventurer."

One of the orderlies showed the Egyptian brand on his rifle and offered to go through his drill. He performed it admirably, but the rebels chose to remain unconvinced.

Jephson was then called. Fadl-el-Mulla asked questions about the expedition until its whole story was told. And why, asked Fadl-el-Mulla, did Stanley bring only letters from the Khedive? Why did he not also bring letters from the friends or relatives of the officers in the province? Such letters would have been more convincing because more difficult to forge.

Jephson admitted the oversight, but said that an expedition coming to rescue men it believed to be in a desperate plight did not expect to be asked for its credentials.

But why did the Khedive not send one of his officers or a pasha with the expedition? The word of such a one would have convinced them all. It was a pity these things had not been thought of. Yes, Jephson agreed dryly, it was a pity.

The letters from the Khedive and Nubar Pasha were then taken and examined closely by clerks familiar with their signature. A long discussion followed. At last a clerk rose, threw the Khedive's letter at Jephson's feet and shouted: "It is a forgery, and you and your masters are impostors."

Jephson tells us: "My first impulse was to knock him down, but with a strong effort I restrained myself. Something in my face must have shown the officers how difficult the effort to control my anger was, for they dragged the clerk away and ordered him to be silent."

In the excited discussion that followed, it was decided to send the steamers up to the lake to capture Stanley. Jephson told them they would be wasting their time. Stanley would immediately ask: "Where is your Mudir, where is my officer?" and at once suspecting the truth, would open fire.

The rebels said they would explain to Stanley that Emin and Jephson were busy in the province and would offer to take him to them.

"You do not know the man with whom you propose to deal," said Jephson, "he will see through the thin covering of your plot like lightning and, moreover, will act like lightning." He demanded to be sent back to his leader, but the officers refused to let him go. He now began taunting them for treating a guest in this way. They were, he said, acting like savages. He had come among them only to help them, and after greeting him on his entry into the country with bows and fine words, they had intrigued against him. His life had been threatened at Laboré; here he had been imprisoned and insulted; and now they refused to let him join his own people.

"Do not," he said, "come before me again with your bowings and protestations, and do not offer me your hands, for I know your hearts are full of treachery against me, your guest, who has come to help you. You are savages and not soldiers."

After this outburst, a tremendous confusion of tongues arose. Some of the officers were for punishing him for his words but others cried "Shame!" He realised he had, by touching on the strict laws of Mohammedan hospitality, roused the more serious-minded of them: "I could not possibly have said any bitterer thing to them. There is, too, in these people, these negroes, a certain rough chivalry. Not only have I noticed it here, but I have seen it in our Zanzibaris. 'Chivalry in a negro!' I hear some people say in a tone of contempt, and I answer: 'Yes, chivalry in a negro, as chivalry in a European.' It may not wear quite the same form as ours, but for all that it is chivalry of the truest kind. Touch that string, strike that chord, and you will be answered by as true a strain of melody as ever you could draw from a European."

High above the uproar rose the voice of Fadl-el-Mulla: "By Allah! he has spoken truly, and he shall join his people. I am the head of the council and I swear it!"

Three days later Jephson set out on the *Khedive* to join Stanley on the lakeside. He left Emin reluctantly but knew he could do more for him by going than by staying and risking Stanley's walking into a trap.

The journey, which those sent to accompany him made as difficult for him as possible, ended in bitter disappointment. At Tunguru Casati came on board and told him that not only the elephants but the whole story of Stanley's arrival had originated in some negro's imagination. He persuaded Jephson to remain with him while the steamer went on to M'swa. Jephson remained, fearing he might be failing in his duty by so doing, but the steamer returned to confirm Casati's assurances that Stanley was not at the lake-end. Indeed the rebels had taken the opportunity to steal the thirty boxes of Remington cartridges which Stanley had left there.

Fadl-el-Mulla had sent to Tunguru asking Casati to Dufilé to see Emin and to attend the meetings of the rebel officers. He agreed to go.

At Tunguru Fadl-el-Mulla's representatives acted as though their master were the new governor. They took possession of the government store-house and their captain ordered the Tunguru garrison to be called together. He addressed the soldiers thus:

"The Mudir has outraged the province for five years by acts of despotism, injustice, violence and extortion, and has favoured people according to his own caprice, to the detriment of others who had better claims, and now, as a culmination of the ignominy, he conspires to sell it to the British—but we have proclaimed a new government which will mean the realisation of order and justice for everybody."

The soldiers applauded as enthusiastically as they would have applauded any change in government that brought a new excitement with possible opportunities for looting and licence.

When the steamer returned downstream, Casati and Jephson were on board. At Wadelai Fadl-el-Mulla's representatives called a council and had little difficulty in persuading the excitable Egyptians and suspicious Sudanese that Emin's imprisonment was for the good of them all.

Jephson visted little Farida, who put her necklace into his hands. She said she had heard that the people of Dufilé were not giving her father enough to eat and she wished him to buy chickens with her beads.

The *Khedive* continued on its way with the rebels on board drunk and jubilant. Jephson was thankful to get back to Dufilé. He rejoined Emin in the compound, but Casati, with some idea of using his influence to aid Emin, accepted an invitation to stay at Fadl-el-Mulla's house. Emin was deeply hurt when he heard where Casati had gone, yet next day greeted him with the words: "I wish I had listened to your advice."

It was now September. The prisoners had been held for six weeks and the council was beginning to feel something should be done with them. Fadl-el-Mulla, head of a provisional government, was moderate in his intentions. His first object when he marched into Dufilé had been to get rid of Hawashi and other such evil influences and supplement

Emin's rule with a responsible council. But the Egyptians, full of personal malice and the terror of slavery, were able, with their little education, to overcome Fadl-el-Mulla's scruples and insist on the impeachment of Emin, Hawashi and Vita Hassan. The few who protested were silenced with threats and accusations of disloyalty to the government.

A meeting was held and the charges against the governor read out. These numbered thirty-seven. The first stated that the brevet from Nubar Pasha raising Emin's rank was a forgery. He was wrongfully calling himself Pasha when in truth he was only a Bey. The second, third, fourth and fifth dealt with his plottings with Stanley; the sixth with a quite newly discovered plot of Emin's to hand over all his people to the Mahdi five years before; the seventh attributed to Emin the wrongdoings of Hawashi Effendi; the eighth disclosed for the first time that Emin had poisoned the major of the 1st Battalion; the remaining twenty-nine became progressively weaker and more absurd and consisted of petty accusations of favouritism, injustice and the taking of presents.

The clerks swore they could prove every one of them. So dazed was Fadl-el-Mulla by the list that he signed the act of Emin's deposition without a murmur. The paper was then sent to Emin for his signature. Jephson begged him not to sign, but as Casati had advised him to sign any papers sent to him, he signed this one, possibly out of a new faith in Casati, possibly out of sheer indifference.

Now, the council asked itself, was Emin to remain a prisoner? or would it be wiser to execute him? That was a question on which no one could agree. The discussions dragged on.

Emin, weary to death of imprisonment, sought consolation from the parched earth of his compound by standing tiptoe on a chair and gazing at a patch of grass and trees a mile and a half away.

Hawashi Effendi, who had been ill when arrested, was led to trial through streets lined with people shrieking aloud their hatred of him. He was over seventy years of age and his downfall and imprisonment had completely undermined him. He wept as he went and his tears drew howls of derision from the crowds. At his trial a very long list of accusations was read out against him. All his household goods were seized and brought before the council. A search was made for his money and some 3,200 dollars were found. His possessions and fortune were confiscated and he was returned to prison. The sum of money combined with 700 cattle and 1,100 sheep and goats proved so satisfactory a haul that the council decided to spare Hawashi's life. He was ordered to be sent in chains to an outlying station.

When Emin heard of Hawashi's sentence, he broke down pathetically. Jephson was sorry for him but impatient: "I wished he could have managed to keep up appearances a little more before his people, on whom this giving way had a very bad effect. I told him the people would go on talking and talking for weeks to come and would settle nothing; but it was of no use, the slightest rumour against him was sufficient to plunge him into the deepest dejection."

Emin's temperament inflicted on him sufferings a young man of action such as Jephson could not well·imagine. He had no appetite for the poor food given him and seldom slept, but by now even Jephson was beginning to feel the strain of their long anxiety.

Hope lay in the fact that the rebels had ceased congratulating one another and were quarrelling violently over the positions and booty allotted them. In the evenings, however, they still got drunk in the square and amused themselves by trying to frighten the listening prisoners.

Jephson was right in supposing the council would not hurry to carry out its sentence on Hawashi. He was left in prison while a new search for money was started through his household. No more could be found. It was decided that some vast sum must be hidden away somewhere. His women and servants, who could not show the hiding place, were flogged in the square. Not only Emin and Jephson but Hawashi himself heard the screams that filled the air for hours. To save his women he at last compiled for the rebels a list of gifts he was supposed to have given Emin.

Although Hawashi was notoriously mean and Emin noted for his stern refusal to accept gifts, the list was believed and Emin was ordered to hand over its contents. Officers were sent to his house at Wadelai. Casati went with them and witnessed their search through the Pasha's private papers. Farida was terrified, wept continually, and begged Casati to return to guard her father. The search party then went on to the house of Dr. Vita Hassan at Tunguru, where they confiscated furniture and provisions and amused themselves by flogging the servants.

When everything lootable had been looted and all the fun was over, the rebellion began to lose its charm for the rebels. The time had come for reconstructive plans. No one wanted the bother of making them, much less of carrying them out. Fadl-el-Mulla, attempting to assign the work that must be done, caused indignation and uproar. The council met occasionally and made a few dispirited enquiries into the villainies of the prisoners, but did nothing about them.

The officers had better things to think of. Private quarrels and jealousies occupied their mornings. In the afternoons it was necessary to sleep. The evenings were given over to feasting on Hawashi's fat cattle, the nights to drunkenness.

The soldiers, who did not share in these pleasures, were beginning to get bored with the rebellion. They were now little more than slaves to a group of self-indulgent tyrants.

In the midst of all this came news that the Mahdists had again attacked the province. This was not a further advance of the troops who had been in occupation of the northern regions for four years. A new force—fresher and fiercer—had come up by river from Khartoum.

An unusual silence fell throughout Dufilé. The feasting ended. The people became filled with fear and dejection. They had no faith in their leaders and they made no attempt to obey the conflicting orders given. They waited in groups about the square to see what would happen next.

The new Mahdists established themselves on the site of the burnt out capital of Lado. From there an expedition of three steamer loads of soldiers descended upon the rebels at Rejaf and mercilessly slaughtered men, women and children. News of this soon reached Dufilé. A panic filled the station.

A few days after the fall of Rejaf three Mahdist dervishes arrived at Dufilé.

The dervishes—handsome and dignified men in the ragged, multicoloured robes of their sect—marched calmly into the station. They brought with them a friendly letter in which their general said he was certain Emin would be pleased to take this opportunity of handing over his province. When asked what they wanted they replied: "We have come to conduct you by the true path to Heaven, and to teach you to pray, as we the true believers, the true Mussulmen, pray."

The rebels, knowing what had happened at Rejaf, were terrified. They put the dervishes in chains and threw them into prison. The panic-stricken soldiers demanded that Emin's advice be asked. The officers, in no better state than their men, sent word to Emin that they would visit him. He prepared for their visit with calm dignity. He had chairs set ready for them and watched them coldly as they filed sheepishly into the compound. He received them in silence and took and read in silence the long letter from the Mahdi general.

It began with a sermon on the transitory nature of life and the unpredictable character of God. These things Emin would no doubt understand, and as he was famous for many virtues, he had been deemed worthy to hear of the true state of things now existing within the Sudan. With the aid of God, who had wiped out his enemies and burnt their bodies with fire from heaven, the Mahdi had brought a vast territory within his just and beneficent rule. His prisoners, known to Emin, including Slatin Bey and Lupton, were said to have sent Emin greetings and letters. Living as they now did, rich and free and "honoured by the Mahdi's grace", they pitied Emin left alone with negroes. This new attack was no more or less than an attempt to rescue Emin from the hands of barbarians, but he must not delay. Mention was made of Emin's early letter of submission sent to gain time, which, Emin now realised, had probably deceived the Mahdi commander, so a number of men had been withdrawn, leaving a handful that had been easily dealt with.

This trick, Emin knew, would be remembered by the Mahdists and make them more eager for revenge.

The officers asked the Pasha if he would answer this letter for them. He refused. They had, he said, put him aside; they had brought the country to this present state, and must now accept the responsibility for its future. He would, however, for love of his people whom the rebels had misled, give them his advice.

They asked then should they surrender? He answered they should on no account do so. The Donagla were noted for trickery and the Egyptians, once in their power, would be ruthlessly destroyed. He advised them to gain time by different prevarications and use it in which to evacuate and burn the northern stations.

The officers were impressed by this advice and Fadl-el-Mulla said excitedly that they had nothing against Emin save his upholding of Hawashi against their wishes.

Emin answered: "When you complained against him in Wadelai, more than a year ago, did I not tell you, if it was the wish of all the officers that Hawashi Effendi should be put aside, they should write an official letter, asking me to remove him, otherwise I could take no notice of it?"

Fadl-el-Mulla replied: "Yes, you did tell me so."

"Then," asked Emin, "why did you not do as I told you? You can have nothing to complain of now."

The rebels did not answer. They made off as quickly as they could.

Their next activity was to question the dervishes. They discovered that the Mahdist force numbered some 1,500. All the stations of the province together could not muster more than 800 men.

The 1st Battalion officers now decided to return to the north and organise their troops against the enemy. Fadl-el-Mulla would have released Emin but he was too old and weak to stand up against the determination of the Egyptians to keep the Pasha in prison and themselves uncontrolled. They continued to eat, drink and squabble as though there was no danger on the frontier. The soldiers, as they became more discontented, became more difficult to restrain. They took to robbing and committing acts of violence, and no one dared attempt to check them. The natives were terrified of the soldiers, terrified of the Mahdists and terrified of being abandoned to slavery.

When at last it became obvious that something must be done to divert the town, the dervishes were brought out and tortured. For days they had been fed on salt food and deprived of water, now more spectacular torments were applied. Either they had no information to give, or would give none. They bore all in silence. Their sufferings became the chief show of the town. The Egyptians found it an entertaining break in the monotonous round of eating, drinking and sleeping.

The enemy had advanced again. As no one else seemed inclined to do anything, the common soldiers themselves started making preparations for the defence of Dufilé. It was known, of course, that the Mahdists were preserved by a charm from ordinary bullets and there was nothing to do but manufacture hundreds of silver ones. In these the soldiers had great faith and every piece of silver in Dufilé went into them.

News came that the 1st Battalion had been defeated outside Rejaf. The commander, major, three captains and a clerk had all been slain. The Dufilé officers were at last terrified into activity. They asked Jephson to inspect the ramparts with them and advise them on repairs and improvements. He did so and his advice showed his good sense. Although the officers were pleased by it, no attempt was made to carry it out. The one activity to which they brought enthusiasm and ingenuity was the torture of the dervishes, who, when all cruelties proved fruitless, were taken to the river, beaten to death with clubs and thrown to the crocodiles.

It was realised at last that there was little point in keeping Emin in prison. If released, he might be persuaded to get everyone out of this muddle.

In November, three months after his arrest, he was taken out of the compound and permitted to board his steamer for Wadelai. Salutes were fired, the Khedivial Hymn played and the soldiers lined up to wish him well. His own flag flew fore and aft. The people of Dufilé obviously regarded the rebellion as a thing of the past.

Delighted by freedom and the sight again of trees, water and mountains, Emin responded charmingly to everyone and forgave all. When he arrived at Wadelai his welcome was the warmest he had ever known.

The Wadelai officials declared they had been disgusted by the incompetence of the rebels. Now the coming of the Donagla had convinced them that the road to Khartoum was closed and Emin had not deceived them. They followed him from the quayside with loud and prolonged cheers. Troops lined the road to salute him. Guns were fired. He seemed surprised rather than affected by all this show of respect.

The officials begged him to resume governorship, but he refused. He had given his promise to the officers that he would remain a private citizen and was determined to keep it. He knew that were he to accept authority again, his position would be weaker than it had ever been and he would not only have to suffer the disobedience of the ex-rebels but be responsible for the chaos they had caused.

In his diary Jephson noted sagely: "It is true that these people are rejoiced at his return, but it is only the coming of the Donagla which has brought them to their senses. They think that their only hope of safety lies with him. Three-quarters of their rejoicing at his return is for themselves, they think he will save them the trouble of thinking."

To Jephson the way seemed clear. The Pasha was now released from responsibility and could escape unimpeded by anyone but his daughter and a few faithful friends. Unfortunately nothing could be for Emin as simple as that. The people may have declared against him, but his sense of responsibility remained. They were, after all, his people and this was the country he had made. Their renewed protestations of love and loyalty were making him forget the rebellion altogether—but, what was more, pneumonic plague had broken out and only he could deal with it.

After the first shock of news of the Mahdist advance, the people of Wadelai had forgotten all about the invasion until fresh news came of enemy successes in the north. At once the town fell into a panic. The officers rushed to Emin and said: "Of course you are responsible for us all, and cannot abandon us, we came from Egypt by the orders of the government to serve under you, and you must look after us."

Emin answered: "Indeed! You seem to forget that I have a paper in which it is written that the officers have deposed me, and no longer desire me to interfere with the affairs of government, or to be their governor; this paper was written at Dufilé and was signed by you all."

"Oh!" said the Egyptians, "that was all nonsense."

"Nonsense or not, I was kept in prison for three months, and had I been free, and allowed to act, we should never have been in this predicament, so I have absolutely no responsibility now."

The people were surprised and shocked at this change in their governor, and the alarm increased wildly. That afternoon all the soldiers lined up in front of Emin's house and begged him to accept the governorship again. Everything, they said, had gone wrong since his deposition and they were lost without him.

Emin soon began wavering. At last he promised that if trouble started near Wadelai, he would give orders. Jephson and Casati, both of whom had begged him not to commit himself, were very annoyed. Emin said he had to be careful with the soldiers, he might yet need their help.

Jephson replied angrily that any promises the soldiers made were meaningless. They would never stand by him when he needed them.

"Mr. Jephson," said Emin with dignity, "I have known my people for thirteen years. You have only known them for seven months, allow me to know them best."

Jephson shrugged his shoulders: "Very well, Pasha. *Nous verrons.*" "It was," he commented, "quite hopeless to try to make Emin understand that his people were not to be trusted, for if anything bad was done by them, and they afterwards came up to express their sorrow for having done so, and assure him of their devoted attachment to him, and promised implicit obedience for the future, he was always ready to forgive and believe in them again. Certainly, for so clever a man, he learnt wonderfully little from experience."

At the beginning of December the Mahdists were pouring upon Dufilé. Every intervening station had fallen. The Dufilé garrison fought for four days. During this time the clerks were advising the people to surrender to the Mohammedans rather than retreat into the hands of the infidel English. When the Mahdists broke into the town the clerks ran to the river and sat up to their necks in water. The garrison broke and fled in every direction until the soldiers, suddenly remembering they had weapons, turned and fought with some courage. The enemy, surprised by this, retreated again outside the walls. The officials at once began evacuating the women and children to Wadelai.

When the first refugees arrived with stories of the fury of the Donagla, the Wadelai officers rushed wailing appeals to Emin. He had not the heart to disregard them and ordered an immediate evacuation of the capital.

Emin and Jephson started packing for departure. They could not take much luggage and Jephson was forced to abandon the clothing and gifts he had been collecting for his friends. Emin was desolated to leave his scientific instruments and the museum of rare beasts and birds that represented the labour of years.

As there were no oars with the steel boat *Advance*, the officers asked Jephson to destroy it so it might not be of use to the Donagla. That evening he unscrewed the sections and threw the bolts into the river.

At daybreak next day all was ready for departure. The soldiers were marched to the store-house and the ammunition distributed among them. As soon as they had got possession of it, they refused to follow Emin. They said they preferred to return to their own countries. Jephson remembered that only two days before the Pasha had said that after thirteen years in the country he knew his soldiers best.

Emin had no choice but to leave men and ammunition behind. There remained the Egyptians with their enormous households of women, children and slaves. They got off by seven o'clock—a long, straggling line of people and beasts. The noise and confusion were bewildering.

Emin and Jephson led the way. Farida followed in a hammock. Gazing back Jephson saw the column stretching behind them for about three miles. Some of the refugees had already fallen out and were imploring help and wringing their hands in despair at being left. Others were dragging along children and animals, shouting, crying, bleating, lowing together in a deafening uproar.

Numbers of stragglers were killed by natives; others returned in despair to Wadelai. Those who remained reached the lake at last. They stopped outside Tunguru. Jephson urged Emin to continue to M'swa, where he could take to the mountains if attacked, but he was afraid of seeming to desert the miserable, exhausted column. A camp was made on the lakeside.

Meanwhile the Donagla had withdrawn from the Dufilé area and some time passed before they reappeared. A false sense of security settled over the town, and the anti-Emin party, regaining confidence, returned to activity. Emin, it was reported, had seized the steamers and escaped the country. Furious indignation swept Dufilé until one of the steamers were seen making its way unharmed down to the station. At once the indignation turned against the mischievous clerks who had spread the report. They, cunning and skilled in flattery, soon regained the soldiers with gifts. They could, after all, prove that Emin had left Wadelai and was now in the neighbourhood of Tunguru.

A highly moral letter, signed by five rebel captains and five lieutenants, was circulated confirming the deposition of the Pasha and making fresh accusations against him. The garrisons of Tunguru and M'swa were ordered to arrest him at the first opportunity and as a result both Emin and Jephson were seized at Tunguru and treated as prisoners.

Dufilé was evacuated and burnt. The rebels settled at Wadelai, where they returned to the much discussed question of what to do with Emin. Decision was not easy. One uproar followed another, and in the end the Pasha was condemned to be hanged. For aiding him and for cowardice in fleeing Wadelai, Jephson and Casati were condemned to the same fate. It was decided that when defence of the province had been arranged, some rebel officers would go up to Tunguru and see the sentences carried out.

Shukri Aga, commander of M'swa, having heard that Emin had been condemned to death, wrote offering to come to Tunguru with 200 carriers and a party of soldiers to rescue the three prisoners and take them back to his station. Casati and Jephson begged the Pasha to accept this offer. He would do no more than think about it until the next day, when he suddenly decided to remain a prisoner. He would not, he said, appear to be running away.

Jephson could scarcely contain his irritation. He was very worried on Stanley's behalf and had hoped that from M'swa he would be able to watch for him and warn him. Emin himself seemed not to give a thought to Stanley's danger and, according to Jephson, "seemed to think that as Stanley had orders to relieve him, he must do it". When Jephson reminded Emin that he had a certain obligation to the expedition that might any day walk into a trap, Emin rounded on the young Englishman for so ungenerously reminding him of the fact. Jephson decided to keep quiet.

Emin's chief worry was that by leaving the province he would be deserting someone. Jephson saw this fear as absurd. The very few who had remained faithful to Emin all during the rebellion were now with him at Tunguru and could, if they wished, follow him to Egypt. Any of the others were free to come too if they wished. If they preferred to stay, they could obviously manage very well without their condemned prisoner.

To Emin the situation was not so simple. He felt for his people as a father for his children. They might be disobedient, but his responsibility remained. They were sure to suffer without his advice, and that advice he knew they would ask again as soon as they needed it. In spite of this attitude, Jephson was sure he could influence Emin had he not to deal with Casati as well.

Jephson had said to Emin: "I presume now that your people have deposed you and put you aside you do not consider that you have any longer any responsibility or obligation towards them."

"Had they not deposed me," replied Emin, "I should have felt bound to stand by them and help them in any way I could, but now I consider I am absolutely free to think only of my personal safety and welfare, and if I get the chance, I shall go out regardless of everything."

Casati, when he heard this, took Emin aside and urgently advised him "that no inconsiderate step should be taken" and that Emin must await the arrival of the officers from Wadelai. This was enough for the Pasha, whose own instinct was always rather to do nothing than something, and he said to Jephson: "I know I am not in any way responsible for these people, but I cannot bear to go out myself first and leave anyone behind me who is desirous of quitting the country. It is mere sentiment, I know, and perhaps a sentiment you will not sympathise with, but my enemies at Wadelai would point at me and say to the people: 'You see he has deserted you.'"

Jephson replied sharply: "If ever the expedition does reach any place near you, I shall advise Mr. Stanley to arrest you and carry you off, whether you will or no."

"Well," said Emin, "I shall do nothing to prevent his doing that."

Jephson decided: "If we are to save him, we must first save him from himself."

According to Casati, Emin doubted whether the expedition would ever return, but no mention of this was made to Jephson.

The situation at Tunguru was not improved for the prisoners by a declaration of war on Equatoria made by Kabba Rega. Retribution for the burning of the salt store was expected daily, but nothing happened.

News now arrived that the rebel council had by drunkenness, debauchery and looting so incensed Wadelai that the people were again crying out for their governor. The rebels were all for hanging Emin straight away, but as their quarrels among themselves usually ended in blows and indecision, the prisoners seemed safe for the time being.

On January 26th Jephson received the letter from Stanley. He learnt that Stanley was furious with him and with the Pasha—he gave them twenty days in which to join him. If they did not come within that time, he would start home without them.

Jephson had promised Emin that Stanley would arrive with extra men, carriers, supplies and ammunition, and would rescue them as soon as he heard of their plight. Instead, it could be seen through Stanley's bluster that his position was not much stronger than their own.

Emin almost wept when he received his letter from Stanley. Instead of friendly encouragement it contained a frigid "official" demand for a receipt for the goods and cartridges he had received. Jephson explained that Stanley no doubt had written in this way fearing his letter might fall into rebel hands—but Emin was not convinced. Jephson urged him to go with him to the lake-end. Emin refused to attempt such a thing. Jephson explained that as he himself had been ordered by Stanley to go, go he must.

Emin agreed at once. Of course Jephson must go. He told the chief of Tunguru to find Jephson carriers. The chief was disconcerted. He had been ordered to hold both white men prisoner, and now one of them was about to start on a journey. He invented one excuse after another for not producing the carriers and secretly wrote to the rebel council at Wadelai. Jephson, guessing what he was up to, sent for him in a towering rage and demanded immediate delivery of the carriers.

The chief cowered before Jephson's anger. Shifting from one foot to the other, in an agony of uncertainty, he protested his good intentions. It was the talk of Tunguru that Stanley had arrived not only with a horde of the fearful Manyuema but a wondrous machine-gun that mowed down people by the hundreds. What might not Stanley do if his officer were held? But, at the same time, what might the Wadelai council do if he went? Jephson shouted that if the carriers were not produced at once, he and his orderlies would shoot their way out of the station—and it would later be the worse for Tunguru. The chief assured him that the carriers were ready and waiting. He had but to command them.

Emin spent the day making preparations for Jephson's departure. In the afternoon the *Khedive* arrived with Hawashi Effendi and other refugees who brought the news that the rebel council had split into six parties and was almost at war within itself. Emin persuaded the captain to continue next day to M'swa and take Jephson with him.

That evening Emin read to Jephson the letter he had written to Stanley. Jephson commented in his note-book: "I do not think he has written very definitely, and I hardly think, however easy and simple the circumstances might be, that it is in the Pasha to give a straight answer. Poor Pasha! long residence in the Orient has made him eminently a man of compromises."

The soldiers tried to sabotage Jephson's departure. The chief, while appearing to assist it, put every difficulty in its way. Jephson, who could imitate Stanley admirably, worked himself up to another rage that got him on board before the station had recovered.

As the steamer moved off, leaving on the shore the lonely figure of Emin surrounded by the treacherous people of Tunguru, Jephson felt a deep pang of pity for him and realised he had grown to love him.

At M'swa, Shukri Aga received Jephson with pleasure. When he heard the young man was on his way to join Stanley, he bribed the captain and crew with gifts of corn and meat to continue to the lake-end. The captain was not easily persuaded. At last, when Shukri Aga had spoken dramatically and at length about the dangers through which the expedition had passed for all their sakes, it was agreed that Jephson should be taken on next day to Nsabé. Jephson, deeply grateful, gave the captain his last fifteen dollars and retired to Shukri Aga's house for a good night's rest. Next morning, awaking and looking towards the river, he saw his luggage lying on the sand and the steamer disappearing towards Wadelai.

He wrote angrily to Emin urging him to leave this miserable people and come at once to safety. He then collected native oarsmen and started for the lake-end in a canoe. After six days of journeying between the shores of a war-ridden and dangerous country, he was back at Kavalli's.

The camp awaited him. The Zanzibaris surrounded him, shouting congratulations and shaking him by the hand. Their headman even embraced him.

As for Stanley, he "received me in his usual calm manner, tempered, however, by a smile; I think he was pleased to see me again, I know I was glad to see him."

No doubt Jephson could now explain his contradictory letters and make clear to Stanley how Emin, after being taken prisoner, had then, apparently, been, at one and the same time, restored to authority, condemned to be hanged and given freedom to leave the province.

Jephson summed up events as best he could: Emin had been deposed and taken prisoner during a panic created by his enemies. He had been held prisoner: (a) to ensure the downfall of Hawashi; (b) to prevent the evacuation of the province; and (c) to leave the officers at liberty to enjoy themselves.

A second panic, created by a Mahdi advance, had caused the officers to release Emin in the hope that he would save them from the chaos they had created. On his release, he had gone to Wadelai, where he had been persuaded to resume a sort of command and had evacuated to the lake-side those willing to follow him.

While this was happening, the Mahdi forces had withdrawn and the anti-Emin faction, newly confident, had regained control. In a spirit of bravado following their earlier defeat, they had condemned Emin to be hanged. Thus he was regarded by one faction as virtually governor of the province and by the other as a prisoner, deposed and sentenced to death. He was now supposed to be under arrest, but if he were determined to escape, who would be strong enough to prevent him?

Probably no one had any serious intention of executing Emin, but if he remained in the province he might spend the rest of his life in a state between freedom and captivity.

Then what, asked Stanley, did Emin intend to do?

Chapter Fourteen

STANLEY DECIDES

The Pasha: If my people go, I go; if they stay, I stay.
Casati: If the governor goes, I go; if the governor stays, I stay.
The Faithful: If the Pasha goes, we go; if the Pasha stays, we stay.
STANLEY: Letter to England written ten months after meeting Emin.

RUMOURS of the imprisonment of Emin and Jephson reached England through letters sent by Osman Digna to General Grenfell, commander of the English garrison at Suakin. His reports that Emin and a white traveller were in Mahdi hands led to questions in the House of Commons and furious discussions in the Press. At last, in 1888, a letter sent by Stanley from Banalya reached home. The House rose and cheered for joy. Its arrival, however, was overlooked in Germany, where Carl Peters was still pushing his project to rescue Emin and, incidentally, seize territory for the German East Africa Company. Two hundred and twenty-five thousand marks had now been invested in an expedition, but, in spite of German "efficiency", its members did not escape delay by the usual arguments and fears of undertaking anything "whose accomplishment might be obstructive or even inconvenient to the Imperial Procedure". Rumours circulated in Berlin— Emin and Stanley had been killed by the Mahdi; Emin was in chains in Khartoum; the whole Equatorial province had been wiped out. Ignoring all these, Peters announced that it had at last been decided that all interests would be served by a second expedition. It set out from Berlin in February, 1889.

A month before that date Jephson had returned to camp.

In reply to Stanley's question, he shook his head. After eight months' close association with the Pasha he simply did not know what that dear, kind man intended to do. To Stanley this was bad enough, but on top of it he had to read Emin's reply to the "official" letter:

Tunguru,
January 27th, 1889

To H. M. Stanley, Esq.,
　Commanding the Relief Expedition.

Sir,

I have the honour to acknowledge receipt of your note of January 14th, Camp Undussuma, and of your official letter of January 17th, which came to hand yesterday afternoon. I beg at the same time to be allowed to express my sincere congratulations to you and to your party for the work you performed.

I have note of your offer to deliver to me, or any person appointed by me, the second instalment of goods brought by you, consisting of sixty-three cases of Remington cartridges, twenty-six cases of gunpowder, each forty-five pounds weight, four cases percussion caps, four bales of goods, one bale of goods for Signor Casati—a gift from yourself; two pieces of serge, writing-paper, envelopes, blank books, etc. As soon as the officers I am awaiting from Wadelai come here, I shall appoint one of them to take charge of these goods, and I shall at the same time instruct him to give you formal receipt for them.

The thirty-one cases of Remington cartridges, which formed the first instalment of goods, have been duly deposited in government stores.

Concerning your question if Signor Casati and myself propose to accept your escort and assistance to reach Zanzibar, and if there are any officers and men disposed to accept your safe-conduct to the sea, I have to state that not only Signor Casati and myself would gladly avail us of your help, but that there are lots of people desirous of going out from the far Egypt, as well as for any other convenient place. As these people have been delayed by the deplorable events which have happened during your absence, and as only from a few days they begin to come in, I should entreat you to kindly assist them. I propose to send them to Nyamsassi, and a first party starts to-day with Mr. Jephson. Every one of them has provisions enough to last at least for a month.

I beg to tender my thanks for the statement of your movements. As from the day you fixed your movements until the arrival of your letter elapsed nine days; the remainder of the time you kindly gave us, viz., eleven days, will scarcely be sufficient. I cannot, therefore, but thank you for your good intentions, and those of the people who sent you, and I must leave it to you if you can await us, and prefer to start after the twenty days have elapsed.

I fully understand the difficulties of getting food and provisions for your people, and I am very sorry that the short time you have to give me will not be sufficient to send you stores from here.

As Mr. Jephson starts by this steamer, and has kindly promised to hand you this note, I avail myself of the occasion to bear witness to the great help and assistance his presence afforded to me. Under the most trying circumstances he has shown so splendid courage, such unfaltering kindness and patience, that I cannot but wish him every success in life, and thank him for all his forbearance. As probably I shall not see you any more, you will be pleased to inform his relations of my thanks to him and them.

Before concluding, I beg to be permitted to tender anew my most heartfelt thanks to you and to your officers and men, and to ask you to transmit my everlasting gratitude to the kind people who sent you to help us. May God protect you and your party, and give you a happy and speedy homeward march.

I am, Sir,

Your obedient servant,

(Signed) DR. EMIN PASHA

"I do not know," commented Stanley, "what induced the Pasha to write in this melancholy strain, for as plain as tongue could speak, and pen could write, I had been endeavouring to explain to him that we considered ourselves as his servants, and bound to render any service in our power to him, provided he but distinctly and definitely stated his wishes."

He sat down and wrote a request for instructions in "a purely business style, which I thought the dullest private in his army might understand" but fortunately showed the letter to Jephson before sending it. Jephson "affected to be aghast at it". So, as Stanley had no intention "to wound the most supersensitive susceptibilities of any person—least of all the Pasha", he wrote another "after a style which probably Chesterfield himself would have admitted was the proper thing" and passed it for Jephson's approval. Jephson declared it "charming", "nice" and "exquisitely sweet" and the couriers were sent off with it.

During the days that followed, Stanley and Jephson often discussed the Pasha. Stanley tells us: "I acquired a pretty correct idea of the state of affairs. There was one confirmed habit I observed that Mr. Jephson had contracted during his compulsory residence with the Pasha which provoked a smile, and that was, while saying several crushing things about the province, he interlarded his clever remarks with: 'Well, you know, the poor, dear Pasha! He is a dear old fellow, you know. 'Pon my word, I can't help but sympathise with the Pasha, he's such a dear, good man,' etc., etc." As for the Egyptians, Jephson racked his brains to describe them—"unmitigated scoundrels, depraved villains, treacherous dogs, unscrupulously vile," etc. etc. The Egyptians were "animals with foxy natures", the Sudanese were "brutishly stupid".

"Men," Stanley concluded, "reap only what they have sown; as the seed is sown, so will be the harvest." Emin he likened to a solitary snowdrop doomed to melt; the power of the Mahdists to a rolling, growing snowball.

Jephson said he believed Casati was a trouble-maker. He seemed to be working on Emin's uncertainties with the intention of gaining an influence over him.

Stanley's comments impressed Jephson, who reflected how satisfying it was to be again with a man of action.

As the strength of Stanley's rear column was rumoured to be enormous, the rebels, who had been plotting how best to trap the whole expedition, were disconcerted to hear that Jephson had escaped. Now Stanley would know the true situation—what would he do? He would certainly avenge any harm done to Emin. The Wadelai council fell into a state of wild alarm. Furious arguments rent the air. Some members were for killing Emin before he could be rescued. The others knew this would be a crazy move. Eventually it was decided that there was only one sensible thing to do—apologise to Emin and reinstate him before Stanley entered the province.

A deputation of fourteen officers hurried to Tunguru, kissed Emin's hands and begged him to lead them to Stanley. They said they represented the officers and officials who wished to leave the province. Emin was overjoyed by their humble desire for pardon, but kept his head sufficiently to ask in what capacity he was to go with them. They answered as their interpreter.

This was too much even for Emin. He refused angrily. The officers were bewildered. Knowing if they visited Stanley without Emin they would not be permitted to enter the camp, they were at a loss what to do. Some were for giving up the project of leaving Equatoria altogether; others blamed Emin for depriving them of the right to be saved.

At this point they were addressed by Shukri Aga, who had come to Tunguru and who painted so lurid a picture of what would befall them at the hands of the Donagla if Stanley left without them that they fell into a panic. Casati now started an intrigue on his own and persuaded the officers in their own interests to beg Emin's pardon and pray him once again to accept the governorship. This was done.

Emin made some show of indifference but in private he wept for joy, seeing this new move as a proof of the rebels' love for him. On February 9th, 1889, he formally resumed the rank of governor and at once promoted officers who had performed acts of valour at Dufilé. Selim Matera, leader of the deputation, now became Selim Bey and vice-governor of the province. A resolution was sent to Wadelai requesting the adhesion of all who intended following Stanley out of Equatoria.

Emin wrote a letter:

To HENRY M. STANLEY, Esq.,
    Commanding the Relief Expedition.

SIR,

In answer to your letter of the 7th instant, for which I beg to tender my best thanks, I have the honour to inform you that yesterday, at 3.0 p.m., I arrived here with my two steamers, carrying a first lot of people desirous to leave this country under your escort. As soon as I have arranged for cover of my people, the steamships have to start for M'swa station, to bring on another lot of people awaiting transport.

With me there are some twelve officers anxious to see you, and only forty soldiers. They have come under my orders to request you to give them some time to bring their brothers—at least, such as are willing to leave—from Wadelai, and I promised them to do my best to assist them. Things having to some extent now changed, you will be able to make them undergo whatever conditions you see fit to impose upon them. To arrange these I shall start from here with the officers for your camp, after having provided for the camp, and if you send carriers I could avail me of some of them.

I hope sincerely that the great difficulties you have had to undergo, and the great sacrifices made by your expedition in its way to assist us, may be rewarded by a full success in bringing out my people. The wave of insanity which overran the country has subsided, and of such people as are now coming with me we may be sure.

Signor Casati requests me to give his best thanks for your kind remembrance of him.

Permit me to express to you once more my cordial thanks for whatever you have done for us until now, and believe me to be,

Yours very faithfully,
(Signed) DR. EMIN

In a separate letter to Jephson Emin said he was bringing ivory to pay the Manyuema and also the steel boat repaired and ready for service.

When these letters arrived Stanley and Jephson were dining. Stanley leant across the table and said: "Shake hands on it, old fellow! we'll be successful after all."

Jephson replied: "If anyone deserves it you do, for you have toiled hard for it."

Stanley announced that at last, two years after setting out, the expedition was going to make its first serious attempt to rescue Emin. The Zanzibaris received it with shouts and cheers, and danced and sang throughout the night.

Emin and Casati with the officers had by now arrived at the lakeside village of Were. Casati had Emin to himself and, filled with the ambition of the weak, seemed determined to pit his strength against that of the Englishman, Stanley. Stanley, he said, would want Emin to leave immediately with those men and their families he now had with him. Casati impressed on Emin that his duty lay towards any officers still at Wadelai who might wish to come too. He must hold the expedition up until they arrived and, if need be, refuse to leave without them. Emin, whose real wish was to remain in the province, agreed readily. The Wadelai contingent must not be abandoned.

Casati, who knew Emin, realised he must be kept out of range of Stanley's influence. He persuaded Emin that it would be better for him to remain independent of Stanley until the caravan of officers and officials was organised for the journey.

With these ideas in mind, Emin set out with the officers to meet Stanley on February 16th. Casati had brought all his possessions to

Were and remained behind to guard them. While alone there he heard
that two of Kabba Rega's chiefs, out on a marauding expedition, had
devastated a large tract of surrounding country. A few days later
Bonny, marching from Fort Bodo with ninety-four men, arrived at Were
and Casati asked him to remain and guard the village against a surprise
attack. Bonny, who intended keeping his men and ammunition intact,
and impressing his chief with his speed and efficiency, replied coldly
that his job was not to fight but to bring over the luggage.

Stanley waited grimly in his tent while Jephson made the journey
down to the lake-shore to meet the steamer. He had been reflecting
on this sudden change of heart of the officers and he regarded it with
the darkest suspicion. He concluded that the whole thing was a
plot to trap the expedition, with Emin as well, and hand them all
over as a gift to the Mahdists. No doubt they thought all white men
were "soft-headed duffers" who would be deceived at once by their
cunning humility. Well, Stanley was going to show them!

Emin arrived in the steamer with about sixty-five followers. He wore
civilian clothes, but Selim Bey and the other seven officers were in their
most resplendent uniforms and impressed the Zanzibaris, who screamed
an excited welcome. Emin stood laughing in their midst. On board
were the officers' possessions. The steamer had to return to Were for
many more loads of stuff. Jephson went back with Emin to the village
and from there wrote to Stanley: "I find Casati more impossible than
ever. I asked him whether he would go with us to-morrow, and he
replied he would rather wait. I then asked: 'How many loads have
you?' 'Oh!' he answered, 'you know I have very few things. All my
things were taken by Kabba Rega; perhaps I may want eighty carriers.'
Vita, the apothecary, wants forty carriers, and Marco, the Greek trader,
wants sixty, so at this rate our Zanzibaris will be killed between here and
Kavalli's. The Pasha remonstrated with Casati for taking all his
grinding-stones, earthen jars, bedsteads for his boys and women, etc.,
upon which he said: 'Mr. Stanley has offered to take all our loads.'
These people have no conscience, and would rather load down our
long-suffering people than throw away a single load of rubbish which
they will eventually be obliged to discard. Casati, so the Pasha tells me,
was averse to their leaving Tunguru, in spite of Shukri Aga's offer of
carriers, and my urgent letter, and did all he could to prevent his
coming down here, as he considered it 'impolitic'. One internally
fumes at the selfishness of these people, and at their inability or aversion

from seeing things as they really are. . . . Casati refuses to move until he has sufficient carriers to take him and all his goods away together. The Pasha is very irritated about it."

For all that, Emin would not order his people to leave their worthless possessions behind. If they would not leave them voluntarily, then he was sorry but the Zanzibaris would just have to carry them up the lakeside to the table-land. Jephson fumed and counted the journeys and made malicious fun of Selim Bey's journey uphill: "I, who was below, occasionally got views of the profile of him and his donkey against the sky-line, which were most ludicrous. This huge fat man, seated on his very small donkey, well over its tail, which hung down directly beneath him, and looked as if it belonged to himself!"

Stanley stood in his camp at Kavalli's and watched the Zanzibaris toiling up with the loads from the steamer. Sixty loads for the Pasha alone! Trunks that took two men to carry, sea-chests, great coffin-like coffers, ten-gallon jars, packed baskets big enough to hold three men! He bitterly regretted having promised to transport this stuff and the Zanzibaris were in revolt against the labour of carrying it.

After the luggage came the old and the sick, some of them unable to ride a donkey without assistance. Then the infants, too small to walk—three or four belonging to one mother! Who was going to carry them? One Sudanese woman gave birth to an infant on the way up from the steamer to the camp. Hundreds of other women were pregnant. It was reported to Stanley that one of the officers had stolen a rifle. . . . Stanley damned the lot of them, but he had undertaken this evacuation and would carry it through.

On February 26th Emin joined Stanley to tell him that the Wadelai rebels, indignant at Selim Bey's independent action, had again deposed their governor and, what was more, had again sentenced him to death. Stanley showed no surprise at this piece of news.

He put up a show of courtesy towards Selim Bey and the others, but he was determined from the first to stand no nonsense from them. He described the elderly Selim Bey as being six feet high, large of girth and as black as coal. "I am rather inclined to like him. The malignant and deadly conspirator is always lean. I read in this man's face, indolence, a tendency to pet his animalism. He is a man to be fed, not to conspire." But Stanley was taking no risks. He presented the officers with a written statement that on the journey transport would be provided only for Emin, Casati and the Greek merchant Marco.

Everyone else would have to provide his own beasts and porters, and should, therefore, be careful not to burden himself with unnecessary goods.

Casati, when he saw the letter, went indignantly to Emin and told him Stanley was usurping his authority. Emin preferred to overlook the fact.

Stanley now told Selim Bey that he might return to Wadelai and bring those who wished to join the expedition. The expedition would wait a reasonable time for them. Selim Bey on his departure said he was determined to make a stand against Fadl-el-Mulla and would return with all haste to the camp.

A month later Selim Bey wrote to say he was sure all the rebels would follow him. Emin was delighted: "What did I tell you?" he said. "You see, I was right! I was sure they would all come."

Stanley grunted his disbelief.

Later Shukri Aga arrived from M'swa and asked Stanley for instructions. Stanley, annoyed by Emin's and Jephson's faith in this man, told him angrily that he had received his instructions ten months before when told of the reason for the expedition's arrival. If he wished to leave with the rest, he had better hurry back and evacuate his station. Hurt and surprised, Shukri Aga hurried back.

Casati and Vita Hassan finally joined the camp in March. Casati immediately observed that the place was completely under Stanley's control. Emin's authority existed only in theory and the fact was underlined by Stanley's saying with some irony that Emin was the man who must make the scientific observations during the journey.

In spite of himself Casati was impressed by Stanley's strength of character, resolution, promptness of thought and iron will. "Jealous of his own authority, he does not tolerate exterior influences, nor ask advice. Difficulties do not deter him, disasters do not dismay him. With an extraordinary readiness of mind he improvises means, and draws himself out of difficulties; absolute and severe in the execution of his duty, he is not always prudent, or free from hasty and erroneous judgments. Irresolution and hesitation irritate him." Even Casati must have realised that such a man could not be expected to submit to Emin's indecision.

A long period of waiting began. As days passed into weeks and weeks into months, Stanley's irritation grew dangerously. He told Emin he was certain neither Selim Bey nor Shukri Aga had any intention of following him anywhere. Emin was quite confident they would come. At last, unable to contain himself longer, Stanley told Emin plainly that every month they lingered here cost the Relief Committee £400. There were also the young officers to be considered. They had to think of their army careers—their leaves of absence had expired long before. The Zanzibaris wanted to return to their homes and all were growing impatient. It was now eleven months since they had warned the province that an evacuation was being organised, with what result? About forty clerks, officers and their families had arrived at the camp. And the baggage of these alone had taken the Zanzibaris a month to cart up from the lake to the camp!

Emin was bewildered by this outburst. Like Casati, he could see no reason why Stanley, working under the orders of the Khedive, should not be content to remain peacefully in the camp until the caravan was ready. His job, after all, was to take back to Egypt those who wished to go.

Fortunately he did not mention this to Stanley, who was working himself into one rage after another. He told Emin that he alone had any faith in the good intentions of the Wadelai officers. Major Hawashi, Osman Latif Effendi and an engineer called Mohammed had all come separately to tell Stanley that neither Selim Bey nor Fadl-el-Mulla would leave Central Africa. Selim might come to Kavalli's and settle in the district, but no more than that. As for the rebels—what reason could anyone have for trusting them? Hadn't they revolted three times, captured Jephson and, by the act of menacing him, insulted Stanley? They had even plotted to capture Stanley himself: "But, Pasha," said Stanley, "let me tell you this much: it is not in the power of all the troops of the province to capture me, and before they arrive within rifle-shot of this camp, every officer will be in my power."

Emin was quite stunned by all this suspicion of his officers. But, if it were justified, what did Stanley intend? Stanley said he intended to decide on a date for the return journey to begin—say, April 10th—and stick to it. To Emin it seemed impossible to desert his officers in that way. To show him his folly, Stanley called together his own officers—Stairs, Nelson, Jephson and Parke—to ask their opinion.

He addressed them at great length pointing out that Selim Bey had left the camp on February 26th. Shukri Aga had gone on March 16th. Both had been told that the march would begin early in April—and what had resulted? Shukri Aga was still at M'swa, Selim Bey had reached Tunguru with about one sixteenth of the expected force. Neither showed signs of moving nearer. Remembering the purpose of the expedition, remembering the state of revolt existing inside the province, remembering the risk the expedition ran in remaining near the rebels—would he, Stanley, be wise in extending the time of delay beyond the date the Pasha had now fixed, April 10th?

One after another the officers answered "No". Nelson alone saw Emin's point of view and agreed with him that he could not abandon those at Wadelai who were still loyal to him. Stanley at once put this aside as foolish sentiment and said: "There, Pasha, you have your answer. We march on April 10th."

Emin, who had sat in silence during Stanley's speech, asked miserably if the Englishmen could in their conscience acquit him of having abandoned his people supposing they did not arrive in time?

"Most certainly," Stanley replied for them all.

Emin, whose one hope of proving to himself that he had not altogether ceased to exist would be in feeling a weight of responsibility, returned in despair to his own tent. It seemed to him that of his life, his work, his province, nothing now remained.

Casati followed him quickly to tell him that he had pledged himself to wait for the others. If he went, he was breaking his pledge. This was exactly what Emin felt himself.

The officers in the camp were told of the departure date and agreed to it with enthusiasm. Next day four of the more enthusiastic were filled with qualms at the realisation they would be abandoning their brothers in Wadelai. At the same time they told Emin they believed Fadl-el-Mulla was plotting to ruin the whole expedition. The Egyptians in the camp alternated between joy at the thought of departure and outbursts of grief over the fate of the Wadelai contingent. Emin had to suffer all their confidences and changes of mood.

Torn between a sense of responsibility towards Selim Bey and fear of upsetting Stanley further, Emin spent sleepless nights worrying over his position. It was settled to some extent by his resentment of the sense of inferiority Stanley forced upon him. He suddenly declared: "I feel it is my duty to stay."

"Where, Pasha?" Stanley pertinently enquired.

"With my people."

"What people, please?"

"Why, with my soldiers."

"Well, now, really, I was under the impression that you wrote me some time ago, with your own hand, besides endorsing Mr. Jephson's letter, that you were a prisoner to your own soldiers, that they had deposed you, that they had threatened to take you in irons, strapped to your bedstead, to Khartoum, and I am sure you know as well as I do what that means."

"That is true," sighed Emin, defeated. "But you must not think I am about to change my mind. As I said to you, I leave with you on April 10th next. That is settled. I wish, however, you would see Casati about this and talk to him."

"I should be most happy to do so, but my French is wretched, and his is still worse."

"Oh, if you will send a boy to call me I will come in and be your interpreter."

Later Stanley visited Casati. As neither could make himself understood by the other, the boy was sent to call Emin. As soon as Emin arrived Casati started to lecture him in the name of honour and duty, telling him he was morally wrong in abandoning his troops.

Stanley, on being told what the Italian was saying, interrupted: "But the Pasha, Captain Casati, never had an intention of abandoning his troops, as no person knows better than you. It is these troops who have deposed him, and made him a prisoner from August 18th to February 8th, or thereabouts, nearly six months. They have three times revolted, they have said repeatedly they do not want him, nor will obey him, and they have threatened to kill him. They would probably have sent him to Khartoum before this, had not the mad Donaglas shown what little mercy would have been shown to them."

"The governor of a fort should never surrender his charge," said Casati.

"I quite agree with you in that," said Stanley, "if his troops remain faithful to him; but if his troops arrest him, haul down the flag, and open the gates, what can the poor governor do?"

"A captain of a warship should fight his guns to the last."

"Quite so, but if the crew seize the captain, and put him into the hold in irons, and haul down the flag, what then?"

"No, I do not agree with you," said Casati with emphasis. "The Pasha should remain with his people."

"But where are his people? The rebels refuse to have anything to do with him except as a prisoner to them. Do you mean to say that the

Pasha should return as a prisoner, and be content with that humiliating position?"

"No, certainly not."

"Perhaps you think they would relent, and elevate him again to the post of governor?"

"I cannot say."

"Do you think they would?"

"It may be."

"Would you advise the Pasha to trust himself into the power of Fadl-el-Mulla Bey and his officers again?"

"No."

"Now, here are your servants. Supposing they lay hold of you one night, and were going to kill you, and you were only saved because your cries attracted your deliverers to the scene. Would you trust your life in their hands again?"

"No."

"Supposing your servants came to you this afternoon and told you they would not obey you in the future, and if you insisted on their obedience would shoot you, would you then consider yourself as morally bound to command them?"

"No."

"Then, my dear Casati, you have answered the Pasha, and what you would not do, the Pasha is not bound to do. Emin Pasha had two duties to perform, one to the Khedive and one to his soldiers. It is because he performed his duty nobly and patiently towards the Khedive that I and my young friends volunteered to help him. The Khedive commands him to abandon the province, and forwards assistance to him for that purpose. He appeals to his troops and requests them to express their views, whereupon they seize him, menace him with death, and finally imprison him for six months. His answer is given him, which is: 'For the last time, we have nothing to do with you.'"

Casati became sulkily silent, Emin much troubled. The two arranged to meet again that night to "argue the moral aspect of the case again".

Stanley commented in his diary: "God knows what their intentions will be to-morrow. Neither of them realise the true state of affairs. I am convinced that their minds are in a bewildered state, as their position would be desperate if we left them to themselves for a few days."

Writing home, he pointed out that the "principal difficulties lay not only with the Sudanese and Egyptians". As for Emin's belief in a duty towards his people—this Stanley compared to a contract between two people. "One party," he said, "refused to abide by its stipulations, and would have no communication with the other, but proposed to itself to put the second party to death. Could that be called a contract?"

A nervous tension, an atmosphere of irritability and continual quarrelling hung over the camp. Because of their contempt for Emin, the Egyptians were always calling on Stanley to arbitrate and he was not unwilling to be called upon. To their cases he brought no understanding, indeed nothing but his determination to maintain a strict discipline, and, by preferring his judgment, they gained only the satisfaction of slighting their governor.

When Emin asked his orderlies, guards, clerks and servants if they would follow him, all except two said they preferred to remain with their "brothers". Emin, oppressed by loneliness and a sense of his own impotence, tried to shut himself off from his own doubts and disappointments and Stanley's dominance by giving all his time to zoology and botany.

Stanley, sending his spies round the camp and gathering in the rumours and plottings that made life for the Egyptians, watching the whispering circles, the packets of letters sent to Wadelai and the packets that came in reply, became sure that between the officers left behind in the camp and those that had returned to the province, some vast conspiracy was taking shape. He believed the Egyptians thought all white men "similar to the Pasha", and he was determined soon to show them their mistake.

Selim Bey, writing to Emin, described the situation in Wadelai as chaotic. The rebels had divided into six warring factions and the town seemed to be peopled by madmen. The soldiers had broken into the government magazines and taken whatever they pleased. The officers were unable to keep order. Selim Bey himself had not yet started to embark his family, but he had a few followers, unruly though they were.

On the night of April 4th, six days before the expedition was due to start, thieves attempted to steal the Zanzibar rifles. Stanley was convinced that the theft of the guns was part of the Egyptian plot and he now determined to leave the camp before any further schemes could be carried out.

On the morning of the 5th he entered Emin's tent without ceremony.

Emin, who was seated at his table stuffing some birds, "pulled himself up with his usual dignity and gravely prepared himself to listen". Stanley plunged at once into the cause of his anger:

"A conspiracy is going on here against the expedition," he said. "Plots are being concocted against the expedition. I know that when the time comes to leave, your party will refuse to go."

Emin was bewildered: "I do not know what you mean. I don't think anyone would be so wicked as to dare to act as you have been made to believe."

"Don't let us evade the question, Pasha," said Stanley, "that is not my habit. I have two proposals to make to you; it is for you to choose, and that without delay. To-morrow morning I mean to make the round of my Zanzibaris and to tell them of our immediate departure. In case of any resistance or attempt at refusal, I am prepared to use force and then start with you and the few who remain faithful to you. Should these strong measures not suit you, then I propose that you should start with a trustworthy escort at once, unknown to everyone; I would soon rejoin you. Choose, Pasha; decide."

Emin seemed stunned. To choose between two such unwelcome alternatives was beyond him. He asked miserably: "May I inform Casati of this?"

"No, sir," replied Stanley.

Emin pulled himself together. He refused to agree to either proposal. He said he could not abandon Casati, Vita Hassan and Marco in this way.

"Don't think of them," said Stanley, "Casati is in no danger; they will not hurt him because he is not their governor or officer. He is only a traveller. He can come the next day, or whenever he is inclined. If he is detained, I will attack the rebel camp and rescue Casati quickly enough."

Emin said he could see no need for all this excitement. The expedition would start on the 10th as arranged.

At this Stanley's anger overcame him. Choking with rage and stamping his foot, he swore: "I leave you to God, and the blood which will now flow must fall upon your head."

Gun in hand, he rushed from the tent and a few minutes later his alarm signal penetrated the camp. The Zanzibaris had learnt to obey. This, they knew, was the signal of departure and they leapt to the work of dismantling the tents.

Casati, supposing the men were being drilled, went to see Emin and found him pale with indignation. His voice trembled as he said: "We are going. To-day, for the first time in my life, I have been covered with insults. Stanley has passed every limit of courtesy, but I have promised not to speak, so I can say no more."

He went out and begged Stanley to listen to one word.

"Certainly; what is it?" asked Stanley.

"Only tell me what I have to do now."

"It is too late, Pasha, to adopt the pacific course I suggested to you. The alarm is general now, and, therefore, I propose to discover for myself this danger, and face it here. Sound the signal please for the muster of your Arabs before me."

Emin sounded the signal. His followers ignored it. Stanley waited ten minutes in silence. A few Egyptians at last ambled from curiosity out on to the square. The Kavalli natives, thinking the preparations were for war against Kabba Rega, crowded round excitedly. Stanley waited, watch in hand, until the last of the ten minutes had elapsed, then he sprang into life.

He ordered Jephson to arm the Zanzibaris with clubs and sticks and set them to driving everyone of Emin's men, without regard for rank, into the square. The Zanzibaris, who had a lot of scores to settle with the insolent Egyptians, set to with a will and drove every male with whacks into position before Stanley.

Majors, captains, lieutenants, clerks and store-keepers, amazed, speechless with indignation, were forced into a line by the Zanzibaris. Stanley, beside himself with rage, insisted that the line must satisfy his sense of order. Then, a Winchester rifle in his hand, a hundred armed Zanzibaris at his back, he shouted:

"If you have the courage point your guns at my breast. I am here alone and unarmed."

The Egyptians gaped at the rifle as Stanley waved it in their faces. They said nothing.

"My orders alone are to be obeyed here," he bawled even more fiercely, "and whoever resists I will kill him with this gun, and trample him under my feet. Whoever intends to start and follow me, let him pass to this side."

The Egyptians looked dazedly at one another. Most of them had been dragged out from their siesta and, in any case, had no idea what had caused Stanley's fury. At last Osman Latif Effendi, Lieutenant-General of the province, spoke up from the ranks: "But we don't wish to fight," he said.

"Then what is this I hear, that one of you is as good as ten of my men, of rifles being stolen, of plots and counterplots each day that you have been here, of your resolve not to follow the Pasha after making us build your houses and collect food for you, and carrying hundreds of loads the last two months up this mountain from the lake, and last night three of our houses were entered, and you laid your hands upon our arms. Speak, and say what it all means."

Osman Latif replied meekly that the thieves, if found, should be executed.

"If found! Will any thief confess his theft and deliver himself to be shot. Will you, who are all of one mind, betray one another, and submit yourselves to punishment? Do you intend to follow your Pasha?"

"We all do," they answered.

"Stay! Those who intend following the Pasha form ranks on that other side, like soldiers, each in his place."

The Egyptians formed ranks like one man.

"So! Is there none desirous of staying in this fair land with Selim Bey, where you will be able to make these natives do your work for you, cook, and feed you?"

"None, not one. La il Allah il Allah!" chorused the Egyptians.

It was then discovered that none of Emin's own servants and orderlies were present.

"Ah, Lieutenant Stairs," said Stanley, "please take a party and roust every man out. On the least resistance you know what to do."

"Right, sir," replied Stairs, who returned a few minutes later with the servants.

"Now, Pasha," said Stanley, "please ask them severally before me what they intend doing."

All except one, named Seroor, replied they were willing to follow their master to the end of the earth.

Emin pointed to Seroor: "That is the chief conspirator in my household."

"Oh," replied Stanley, "it will only take one cartridge to settle his business."

Emin grew pale: "But I hope, for God's sake, that you will try him first, and not take my word for it."

H*

"Undoubtedly, my dear Pasha. We invariably give such people a fair trial."

Seroor and three other suspects were placed under arrest. Two of these, for failing to obey the summons, were flogged; others were put in irons and under guard.

"Now, Pasha," said Stanley with some satisfaction, "this business having been satisfactorily ended, will you be good enough to tell these officers that the tricks of Wadelai must absolutely cease here, and that in future they are under my command. If I discover any treacherous tricks I shall be compelled to exterminate them utterly. No Mahdist, Arabist, or rebel can breathe in my camp. Those who behave themselves and are obedient to orders will suffer no harm from their fellows or from us. My duty is to lead them to Egypt, and until they arrive in Cairo I will not leave them. Whatever I can do to make them comfortable I will do, but for sedition, and theft of arms, there is only death."

Emin translated and the Egyptians, bowing understanding, vowed that they would obey their "father" religiously.

"Good," replied Stanley, "and now that I assume command, I want to have a list of your names and exact number of your families, and carriers will be allotted to you according to your number. Bear in mind that the departure is irrevocably fixed for the 10th."

"Poor Pasha!" commented Stanley. "It was as clear as the noonday sun why 10,000 followers had dwindled in number to Bilal, the solitary ONE! After a patient and scrupulous analysis of the why and wherefore of these events, the result is manifest, and we see the utter unfitness of the scientific student and the man of unsuspecting heart to oppose these fawning, crafty rogues, who have made fraud and perfidy their profession. At the same time, it is not so clear that, had he penetrated their dissimulating wiles, and grappled with these evil men boldly, and crushed the heads of these veterans in falsehood and craft, that his position would have been safer than it was. Each man, however, follows his own nature, and must abide the consequences of his judgment and acts. But all must admit, that what is so far written does infinite credit to his heart."

Emin's heart must have suffered considerably as he stood on one side and watched the people whose susceptibilities he had considered so tenderly springing to obey Stanley's orders.

Osman Latif Effendi, the Lieutenant-Governor, had displayed a sudden amazing energy, and, Stanley tells us in his journal: "His mother, an old lady, seventy-five years old, with a million of wrinkles in her ghastly white face, was not very fortunate in her introduction to me, for, while almost at white heat, she threw herself before me in the middle of the square, jabbering in Arabic to me, upon which, with an impatient wave of the hand, I cried: 'Get out of this; this is not the place for old women.' She lifted her hands and eyes up skyward, gave a little shriek, and cried 'O Allah!' in such tragic tones that almost destroyed my character. Everyone in the square witnessed the limp and shrunk figure, and laughed loudly at the poor old thing as she beat a hasty retreat."

Emin must in his own mind have contrasted Stanley's attitude towards the old and helpless with that of Gordon, who wrote during his early days in the Equatorial province: "I took a poor old bag of bones into my camp a month ago, and have been feeding her up, but yesterday she was gently taken off and now knows all things. I suppose she filled her place in life as well as Queen Elizabeth"; and of another old woman: "I have sent her some dhoora, and will produce a spark of joy in her black and withered carcass."

Emin—once the poor doctor of Khartoum forced to accept charity because he had given away what he earnt—was not a man to be comprehended within the limits of Stanley's understanding. Stanley saw only that Emin could be overridden, not that Emin, when overridden, hid beneath his dignified silence a bitter, resenting hurt. Stanley's own picture of this whole incident draws a Governor of Equatoria humbled and awed before Stanley's wisdom and knowledge. But Emin, returning to his tent, wrote no record of this for posterity. Indeed, he could scarcely bear to remember the incident. He noted briefly in his diary that that day, for the first time in his life, he had been insulted in his own house.

Chapter Fifteen

THE RETURN

"I was compelled, as I had pledged my word—with a heavy heart it is true—to march, without knowing where the people were, or what had kept them back. All my hopes are shattered, and I return home half-blind and broken down. I indeed hope that I shall not be judged too hardly."

EMIN: Letter to Felkin

AT daybreak on April 10th, 1888, Stanley's alarm signal—"the well known whistle" as Casati described it—pierced the camp. That was the signal for departure.

There was no sign of Selim Bey or the Wadelai officers. Emin was uneasy that no word had come from them and wretched at the need to go without them. Although he could know nothing of Gordon's determined "insubordination" in remaining with the people of Khartoum instead of saving himself, Emin, who for years had tried to emulate his hero, knew instinctively that were he governor here still, Gordon would not be the first but the last to leave Equatoria. Casati's *cliché* about the captain and the sinking ship must have been in Emin's mind as, with a mere 600 of his people, he followed Stanley from the camp.

The caravan was in position by seven o'clock. Stanley then gave an order for the camp to be fired, and the Egyptians, who had supposed it would stand as a refuge for the Wadelai contingent, set up a despairing wail.

In profoundest gloom the evacuees started on the road, saved in spite of themselves. Next day Shukri Aga, deserted by all but two of his soldiers, caught up with the caravan.

Three days later Stanley developed inflammation of the stomach. The journey came to an abrupt stop. A new camp was made. For nearly a month the leader lay in acute pain that could only be eased by injections of morphia. Emin, although the fact was not mentioned by the patient, assisted Parke in saving Stanley's life.

The caravan at a standstill, all the old dissensions broke out again. It was rumoured that the Wadelai officers had gathered an army which was advancing on the camp—no one knew for what purpose. The constantly circulating stories of the starvation and horrors ahead brought the refugees to the verge of panic. As the caravan had halted at an unhealthy spot, its members were soon complaining of agues, fevers and rheumatism, while, to increase their discomfort, a hurricane overturned the tents and tore away every movable object. One after another the Egyptians deserted with their families to join a mythical party of rebels said to be only a few miles behind.

Disruption reached such a pitch that Emin decided something must be done. He tracked down the chief rumour-monger, tried him and condemned him to death. The question then was who would carry out the sentence. Emin asked the English officers to provide him with a firing squad.

Stairs went to Stanley with the request. Stanley's moral indignation enabled him to raise himself from his sick bed and whisper hoarsely: "No detail of Zanzibaris can be sent. Let the Pasha shoot his guilty men with his own people. If he needs a guard for protection, let him have the men, but we came to save life, not to destroy it."

So Emin, in his one attempt to adopt Stanley's methods, was utterly frustrated. Having no one he could trust to carry out the order, he was forced to spare the man's life.

A few nights later a young Sudanese, Rehan, made off with twenty followers and as much ammunition as they could carry. Then came down the might of Stanley's wrath. Rehan was captured by Stairs. Stanley was carried out to preside at the trial and condemned the man to death. A Sudanese who had been his friend was forced to hang Rehan from a tree, and Stanley, collecting all his strength, cried aloud: "Pass the word, Mr. Stairs, throughout the camp among the Pasha's people, and bid them come and look at the dead Rehan, that they may think of the serious scene, and please God mend their ways."

Daily it was brought home to Emin, since Stanley by his *coup d'état* had forced the camp to realise it was powerless, that he was of no more consequence than one of the Egyptians. He bore the situation without comment or useless complaint, and intruded upon the running of the camp only to offer his knowledge and medical skill where it was required; but at times his resentment broke out in displays of hurt, anger and even spite that the English found ridiculous. Stanley, brutal in his irritation and incomprehension, responded by slashing right and left at any illusion of authority Emin might still retain.

Before the caravan moved on, a letter was found written by one Ibrahim Effendi Elham that seemed to prove that Selim Bey, still at Wadelai, was plotting with the officers in the camp to get possession of the expedition's arms. The letter contained the words: "I beseech you to hurry up your soldiers. If you send only fifty at once, we can manage to delay the march easily enough, and if you can come with your people soon after, we may obtain all we need."

"This is a discovery, Pasha!" said Stanley who was now almost recovered. "Now are you satisfied that these people are incorrigible traitors?"

"Well," replied Emin, "I should not have expected this of Ibrahim Effendi Elham. I have been constantly kind to him. As for Selim Bey, I cannot see what he can want."

"It is this, Pasha. In reality few of these men wish to go to Egypt. Even Selim Bey, despite all his promises, never intended to proceed to Egypt. They were willing to accompany you until they reached some promising land, where there was abundance of food and cattle, and removed from all fear of the Mahdists; they then would tell you that they were tired of the march, that they would die if they proceeded any farther, and you, after conferring with me, would grant them ammunition, and promise to send some more to them by and by. But this ammunition would not be sufficient in their eyes, however liberal you were. Their rifles would be too few, nothing would satisfy them but all the rifles and ammunition and everything we possessed. Wait a moment, Pasha, and I will reveal the whole plot to you.

"After Mr. Jephson received my order last January, of course the news soon spread as far north as your farthest station that I had arrived with all my people and stores. They knew, though they affected to disbelieve it, that the Khedive had sent ammunition to you. But they were clever enough to perceive that they could get nothing from me without an order from you. But as Jephson had fled and conveyed the news of your deposition and imprisonment to me, even an order would scarcely suffice. They, therefore, knowing your forgiving disposition, came to you, a deputation of them, to profess regret and penitence; they kiss your hand and promise greatly, which you accept, and as a sign of amity and forgiveness of the past accompany them, and introduce them to me. You ask for a reasonable time for them, and it is granted. But so strong was the temptation, they could not resist stealing a rifle. If they intend to go with us, what do they wish to do with this rifle while steaming on the lake? Is it not a useless encumbrance to them? I suppose that the varying strength and influence of the factions have delayed them longer than they thought, and we have been saved from proceeding to extremes by dissension. . . . These people . . . can understand only what they feel, and to make such as these feel they must receive hard knocks. When I had thoroughly sounded the depths of their natures my mind began to discover by what method I could master these men. There were half a dozen methods apparently feasible, but at the end of each there was an obstacle in my way. You could not guess what that obstacle was, Pasha?"

Emin shook his head.

"This obstacle that presented itself constantly, at the end of every well-digested method, was yourself."

"I! How was that?"

"On April 5th you ceased to be so, but until then, I could not carry any scheme into execution without reference to you. You were in our eyes the Pasha still. You were the governor and commander of these people. I could not propose to you to fight them. You believed in them constantly. Each day you said: 'They will come,' but it never came across your mind to ask yourself: 'What will they do after they do come, if they find they outnumber us three to one?' Had they come before April 5th, my plan was to separate from you and leave you with them, and form camp, with every detail of defence considered, seven or eight miles from you. All communications were to be by letter, and guides were to be furnished after we had gone in the advance a day's march, to show you the road to our last camp. No force of any magnitude would be permitted to approach my camp without a fight.

"But after April 5th this method was altered. I should have been wrong were I to separate from you, because I had a proof sufficient for myself and officers that you had no people, neither soldiers nor servants; that you were alone. I proposed then as I propose now; should Selim Bey reach us, not to allow Selim Bey, or one single soldier of his force, to approach my camp with arms. Long before they approach us we shall be in position along the track, and if they do not ground arms at command—why, then the consequences will be on their heads. Thus you see that since April 5th I have been rather wishing they would come. I should like nothing better than to bring this unruly mob to the same state of order and discipline they were in before they became infatuated with Arabi, Mahdism, and chronic rebellion. But if they come here they must first be disarmed; their rifles will be packed into loads, and carried by us. Their camp shall be at least 500 yards from us. Each march that removes them farther from Wadelai will assist us in bringing them into a proper frame of mind, and by and by their arms will be restored to them, and they will be useful to themselves as well as to us."

So it was made clear to Emin that he was governor no longer; he was not even leader of the few hundred men who had come with him from the province. Without position or followers, he was returning to the world in his middle-age as empty-handed as he had left it in his youth.

Before camp was struck Stanley ordered the sixty-three cases of ammunition which he had not offered to Emin, to be buried. This was the ammunition which Stanley's officers, when sick and starving, had held against all temptations. Several months later Selim Bey, arriving at the site of the camp, stumbled by accident on the buried ammunition and used it for its original purpose, the defence of the province.

Now that there was no ammunition to lose and no risk of Zanzibar desertions, Stanley decided that the return journey would not be back through the forest which two years before he had declared the only possible route, but would cover the condemned route to the east coast. The caravan might, by a detour round the Albert Edward Nyanza, have avoided the dangerous Unyoro country but Stanley had decided to cross the foothills of Ruwenzori in order to study the mountain. When the risks entailed were pointed out to him, he said he wished to avoid the greater danger of the caravan being overtaken by Selim Bey. He said: "I shall put between me and them such a series of obstacles the expedition will have no longer any cause for fear."

The road that had at first run through flat, swampy woodland, began to rise and fall precipitously. The caravan was continually being brought to a pause by violent, icy rivers that could not be forded. Long journeys had to be made to find a crossing. Already many refugees were complaining of exhaustion and foot sores. When they begged Stanley to bring the caravan to a standstill so they might rest, he referred them to Emin, who usually replied that as they could not stop long enough to allow people to recover they had better not stop at all. So they dragged on. At the beginning of June they were 3,513 feet above sea level on the lower Ruwenzori slopes.

On the way, Stanley tells us, he made a study of the curious man whom he had rescued "from himself" and "in spite of himself". Unlike Jephson, Stanley did not admit any man to be beyond his understanding. He summed up the Pasha without difficulty and his disappointment in his ideal governor was expressed with equal sorrow and anger.

He said that when he planned to rescue Livingstone he was told that the great missionary was a misanthrope, a recluse, was married to an African princess and would not welcome a European intruder: "I proceeded to him with indifference, ready to take umbrage, but I parted from him in tears."

How different this second rescue! Emin had been described as a great hero, another Gordon, "a tall, military-looking figure, austere in manners, an amateur in many sciences, who, despite the universal misfortune hovering over a large part of North-Central Africa, maintained evenness of mind, tranquillity of soul, and governed men and things so well that he was able to keep the Mahdi and his furious hordes at bay."

Instead the Pasha "was not a tall, military figure, nor was he by any means a Gordon". He had failed to come to the lake to meet the expedition. He treated his men with absurd consideration and unnecessary politeness. Behind his back they spoke of him not only with contempt but even with passionate hatred. Added to this was his failure to describe frankly the true state of affairs in the province, a failure that had endangered Jephson's life.

"Was it delusion on the Pasha's part, or was it his intention to mislead us? I believe it was the former, caused by his extraordinary optimism and his ready faith in the external show of affectation of obedience. Even the crafty Egyptians had become permeated with a high sense of their power by the facility with which they gained pardon for offences by ostentatious and obsequious penitence. Is this too harshly worded? Then let me say in plain Anglo-Saxon, that I think his good nature was too prone to forgive, whenever his inordinate self-esteem was gratified."

Stanley decided that Emin suffered from spiritual as well as physical myopia. He had no understanding of the mind of man. Stanley had tried to discover during their daily talks whether Emin was Christian, Moslem, Jew or Pagan, and came to the conclusion that he was nothing but a Materialist. Why, he wondered, were scientists, in comparison with Christians, guilty of a certain hardness, an indelicacy of feeling?

"If one talks about the inner beauty," said Stanley, "which to some of us is the only beauty worth anything, they are apt to yawn, and to return an apologetic and compassionate smile."

Stanley might have been surprised had he realised that the myopic Pasha was summing him up as critically as he summed up the Pasha. Emin did not write a book or express his views in a series of lectures, but he did have an opportunity to unburden to one sympathetic listener his opinion of his rescuer, and that listener gave Emin's opinion a voice as penetrating as Stanley's own. But all that was still in the future. On the journey Emin maintained, as best he could, the show of good manners and gratitude he felt required of him.

As the danger from Kabba Rega's forces increased, Stanley ordered all servants armed with guns to join the rear guard with the Zanzibaris and Manyuema. This raised a protesting wail from the Egyptians, who needed the servants to carry the children and baggage and help the sick. The caravan nearly revolted.

Emin, deprived of his six armed men, complained to Stanley. Stanley flew into a rage and blamed Emin for every misfortune that had so far befallen the caravan. As he could not very well arrest the Pasha, he arrested Vita Hassan and Marco the Greek as an example to everyone who failed to obey orders instantly. This merely increased the uproar but Stanley came out of it on top as usual and got his own way.

Jephson's dignified description of the incident shows that Emin was now displacing Stanley in the disapproval of the young Englishmen: "On reaching the open country, the names of all men available for the service were taken, and they were enrolled into a company, and Shukri Aga, as the fittest officer, was appointed captain. Rifles and ammunition were then served out, and a new company, well armed and equipped, had been added to the expedition for the common good. But without a word of warning that anything out of the way, or that any slight had been put on him, the Pasha came in an excited state to demand that his people should be restored to him. He had no orderlies, and insisted on having them, he had no guards, and he would have them; he resolved that he should have four guards in front, and four in rear, two to attend to his daughter, besides two orderlies and servants for his tent, and then cried out to Mr. Stanley, 'I am sorry that I ever agreed to go with you.' We could not help thinking that this was most intemperate language and utterly uncalled for, because the position of himself and family on the march was always in rear of No. 1 Company, and three companies immediately followed his family; while another company acted as rear guard of the column. Besides this, two of the most respectable Zanzibari chiefs had the honour of conveying his daughter in a hammock, and several armed porters had been detailed to help his servants carry his luggage. The country we were now about to enter we expected would prove hostile, as it swarmed with Kabba Rega's bandits, and any moment an attack might be made on us. In such an event it was natural to expect that the able-bodied of the refugees would assist in their own defence, since we had so many rifles and so much ammunition to serve out. We were glad to hear the Pasha apologise for the warmth of his manner the next day."

In a speech to the English officers and the more important members of the expedition, Stanley made it clear that he regarded Emin as a simpleton. Not only as a simpleton but an outcast, for Stanley spoke of himself and other English, and even Casati, as Christians, but this governor who had no one to govern, who had been thrown out and jeered at by his people, who would have been almost certainly hanged but for the good sense of his rescuers, was referred to as Mohammed Emin Pasha.

At this time Emin's behaviour seemed to Stanley outrageous. Emin said he intended boiling the heads of any dead Unyoro natives they passed in order to preserve the skulls for a museum. Stanley was shocked and said the Zanzibaris would object to such a thing. Emin merely smiled, saying: "All for science."

"This trait in the scientific man," wrote Stanley, "casts some light upon a mystery. I have been attempting to discover the reasons why we two, he and I, differ in our judgments of his men. We have some dwarfs in the camp. The Pasha wished to measure their skulls; I devoted my observations to their inner nature. He proceeded to fold his tape round the circumference of the chest; I wished to study the face. The Pasha wondered at the feel of the body; I marvelled at the quick play of the feelings as revealed in lightning movements of the facial muscles. The Pasha admired the breadth of the frontal bone; I studied the tones of the voice, and watched how beautifully a slight flash of the eye coincided with the slightest twitch of a lip. The Pasha might know to a grain what the body of the pigmy weighed, but I only cared to know what the inner capacity was."

But, in spite of the fact that no one had suggested making him a Pasha or a governor, Stanley could show forbearance and in his book described frequent friendly intercourse between him and the Pasha, and their exchange of "presents and choice dishes". He tells how Emin planned to supervise the education of his little daughter; spoke of his intention to devote himself to a book on his twelve years in Equatoria, to present himself to the Emin Pasha Relief Committee and express gratitude for their kindness, to read a paper before the Royal Geographical Society—and did no more than mention the fact that Emin failed to do any of these things.

All might have been well had it not been that Emin, in his last struggle to hold on to an illusion of authority, was liable like a trapped animal to spasms of self-hurting temper or sulks. According to Stanley he counteracted reasonable orders or refused to give them. He quarrelled, broke promises, and even told lies.

The time came when Stanley felt it necessary "to seize the opportunity of giving him a little lecture upon the mode of conduct becoming a Pasha and a gentleman".

Emin apologised at once for his bad behaviour.

"I frankly accept your apology, Pasha," said Stanley, "but I do hope that from here to the coast you will allow us to remember that you are still the Governor of the Equatorial province, and not a vain and spoiled child."

"Ah, Mr. Stanley," replied Emin, "I am sorry I ever came on with you, and, if you will allow me, on reaching Mr. Mackay's, I will ask you to let me remain with him."

"But why, Pasha?" Stanley asked, all surprise. "Tell me why, and what is it you wish. Has any person offended you? I know of everything that transpires in this camp, but I confess that I am ignorant of any offence being done towards you intentionally by any person. Down to the smallest Zanzibari boy I can only see a sincere desire to serve you. Now, Pasha, let me show you in a few words for the first time how strange your conduct has appeared to us."

Here followed a long list of Emin's many faults. He had failed to come up to expectations and with frightful results. Among other things he was blamed for Barttelot's death. Stanley said: "We reached Kavalli on December 14th, 1887. You did not reach Kavalli before March, 1888. That omission on your part cost us the life of a gallant Englishman and the lives of over a hundred of our brave and faithful followers, and caused a delay of four months."

It was not surprising that Jephson, who had been most in contact with him, thought that Emin on this journey had become a changed man. Jephson wondered was it possible that Emin was harbouring resentful thoughts about them all? Surely not, when he could have so little cause for doing so!

Sad news followed them from Selim Bey. At first it had looked as though Fadl-el-Mulla would join the expedition and Selim had enthusiastically rounded up a number of officers, their families and all possible ammunition at Wadelai. But Fadl-el-Mulla changed his mind. In the middle of the night he and his men got possession of all the ammunition and disappeared with it. Selim awoke to find his party unarmed save for the forty rounds per man which had been served out to the soldiers. He then journeyed with his party to M'swa, where they settled down in a sort of muddled daze. During a momentary wakefulness he suddenly wrote to Emin and Stanley:

"We wish to know why you convert Egyptian officers and soldiers into beasts of burden. It has been reported to us that you have cruelly laden all with luggage, and that you convert the soldiers into porters. This is most shameful and we shall strictly inquire into it."

He had then, apparently, sunk back into a coma until news reached him that the caravan had set out from Kavalli's. He at once sent messengers with a letter that told of Fadl-el-Mulla's treachery and begged Stanley to wait for him so that he and his men might not all be destroyed by Kabba Rega.

To Emin he wrote that if the expedition did not wait for him and a misfortune resulted, Emin would have to account for it before God.

"But, my friends," Stanley asked the messengers who brought these letters, "how can we be sure that Selim Bey intends coming after all?"

"He will be sure to do so this time," they replied.

"But why is he waiting at M'swa? Why not have come himself with his steamer to the lake-shore camp? It is only nine hours' journey."

"He heard through some deserters that you had gone on."

"It might have been easy for him to have overtaken such a big caravan as this, with the few people whom he leads."

"But everything is going wrong. There are too many counsellors with Selim Bey, and the Egyptian clerks fill his ears with all kinds of stories. He is honest in his wishes to leave the land, but the others bewilder us with their falsehoods."

"Well, we cannot stay here to await Selim Bey. I will go on slowly—

a couple of hours a day. I must keep these people marching, otherwise the Pasha will be left alone. . . . If Selim Bey is serious in his intentions, he will soon overhaul us; and, besides, when we reach the river we will send him a guide that will enable him to travel in four days what will take us twelve days."

The soldiers returned, taking with them a sick officer and his family, and that was the last that Stanley ever heard of Selim Bey.

The Egyptians, Stanley's "guests", now found themselves making the journey practically under arrest. At the first show of recalcitrance, Stanley issued the order: "Upon any insolence, whether from Egyptian officer, private soldier, or follower, the officer in charge will call his guard and bind the offender, and bring him to me for punishment. If any violence is offered it must be met by such violence as will instantly crush it."

Casati, complaining against the harsh treatment of Emin's people, said: "To this . . . was added the disdainful and insulting behaviour of the Zanzibaris, who also believed themselves authorised to assume the character of liberators and to commit any act of oppression they pleased."

The caravan had been for some time skirting the Ruwenzori range while to the right could be seen the black, undulating edge of the forest that stretched westwards for over five hundred miles. The people of this district, the Wakonju, belonged to a hardier race than the lowland negroes although they bore no resemblance to the mythical people mentioned by Casati. Some of them had built their villages as high as 8,000 feet above sea-level. At times they had been driven by other tribes to retreat higher and it was said that fifty men once took refuge in the snow region but only thirty of them survived the cold.

The Wakonju treated the caravan kindly and supplied it with goats, bananas and honey.

The going was hard and proved too much for many Egyptians. Mothers began abandoning their infants; the sick were falling out one by one; a soldier, neither sick nor overloaded, suddenly lay down to die and was left behind, but a day or two later reappeared "looking rather sheepish". Continual attacks by Kabba Rega's guerrillas had to be beaten off.

Whatever cause for complaint Emin might think he had on the march, Stanley felt himself to have very much more. The Egyptians with their laziness, their whining discontent and cowardice infuriated him. He said they were all syphilitic and "had led such a fearful life of debauchery and license in their province that few of them had any stamina remaining, and they broke down under what was only moderate exercise to the Zanzibaris". Their crowds of children kept him awake at night: "These wee creatures must have possessed irascible natures, for such obstinate and persistent caterwauling never tormented me before. The tiny blacks and sallow yellows rivalled one another with force of lung until long past midnight, then about 3.0 or 4.0 a.m. started afresh, woke everyone from slumber, while grunts of discontent at the mee-awing chorus would be heard from every quarter."

The Pasha infuriated Stanley. Bored with the whole expedition by now, Stanley only wanted to get back to civilisation. Emin, who could see no need for haste and indeed dreaded his return, wanted to linger on the road and collect beasts and birds. He begged Stanley "to take it easy".

"But we are taking it easy for manifold reasons. The little children, the large number of women burdened with infants, the incapable Egyptians, the hope that Selim Bey will overtake us, the feeble condition of Jephson and myself, and Stairs is far from strong."

"Well, then, take it more easy."

"We have done so; a mile and a half per day is surely easy going."

"Then be easier still."

"Heavens, Pasha, do you wish us to stay here altogether? Then let us make our wills, and resign ourselves to die with our work undone."

At such a point as this Stanley would realise that "another explosion was imminent" and would conclude that their natures were "diametrically opposed". He was disgusted with Emin's "mania" for collecting natural history specimens. "He would slay every bird in Africa; he would collect ugly reptiles, and every hideous insect; he would gather every skull until we should become a travelling museum and cemetery, if only carriers could be obtained."

His people were developing "rabid ulcers, syphilis had weakened their constitutions, a puncture of a thorn in the face grew into a horrid and sloughy sore; they had pastured on vice and were reaping the consequences"; the camp was becoming filthy; carriers were dying from ill-treatment—but all Emin could care about was some horrid, crawling creature. Stanley concluded vehemently: "The continent of Africa was never meant by the all-bounteous Creator to be merely a botanical reserve, or an entomological museum."

But Ruwenzori—which excited Stanley very much—produced no unusual interest in the Pasha. To him it was merely a possible source of new specimens. Stanley roared poetically in indignation at such an attitude: "He—the Maker who raised these eternal mountains and tapestried their slopes with the mosses, and lichens, and tender herbs, and divided them by myriads of watercourses for the melted snow to run into the fruitful valley, and caused that mighty, limitless forest to clothe it, and its foliage to shine with unfading lustre—surely intended that it should be reserved until the fullness of time for something higher than a nursery for birds and a store-place for reptiles."

Ruwenzori, he decided, must be the fabled Mountains of the Moon. Although authorities later decided that the Mountains of the Moon were more probably the vast range of Kilima Njaro, they named the central Ruwenzori peak Mount Stanley, which must have compensated its namesake for much.

Casati, a not unknown explorer and liable to all the jealousies and rivalries that agitated the supermen of the period, made it clear in his book that he did not regard Stanley as the discoverer of a mountain that he himself had seen first, but to Stanley the discovery was the triumph of the trip. When a suitable point was reached he brought the caravan to a standstill and suggested that someone might like to climb the mountain. He pointed out that he was not yet well enough; Bonny and Jephson had fever and Casati was also ill; Parke could not leave his patients and Nelson said he could see no practical use for such a climb—but the Pasha now, that man of science, might like to seize the opportunity! Emin politely expressed "rapture at the very thought". Stairs was willing to go with him and they set out early next morning with forty Zanzibaris. The Zanzibaris were full of excitement as they hoped to get some of the white stuff—believed by the natives to be silver—which they could see at the top.

Emin, who had probably merely made a start to satisfy Stanley, returned to the camp exhausted after getting up 1,000 feet. Stairs went on alone. At a height of nearly 11,000 feet, he realised that three enormous ravines lay between him and the snow mountain proper. Having neither the equipment nor time to proceed, he had to make his way back, but he had touched on that fantastic, mist-clad region described by the Duke of Abruzzi, who, with the help of expert Alpine climbers, reached the summit in 1906. He brought back to the camp specimens of heather, blackberry and bilberry, all of giant size. Casati noted with some satisfaction that, in spite of Stanley, the great mountain still held its mystery.

Stanley, however, made the most of his discovery. He filled two chapters of *Darkest Africa* with descriptions and legends, and quoted from an old manuscript: "Some say that people have ascended the mountain, and one of them began to laugh and clap his hands, and threw himself down on the further side of the mountain." "I have not," he commented, "learned that Lieutenant Stairs in his ascent was guilty of such extravagance."

At last he was forced to turn his back on his discovery. There was no excuse for holding the caravan up any longer, but the continued journey was enlivened by another discovery. As the caravan made its way southwards a new lake came into sight. The natives said it was called Muta Nzige but Stanley decided to rename it the Albert Edward "out of respect for the first British Prince who had shown an interest in African geography".

After these discoveries, the rest of the journey must have seemed dull. It was mostly a record of miseries and misfortunes endured by individuals on the way. Each day one or two men, women or children, too ill to continue, had to be abandoned. The caravan passed out of the gloomy forest fringe into the beautiful and rich Uganda country. Food became more plentiful and the brilliant park-land raised everyone's hopes, but a new danger threatened. Kabba Rega's men, who had pursued the column for miles, were now falling back, but this new country was one in which Christians were suffering severe persecution.

The mad king, Mwanga, had been deposed by the Zanzibar Mohammedans for plotting against them. They had put in his place a simpleton named Karema and, naming Karema as their authority, had burnt every Christian convert they could rout out of hiding. The English officers awaited trouble, but the Uganda natives did no more than capture stragglers to use as slaves.

Mwanga, who had fled to a small island on Lake Victoria, had now become a Christian himself in the hope of getting Christian support. A group of his followers came to the expedition's camp and begged Stanley to help them put the old tyrant back on the throne. Stanley was in a difficult position. He ran considerable risk in offending either faction. Emin complicated the situation and annoyed Stanley by pressing him to help the Christians.

"We are much too weak," said Stanley angrily. "You do not

know Uganda if you think that our force would be sufficient."

Emin then rashly offered to go himself with his own people to help the Uganda Christians. At this Stanley had one of his outbursts of fury and threatened to have Emin put under supervision if he tried to carry out such a plan. He (Stanley) was responsible for the safe return of the Pasha to the coast and without the command of the Queen of England did not choose to mix himself up in Uganda's affairs. He got rid of the waiting deputation by promising to return to fight for Mwanga once he had safely deposited the refugees.

Emin's offer to aid the Christians probably had a motive other than a desire to give help. The caravan was now skirting the Victoria Nyanza. It was in this region that Emin had hoped to make a new settlement from which to reconquer his province with men and ammunition sent to him by Stanley. It had actually at one time been agreed that the refugees should be taken round the lake to settle at Kavirondo, and this plan had remained in Emin's mind despite later events. To Stanley it had become merely ridiculous; the rebellion had put an end to all that. Emin was no longer a governor, he had no people to populate a new province, and, as for the old one, he would have to reconquer it not only from the Mahdi but from his own army.

Stanley had marched on day after day without any mention of a stop until at last Emin was forced, in spite of his natural diffidence, to bring it up himself. Stanley at once made it clear that he had no intention of putting Emin down anywhere. He must come to the coast. When Emin protested, Stanley said that in any case the question of new territory for the refugees could only be settled at the coast. To Emin the Mwanga incident must have seemed to offer a loophole of escape— and who knew but that throwing in his lot with the Christians he might not once again become an influence for good in these regions? Stanley, having put a stop to such nonsense, carried Emin on virtually as a prisoner.

The Egyptians, who had half expected to remain at Victoria Nyanza, continued with even less heart than before. They gave themselves up to their ailments without a struggle. Whole families, too weak to continue, were left at native villages. During the month of July as many as 141 refugees fell out of the column. At one stop on the journey everyone drank of some water in a pit and hundreds developed a fever that for some ended in paralysis and death. Wild beasts, as well as sickness, menaced the caravan. One night the camp was awakened by the screams of a young girl carried off by a leopard. When they climbed to the cold, rainy upper regions, men would fall seized by sudden paralysis and have to be massaged back to life before fires.

Casati, suffering from fever, was carried most of the way in a litter. Stanley made no secret of his dislike and contempt for this man, and Emin, too, found him exasperating. At one time, while Casati was too weak to walk, Emin found him lying in the hot sunshine. Why, asked Emin, did he not set his six servants to building him a shelter of banana leaves?

"I have no servants," replied Casati.

"But you have four stout female servants that I know of."

"Yes, but I do not like to ask them to do anything lest they should say I work them like slaves. They are widows, you know, and their husbands are dead."

Stanley's snort of disgust when told this story must have expressed more than *Darkest Africa* could say.

At last in a bleak stretch of country near the lake, where food was short, the caravan came upon the mission house of Mackay, who had laboured in this region, against unceasing persecution, for twelve years. He welcomed his visitors with delight and fed the caravan with everything his store-room could provide.

Mackay was a man whom Mohammedanism could not break. Although the Zanzibar agents had been afraid to touch him, they had forced him to watch the burning to death of a young Christian boy who had been his especial charge. Hundreds of his converts had suffered death at the stake and he had had to realise that when he offered the natives salvation, he offered them also almost certain martyrdom.

The caravan spent nineteen days resting and recuperating on the good food Mackay provided. He had taught his followers cooking and gardening, the English language, and the use of tools and machinery, and his mission had become an oasis of industry and prosperity in a vast region almost depopulated by wars and persecution. When they separated, Stanley tried to persuade Mackay to go with him on a visit to the coast. He refused, and a few months later the caravan received news of his death.

It was early in September when Stanley's whistle sounded again. The refugees pulled themselves together and started out unwillingly for another long stage of the journey.

In the Usukuma country, below the Victoria Nyanza, the natives became troublesome again. The caravan was now crossing flat grass-land where it could not be ambushed, but one serious concerted attack was made and driven off.

On October 18th the column was joined by a missionary, Father Augustus Schynze, who had been driven out of Uganda. Schynze was a German and later not unwillingly wrote confirming the German view of the whole expedition. He said he had noted in his diary remarks he often heard made among the English officers: "Two years and a half have we spent in misery—and what for? We are bringing a lot of use-less, rotten Egyptian clerks, Jews, Greeks and Turks out of the interior; people who don't as much as thank us for doing so; Casati even wasn't worth the trouble, and the Pasha, although a man of honour, is, after all, merely a scientist." Schynze was convinced that Emin was "too well versed in human nature to deceive himself in the least about the true motives of the expedition". Why, asked Schynze, should the donors to Emin's cause suddenly decide to spend vast sums in extricating an Egyptian official whom until that moment they did not even know by name? The expedition, he decided, was not intended so much for Emin Pasha as for his province and his ivory.

It is possible that Emin, in his growing bitterness against Stanley, sometimes shared these conclusions.

For Emin himself Schynze was full of the admiration which was being accorded the Pasha in Germany at the time these revelations were made. He records how, when early in November Emin fell ill, he offered him some wine he had been keeping for the celebration of mass. Emin refused it, saying: "I shall ask you for it again one of these days, on behalf of some sick member of the caravan; till then, please keep it for me." Schynze wrote in his diary: "It is an enigma to me how he lives and stands the journey."

In the morning Emin took nothing but a cup of coffee. He would then remain all day on his donkey, eating nothing until his people prepared his evening meal. "I have never," said Schynze, "met with any European in Africa who could make so little suffice. But his table and chair were important to him. He always wished to find them ready in his tent—without them he could not work. His time was divided between science and his little daughter, whom he had carried before him in a hammock so that, in spite of his failing sight, he could keep watch over her."

As the caravan approached the coast it came to areas where the Arabs had introduced hashish. One day a hundred hilarious, drunken natives insisted on giving the refugees the pleasure of their company. In the Unyamwezi province, the caravan came upon the tremendous Adamsonia, the largest of large plants, and acacia woods filled with lions, leopards, hyenas and monkeys. Herds of giraffe swept away in soft undulations over the open country as the column approached. From these charming regions it passed into thick mimosa woods where water was hard to find. The refugees had been warned of the danger of thirst but, improvident as ever, had taken no precautions.

West of Unyamwezi was the Ugogo country. The Ugogo, according to Father Schynze, "are troublesome and saucy, and it is difficult to get rid of them; besides, they are very dirty". These Ugogo had grown rich on tribute extracted from caravans passing through their territory, and Stanley was ordered by the prince of the country, in lieu of the usual tribute of ivory, to heap up sufficient wood to build a royal house. Stanley, intensely irritated but aware that by now the caravan was in no condition to fight, paid up with a quantity of cloth.

On the last day of October came a breath of civilisation. A messenger met the caravan with a letter to Emin from Major Wissman, the German Imperial Commissioner, a noted explorer. Wissman had been at the German station of Mpwapwa, and although he had now returned to the coast, he had left his lieutenant Schmidt with troops to await his countryman.

Everyone's spirits rose—Emin's most of all. They were entering the German sphere of influence and it was obvious that he felt an excitement, a sense of home-coming, in a country where his native language and customs were being introduced. In this new atmosphere, Emin wrote in his diary: "It is curious to observe how little Stanley can rid himself of his English prejudices. He is fond of acting the cosmopolitan; and, therefore, in speaking to us, approves of the extension of German dominion, but in unguarded moments, when we are alone, he reproaches me with my German proclivities. The officers of the expedition are superlatively English and look down upon us Germans from a sublime altitude. Lieutenant Stairs, for example, only the other day expressed the opinion that it would be wrong to make use of Wissman's German steamers for the passage to Zanzibar; that ours was an English expedition, and should terminate as such! And then people talk about German narrow-mindedness and particularism!"

The era of the great wars was indeed at hand. Stanley noticed the intense political rivalry existing between Germany and England for superior influence over the Sultan of Zanzibar and his Arabs. As he had rescued a German national, he was received with some evidence of good will, but he felt it to be strained. The young officers noted resentfully that the natives greeted them with "Guten Morgen" and even the women had learnt to salute with Prussian exactness.

Ten days after meeting with the messenger, Stanley sighted the German flag flying in the distance. It was Schmidt at the head of his men, come to lead the caravan to Mpwapwa Station. The German officers vied with one another in affability towards Emin. He, so long forlorn and unconsidered, controlled and lectured on his behaviour, snubbed daily during the whole miserable journey, now found himself the centre of attention. His manner regained its charm, he laughed happily and his eyes shone. It was evident how his spirits had risen and Stanley felt it necessary to administer a rebuke:

"Within a short time, Pasha," he said, "you will be among your countrymen, but while you glow with pride and pleasure at being once more amongst them, do not forget that they were English people who first heard your cries in the days of gloom. That it was English money which enabled these young English gentlemen to rescue you from Khartoum."

Emin answered that Stanley need have no fear of that.

At Mpwapwa the English officers were given a year's issue of the *Weekly Times* so they might read of the events that had occupied Europe while they themselves were buried in the dark forest. Two days later Stanley ordered departure. Emin said he wished he might stay longer to continue treating those who were sick of dysentery. To his surprise Stanley, "who seemed quite altered", agreed, but next day Stanley, become his old self again, insisted they must continue. Emin was forced to leave his patients.

But, as far as Emin was concerned, Stanley's rule was coming to an end. The caravan now fell in with Captain Gravenreuth, "the lion of the coast", and this important individual treated Emin with great deference. He had with him two American newspaper men who had brought provisions for Stanley, and they were all eagerness for Emin's story. A few days later, on the Kingani river, Major von Wissman himself waited upon Emin with full military splendour. The Governor of Equatoria was welcomed on board the cruiser *Sperber* in the name of the German Emperor, who had sent telegrams congratulating

Emin on his "true German fidelity and devotion to duty".

On December 3rd, at the sunset, the sound of a cannon was heard. It was the evening gun at Zanzibar. The Zanzibaris screamed their delight, for they were home again.

Of the 620 of them who had gone to the east coast with Stanley, only 225 had returned. Of the sixty Sudanese enlisted at Cairo, only twelve, and of the thirteen Somalis engaged by Barttelot at Aden, only one, survived. Of the 570 refugees who had followed Emin from Equatoria, 290 reached the coast. Eighty of the missing were known to have died, the rest were abandoned along the way. The return journey had taken eight months, less ten days, one month of which had been given up to Stanley's illness.

The members of the expedition had been travelling for over two and a half years.

Chapter Sixteen

THE BANQUET

"You may imagine the frame of mind I was in; anxiety about my own future, anxiety as to the preservation of my people, sickness, the indifference of the Egyptian government, Stanley's invectives. . . ."

EMIN: Letters

ON the afternoon of December 4th the caravan reached Bagamoya on the coast. The authorities had prepared for the refugees huts on the beach facing the Indian Ocean.

Wissman had arranged a banquet for the Governor of Equatoria and the leader of the expedition, to which the English officers, Casati, the officers of the warships that lay flag-decked at sea to welcome the travellers, and all the important people of the district were invited.

Wissman had been noting with surprise Stanley's manner towards Emin. It was, he said, that "of a military superior and a man of few words towards his subordinate", while Emin "avoided opposing Stanley and gave way whenever the latter had personal transactions with him". There was also the incident when Wissman had given Emin precedence on boarding his boat, and Emin, drawing back quickly, had begged him to let Stanley go first.

The Germans, hypercritical of the British at the best of times, were soon fully aware of the situation. At the banquet Emin was invited to sit on the Commissioner's right. He at once refused and asked that the place be given to Stanley. One might have supposed that, by an excess of humility, he was underlining the situation, but from what happened later there is little doubt that Emin had been brought by Stanley's fits of rage to a state of neurotic fear of displeasing him.

During the meal it was noticed that Emin's sight, that had been failing for a long time, was very bad. He had to take his food to within three inches of his eyes before he could see it. He was delighted with the sentimental music of the German orchestra and asked if he might hear "Heil Dir im Siegerkranz!" Stanley, on the Commissioner's right, was talkative. His voice was described as "sonorous", his delivery "good". He was indeed the successful Welshman with plenty to say for himself and no hesitation in saying it. In his speech he used fine dramatic, rolling phrases full of religious references, such as many a favourite Welsh preacher uses to this day.

Replying to a toast Stanley said he suppressed a tear at his remembrance of the bones of some members of his expedition now bleaching under the African sun—at which the captain of the *Schwalbe* whispered to his neighbour: "Stanley is said to be the most ruthless African explorer in existence."

Emin was described as being "effusively grateful" to each member of the expedition. He embraced Stairs, Nelson, Jephson and Parke, and stood between Wissman and Stanley "expressing his gratification at rescue", then "went away and fell over the balcony to the dismay of the company".

How this accident happened will never be known. Emin had just reseated himself after proposing the health of the German Emperor, when he rose again, unnoticed by anyone, and went into an adjoining room. No one knew why he left the table, but the Germans later suggested that Emin wished to leave the field in favour of Stanley "the ruthless one", and said that "Stanley always excited on Emin an influence that induced him to avoid anything that could have aroused the former's displeasure, as he did not feel himself Stanley's equal in an open contest".

A short while after his departure, an agitated messenger entered the banqueting hall to tell the guests that Emin had fallen twenty-five feet from a window heavily on to his head. He had been taken unconscious to the hospital before the messenger spread the news.

The only explanation of the accident that could be given was that Emin in his half-blindness, had mistaken a window for a door. Emin himself seems never to have given any other. It is an explanation that leaves out of account the fact that outside the window there was a railed balcony. The accident became the mystery of the moment, the more mysterious from the certainty of everyone that the fall was accidental. Those who had seen Emin at the banquet, charmingly entertaining, gracious and grateful for rescue, discussing until the last minute plans for his future, saw no reason to suspect anything else.

Yet Madame Hakki Pasha, until the moment she awoke to find herself deserted, probably saw nothing of the growing desperation that was eventually to give Emin ability to act. His growing determination to escape from a rescuer become a tyrant may have brought him to the unconsciously deliberate act of escape. Added to this was the fact that Emin from his school-days had been morbidly self-critical, morbidly capable of self-punishment for faults he felt inexcusable. Stanley had not only forced him to what he believed was a betrayal of a trust, but had also forced upon him a sense of guilt for the unreasonable behaviour with which he had fought against his impossible position in the caravan. He had been made ashamed of himself and only a violent action, whether fatal or not, could cut him off from the memory of ignominy.

Whatever the cause of the fall, Emin, when he regained consciousness, had come to a decision. He said he did not wish to see Stanley again.

It was at this point that Stanley said "the operations of the Germans commenced", proving "how little the Germans understood tact and finesse".

Emin's skull was not fractured and although he was in great pain, he was soon out of danger. Stanley, visiting him next day, said heartily:

"Well, Pasha, I hope you don't mean to admit the possibility that you are to die here, do you?"

"I'm not so bad as that," replied Emin.

"By what I have seen, Pasha, I am entirely of the same opinion. A person with a fractured head could not move his head after that manner. Good-bye. Dr. Parke will remain with you until dismissed by you, and I hope to hear good news from him daily."

To Stanley's amazement, he was not admitted to see Emin again. Parke was made to feel an intruder at the hospital and every excuse was given to keep English visitors away. Stanley wrote repeatedly urging Emin to cross with him to Zanzibar and from there continue to England. Stanley would no doubt have got his way had not a new influence come into Emin's life. Wissman was befriending him "in the most generous manner" and guarding him against the ruthless Stanley.

At first Stanley's letters were unanswered, then refused. Stanley, convinced that all this was the result of German double-dealing, instructed his cunning, agile boy, Sali, to creep unnoticed into Emin's room with the letters. Wissman was furious and said Emin's wound might reopen if he were worried and pestered in this way. As for crossing to Zanzibar, such action would endanger his life. Wissman told Sali he would have him hanged if he came near the hospital again.

Stanley was very indignant. He complained widely of his boy being threatened in this way when trying to deliver a note of condolence.

Emin, who had planned to accompany Stanley to Egypt, where he would present Casati, Shukri Aga and others to the Khedive, and then proceed to Naples and write a book about Equatoria, now refused to leave Bagamoyo. Was it not obvious that German influence was at work?

Wissman responded with the accusation that Stanley was angry because he could not take Emin with him to Egypt and "carry him triumphantly through every country as one who had been saved from a dreadful fate".

As for Emin's followers, who had been encamped on the beach at Bagamoyo, Stanley put it round that the Pasha had abandoned them. Emin himself wrote: "On the day after my unfortunate fall, Stanley insisted on my men embarking, threatening to put them in chains if they resisted, and had them conveyed via Zanzibar to Mombasa, without permitting them to communicate with me in any way." The men were then taken to Suez and it is doubtful whether Emin ever saw any of them again. Before he discovered why they had apparently deserted him, he wrote indignantly to say he would have nothing more to do with them. Stanley records this with no explanation but the usual bewilderment at such extraordinary behaviour. He also said Emin quarrelled with the Egyptian government and declined to send to Egypt the pay accounts of his men, while Emin wrote that the government "never enquired whether I was in need of anything, or troubled about me in any way", and said that when his creditors applied for money from Egypt through the British Consulate they were refused.

Stanley had another matter with which to deal while in Zanzibar. He commenced on behalf of the Emin Pasha Relief Expedition an action against Tippu-Tib for his breach of agreement, claiming £10,000 damages—the sum lying to Tippu-Tib's credit at Zanzibar. The result of this action is not known.

When Stanley packed up and left Zanzibar, Emin was still in Bagamoyo hospital. When he came out he took a house, engaged servants and settled down to recover from his accident. He made it clear that he had severed himself from the members of the expedition and wrote to Germany to say so. For a month he negotiated with the British East African Company for employment in their territory, then he suddenly announced that he had taken service with Germany at a salary of £1,000 a year—a third or quarter of what he had been offered by the British concern.

He was finished with Britain. As the British, in the shape of Gordon, had once seemed to him a people possessing all the virtues, so, seeing them in the shape of Stanley, they had become for him a nation of repulsive bullies. Peters concluded for him in print that "even the Mahdi could not have been more injurious to the civilising of the Upper Nile than Stanley had been in reality".

Emin's family now heard from him for the first time since his flight from Madame Hakki Pasha. Perhaps his sister Melanié had not known before that the famous Emin Pasha of which so much had been written in the papers was none other than her long lost brother Edouard. She began to receive from him excited letters full of plans for the future. When Emin returned from his German mission he would, he said, build a house at Bagamoyo and Melanié would come out as house-keeper and foster-mother to Farida.

At the beginning of the year 1890 the future had become again for Emin a source of pleasure and new hope.

About the same time, Peters, leading the German Emin Pasha Relief Expedition, was following a route north of Victoria Nile to Wadelai. In February, 1890, he had reached the Wasoga country to the north of the Victoria Nyanza, when a native handed him a letter from Stanley to the Relief Expedition Committee. Opening it, he discovered that Stanley had evacuated the province several months before and was returning with Emin to the coast. Peters, unaware that during his absence from Europe Uganda had been ceded to Britain, believed "that the prize of the contest was still there, and would fall to the lot of the boldest". He continued to Uganda with the ostensible purpose of aiding the Christians and there drew up a treaty with Mwanga in which the deposed king and the German Emperor swore eternal friend-ship. The German people were to have the right of free passage, trade and settlement in Uganda, while the Uganda natives were to have the right of free passage, trade and settlement in Germany.

Chapter Seventeen

CONTROVERSY

"The expensive and superfluous relief of Emin has brought no advantage either to the rescuers or to the rescued. On the contrary the rescuers now find out that their money and their enthusiasm have seriously prejudiced national interests. Although, perhaps, it may have been worth while to relieve Emin in order to afford Stanley an opportunity of still further adding to his great deeds as an explorer, it was certainly not worth while to relieve him for the purpose of presenting the German government with a new and experienced leader of expeditions calculated to open a route into the centre of Africa. If Emin succeeds in re-establishing himself in his old province, the consequence will be that the frontiers of Germany in Africa will be considerably advanced to the north-west."

St. James's Gazette

"We cannot conceal from ourselves that a keen competition exists in Central Africa between Germany and England; and that if Emin is not acting for England he is acting against her. His well-known irresolution can scarcely be held to mitigate a conduct which borders on treason."

·The Evening Standard

IN Egypt, Stanley had an audience with the Khedive at which he praised Emin as a governor but said he had one fault, he was not strict enough. He might successfully act as a civil governor but would require a military governor over him. He would, Stanley suggested, do very well at Wady Halfa or Suakin—both posts being regarded in the Egyptian service as second only to being shelved altogether. On this advice, the Khedive wired offering Emin an undefined appointment but making it clear that wherever he went he would be, as a civil governor under a military one, in a subordinate position. This was so much the kind of offer that Emin had foreseen and feared that it was fortunate that he had previously received the German one.

During the year 1890 the Emin-Stanley battle raged. Stanley's main defence and prosecution was to be his book and, after receiving first honours in Cairo, he retired from Shepheard's Hotel to the Villa Victoria and wrote it. He worked day and night, at a great speed. Guarded from intruders by his boy Sali, drinking only Apollinaris water, he paused for nothing but to sit for his portrait to Miss Meyrick. His publisher was invited to Cairo to admire this industry and abstemiousness, and so great was public interest in the book that the publisher thought it worth writing another to describe Stanley's surroundings and life while writing it.

When it was completed, Stanley returned to England to begin his lecture tour. It was a great success. Each lecture started off with some such words as:

"It is to Dr. Felkin of Edinburgh that we are indebted for the beautiful and inspiring picture of a governor at bay in the far Sudan, defying the victorious Mahdists and fighting bravely inch by inch for the land which he had been appointed to rule by General Gordon." He then described his own imagined picture of Emin—a tall, military figure of severe aspect, of rigid morals, inflexible will and scientific attainments; a brave man, straitened in means, battling against immense odds in the remote heart of Africa. This picture, he said, he found so inspiring that when asked to lead the expedition to Emin's relief "in a reckless mood, I answered in the affirmative". Those equally inspired to give their help "might have emptied the barracks, the colleges, the public-schools—I might almost say the nurseries". And all to what purpose? To rescue a governor without a province; a near-sighted, faithless, ungrateful little man who had, at the last, even abandoned the people over whom he had worried like a mother; who had taken offence at the fact that $200 due to him from the Egyptian Government had been made payable through the British Consul-General at Zanzibar, and who had cabled peevishly in reply to the Khedive's generous offer of a new appointment: "Since you cannot treat me better than this, I send my resignation."

People waiting to welcome Emin in England had felt themselves snubbed when he refused to come, and the subscribers to the Relief Fund were indignant that Emin chose to take service with Germany. Emin's name became a synonym for ingratitude. People felt more bitterly about Germany than before. Stanley was applauded when he mentioned another German, Dr. Peters, who had "raided a broad track through British territory under the guise of assisting Emin". He had reached Uganda and there made treaties at the same time as Emin himself was preparing to return there to annex the whole of East Africa for Germany. Fortunately a stop had been put to these little games by the fact that the two powers had reached an agreement fixing their boundaries to their respective spheres of influence.

Some curious suspicions were cast on Emin in Stanley's lectures and in the Press—that he was a Jew (this, probably, to annoy the Germans), given the name of Isaak in the register of the Jewish congregation, and that of Edouard in the civil register; that his mother was the daughter of a Jewish banker and became Christian when widowed; that Emin had turned Mohammedan to marry the daughter of the Governor of Janina and had deserted his wife (taking with him to Egypt a daughter who would, if anyone had bothered to compute the years, have been, not a child, but a young woman at the time of the rescue); that he had been expelled from Turkey for publishing the seditious paper *Hakikal* and taking part in the "Young Turk" agitation, and had possibly been implicated in the assassination of the Sultan Abdul Aziz. . . .

But, Stanley reminded his audiences, Emin was still alive and "every whisper or insinuation derogatory to him cheapens somewhat the man for whom we ventured our lives". Emin might lack all the virtues known to be Stanley's own, but he was a good man, one "worth all the sacrifices which we have made". Also, even if Emin himself had been a disappointment, his rescue had led to the discovery of the Mountains of the Moon, the sources of the Albertine Nile, Lake Albert Edward and an important extension of the Victoria Nyanza. Stanley chose also to take credit for the fact that the British, German, French and Portuguese Governments had been induced to agree about their spheres of influence—so it could be seen that, altogether, the expedition had not set forth in vain.

The music-halls were having a lot of fun with this major interest of the moment. Stanley, said the comedians, had gone to find Emin and had found him out. And why had Stanley been unable to find Emin Pasha? Because there is no M in Pasha. While a Mr. Gerald Massey was writing with possibly more serious intentions:

> "He strode o'er streams and mountains
>   To free the leaguered band:
> He stood by Nile's far fountains,
>   Lord of the Old Dark Land!
> Where Death the forest haunted,
>   And never dawned the day,
> He pierced the gloom undaunted—
>   For that was Stanley's way."

But the fun was not all in Stanley's favour. A satire on *Darkest Africa* was published that said among other things: "Livingstone didn't want to be found, and could have been perfectly happy if I had let him alone. However, if there is someone to be found, I'm the man to find him, and I don't care two straws whether he wants to be discovered or not. Business is business, and while you are looking for a chap you pick up a lot on the way." A list of equipment for the fantastic journey described included: "Two dozen white double-stiff masher collars to be photographed in."

The young officers of the expedition were busy publishing their own experiences and their attempts to be impartial did not always throw the best light on their leader. Stanley was also being criticised elsewhere. He was accused of putting the "little commissions"—such as the matter of Tippu-Tib—which he had undertaken for his old employer, the King of the Belgians, before the chief object of the expedition. An action "Stanley v. Troup" was entered in the Chancery Court but was withdrawn on terms that left no doubt but that Stanley lacked confidence to go through with it. There was also a bitter controversy over the rear column. When Stanley's accusations against Barttelot and Jameson appeared in print, the relatives of the young men made counter-accusations. Stanley wrote furious letters to the Press blaming his dead officers in unsparing tones and the relatives replied indignantly. All Stanley's bluster could not persuade a strong faction that he was not at fault in leaving these inexperienced men alone at Yambuya to the mercies of Tippu-Tib. His explanations were full of exasperation at the stupidity of people who could not see that Barttelot, the senior officer, was the best, the only possible person to be left behind.

Admitting that Barttelot was "lacking in forbearance", Stanley said: "I promised myself he would have little chance to exercise combativeness. . . . I had to interfere twice between fire-eating young Arabs, and strong, plucky, young Englishmen, who were unable to discern the dark-faced young Arab from the "nigger", before we reached Yambuya. Well, it just happened that the Major, forgetting my instructions as to forbearance, met these Arab fire-eaters and the consequence was that the Major had to employ the Syrian Assad Ferran to interpret for him. Whether the man interpreted falsely, I know not, but a coolness arose between the high-spirited nephew of Tippu-Tib and the equally high-spirited young Major which was never satisfactorily healed up, and which in the long run, led to the ever-to-be-regretted death of poor Barttelot.

This acknowledgment that Barttelot's fate had been written by his own imperious nature did not do much to convince Stanley's critics that Barttelot had been the best choice.

While this controversy was in full swing the Rev. Wilmot Brooke wrote to *The Times* of cannibalism in the Yambuya camp: "Eye-witnesses, both English and Arab, have assured me it was a common thing, which they themselves have seen on passing through the Manyuema camp, to see human hands and feet sticking out of their cooking pots."

"Who were the English who had seen this curious sight?" asked Stanley, and the clergyman did not find it easy to reply.

In Germany, where Emin was receiving a great deal of belated appreciation, the papers spoke of Emin's "forcible abduction by Mr. Stanley" and of the expedition as no more than a huge ivory-hunt. As the ivory in the province was the property of the Egyptian Government, the German Press thought Stanley's interest in it misplaced, but admitted he might justifiably have claimed sufficient to cover the expenses of the expedition.

Emin, in England the symbol of ingratitude, incompetence and false appearances, had become in Germany "the solitary warrior on the abandoned watch-tower in Central Africa". "Every German heart must throb more quickly at the thought that he alone—he, the German —could accomplish great things in Africa." British incompetence alone had brought about the Mahdi rising, while Stanley's indignation was described as no more than that of a "disappointed place-hunter".

Chapter Eighteen

THE LAST JOURNEY

"Emin may be far more intellectual than Wissman, and that he is a great scholar is beyond dispute, but if I had his profile before me, it would show the back of his head to be insufficiently developed, betokening a want of that brute energy which cannot altogether be dispensed with in Africa."

BISMARCK

EMIN, who made no attempt to contact the civilised world he had left long before, knew almost nothing of the uproar to which he had given rise. He was absorbed in preparations for his return to the dangers from which he had been rescued. Rumours may by now have reached the coast that the rebels of Equatoria had driven the Mahdi forces back to Rejaf. If so, his self-condemnation must have been bitter. These men whom he, "the Faithful One", deserted had done his duty for him. He became possessed by the desire to return. His arrangements were those of a man who saw this journey as his last.

He caused Farida's birth to be legitimised, saying: "As I have never been married up to the present, there can be no legal bar to adoption." His will was made in her favour and he left her with friends.

On April 26th, 1890, in the desolating rainy season, he set out again for the interior. The black sky, the cold and tearing rain, seemed to foreshadow the tragic failure of the whole expedition.

Emin had been asked by the German Government "to secure on behalf of Germany the territories situated south of and along Victoria Nyanza up to Albert Nyanza".

Peters, forced to return to the coast from lack of funds, and Emin, *en route* to Uganda, met at Mpwapwa. Peters was charmed by Emin, who, with all his old generosity, pressed on him gifts of which he himself, going inland, would have had greater need. Emin's gratitude for anything done for him seemed to Peters heart-moving. The two men, joined by a racial understanding, talked for hours together, and Emin, for the first and last time, spoke freely of his rescuer. He might have spoken less freely had he known that Peters intended on his return to rush everything said (and possibly much that was not said) into print. Many of the statements have the flavour of being rather what Peters thought Emin should have said or would like to have said and did not. Among other things he reports as Emin's words: "When Stanley came for the first time to Lake Edward, he would have been lost if Casati and I had not gone to him. Stanley did not come to us, we went to him. He did not reach the Equatorial province any more than you did. When he first arrived at Kavalli's and found no tidings of us, he did not venture to make an advance along Lake Albert to Wadelai, but went back for four months to bring up a boat. Then the expedition came back and we sought them out, brought them provisions and clothing, and in this way the expedition was saved from destruction. Then he began to press me to give up my post. He told me the Khedive had sent him hither, for the definite purpose of delivering to me the order commanding me to evacuate the Equatorial province. Stanley gave me to understand that he was empowered, in case of need, to carry me away from the province by force."

He then described the proposal that he and his troops should establish themselves at Kavironda, but even this "he did not carry out. When we had arrived in the south of Lake Victoria, he suddenly found that he did not care to lead me round the lake and to take me to Kavironda from whence, as had been expressly agreed, I was to reconquer my territory with the reinforcements Stanley was to bring up; on the contrary, he suddenly declared that I must go with him to the coast to complete the affair. In this manner I have been compelled to march with him to the coast whereas originally the question was only that of a transfer of my capital from Lake Albert to Lake Victoria."

"If," Emin is further reported as having said, "at any time Stanley suffered from a slight illness, as for instance, from catarrh, we used to be kept waiting for weeks in one spot. On the other hand no particular notice was taken of the state of health, good or bad, of the other members of the expedition. But what distinguishes this man is the extraordinary presence of mind and the merciless resolution with which he carried out what he had made up his mind to do. If any unexpected incident occurred, very little time elapsed before Stanley had resolved upon his measures, which were then put into operation, let the cost be what it might."

Peters could not reconcile his own opinion of Stanley with Emin's last remarks. He thought Stanley had made a muddle of the whole expedition and that his decisions were not only incomprehensible but confused. More loudly than anyone, Peters asked all the questions that had been going round for months. Why had Stanley not chosen to take the convenient east coast route which he (Peters) had followed easily and safely enough? Why, when Stanley knew Tippu-Tib to be a faithless man, did he have dealings with him? Why when he reached the lake did he not spend another fifteen days in continuing to Wadelai? Why, if he had to leave the steel boat 190 miles from the lake and waste four months returning for it, did he not return for the rear column at the same time? All this muddle, this lack of planning, this incompetence, had dragged out the journey to three or four times its length. Even the maps he made were slapdash and inaccurate while Emin's were models of accuracy.

Peters seized on Emin's remark that Stanley "often made wide circuits to keep out of the way of tribes he considered warlike" to explain his belief in Stanley's cowardice. This, he said, accounted for all the wonderful bends and twists to be found in the route of the expedition. He could see no reason why Stanley should not have taken up a strong line with the Wagogo king. He himself had taken up a strong line and, when attacked by two or three thousand warriors, had put them to flight with the shots of twenty men. There was, Peters concluded, no doubt at all that the whole of Stanley's plan to acquire for England the countries of the Upper Nile—cunningly disguised, of course, under a pretence of rescuing Emin—had failed entirely as a result of Stanley's irresolution, blunderings and cowardice. He had not even had the good sense to seize the opportunity in Uganda offered by Mwanga. Exactly what Stanley thought he was up to during the expedition it was beyond Peters' powers to understand.

And what resulted from it all? Emin, who had once been a sincere friend of Britain, had been turned into an enemy and was now on his way back to acquire for Germany all the territory Stanley had let slip through his hands. Peters believed that if Stanley had stuck fast in the swamps of the Aruwimi, Emin would in 1890 have still been in Wadelai in a secure position while the German Emin Pasha Expedition would be establishing for him communication, through Uganda, with the German East Africa Company.

Emin no doubt by now thought so too. When he parted from Peters, he was inspired by the imperialistic race for power and territory in Africa. He marched on towards Uganda, where both the British and German East Africa Companies were intriguing wildly with Mwanga. All the excitement came to an end for Emin when he received news of the Anglo-German agreement which was signed on July 1st, 1890.

Lake Albert was excluded from the German sphere of influence.

Emin, no imperialist at the best of times, lost all interest in his mission and gave himself up to natural history. The past faded so completely that even England began again to receive from him parcels of birds and skins. The German authorities were disgusted. They repeatedly ordered him to report more fully on his activities and in the end began to wonder if Stanley's estimate of the Pasha had, after all, been so unjust. They decided to recall him but could not contact him. If he received their letters, he ignored them and pushed on towards Lake Albert seeking his old associates—Selim Bey and the soldiers. At last he met them again. He accepted with joy their assurances that only a few traitors, in Mahdi pay, had revolted against him; the rest were still loyal. Fadl-el-Mulla had turned out to be the chief Mahdi agent and had tried to persuade the soldiers to surrender to the Donagla. They had rebelled at the suggestion and in the end had killed most of their officers. Emin asked after the two steamers—the *Nyanza* had been destroyed during the last revolt and the *Khedive* had become unserviceable when her captain was killed.

The great store of ivory, worth £100,000, the wealth of the province, had been looted by Kabba Rega and much of it burnt. The province was in confusion.

Emin, ill, exhausted, half-blind, had not the heart then to try and reclaim it. He stayed for a while on the outskirts of what had once been his territory. His old housekeeper, Hadje, fallen on evil days, visited the camp and was welcomed back into his service. When he decided to leave, he asked Selim Bey and the soldiers to go with him. They refused. Emin, deeply hurt, accused them of ingratitude and, with a caravan of only thirty-five people, turned westwards away from them.

He seems to have planned to march through the Congo to the Cameroons, then German territory.

The little caravan took a south-western course and Emin became the first explorer of the south and western shores of Lake Albert Edward. In October, 1891, he was in the Ituri Valley. Exhausted by unceasing misfortune, he wrote in his diary: "Would that I had died after my fall on the stones of Bagamoyo."

Indeed on the journey he had met with hardships comparable with those that had hindered Stanley, and he had countered them with a resolution as firm as Stanley's own. He had with him as a lieutenant Dr. Stuhlmann, a man who had become so deeply attached to him that he chose to remain with the caravan rather than obey the repeated commands of the German authorities to return to the coast.

Near the Victoria Nyanza Emin had rescued some slaves and had handed their Arab masters over to the natives for punishment. These were executed with great cruelty. That Emin, Arabic-speaking, said to be Mohammedan, understanding their contempt for the natives, should have betrayed them in this way, infuriated the slave-traders of the whole region. The word was passed for revenge. Emin's death must have been close behind him for many months before it caught up with him.

He was worn out. Although only fifty years of age, the Equatorial climate had aged him prematurely and undermined his health. The cataract on his eyes was slowly blinding him. He was suffering from a painful illness.

An epidemic of smallpox had broken out among the men. As one man after another contracted the disease, Emin ordered Stuhlmann to take the healthy men and stores to the coast while he remained with the rest. Stuhlmann went unwillingly. Emin remained alone with a camp of sick men who, demoralised by hunger and disease, were continually drunk. The natives of the area were hostile. The Arab slavers, being steadily put out of business by Leopold on Stanley's advice, were in revolt against the white men.

Vultures crowded over the camp; hyenas unearthed the dead. A few days after Christmas Emin was writing in his diary: "The hyenas have once again raked up a corpse and made off with it. I wonder whether they will do the same with mine? Everybody has been drunk from an early hour in the morning and remained so throughout the day." In spite of his own illness and the mutinous insults of his officers, it did not enter his head to make his own way to safety. This time there would be no question of desertion. In his last letter to Stuhlmann, describing the horrible conditions of the camp, he wrote: "If you get to Bagamoyo, give my love to my little one."

He was making his own way westwards towards the Stanley Falls area, perhaps still with some idea of reaching the Cameroons, perhaps merely seeking the last escape of death that he had failed to find on the stones of Bagamoyo. As soon as he could, he moved camp with the survivors of the epidemic. The misery of the march was relieved for him only by a few scientific discoveries that had still the power to make him jubilant.

He survived until the following October, when he reached a village eighty miles east-south-east of Stanley Falls named after its chief, Kinena. There, without the elementary necessities of life, suffering from hunger and illness, he camped with his handful of men. Unconscious of the enmity around him, he sent to Kibonge, the chief of the Manyuema district, for a letter of safe-conduct to the main village. While awaiting it he sat at his table surrounded by his natural history specimens, and recorded the heavy weather and increasing heat.

It was on a Sunday, October 23rd, a day of thunderous and nervous gloom, that the letter arrived. While Emin received it in his tent, Kinena was reading another that came with it.

The chief, with a number of his men, found Emin at his table. Before him were dead insects and the skins of birds. When they entered he was bent over the letter so that his eyes were no more than an inch or two from the paper. Kinena suggested that now Emin had received the safe-conduct, he should send his men to the plantation to cut bananas for the journey. He agreed gratefully and sent them off at once. As they went, Kinena expressed regret that the Pasha must soon leave them—then he gave a signal.

Two Arab captains, Ismaili and Mamba, who had been standing close to Emin, now seized his arms. He asked them with surprise what they wanted.

"Pasha, you must die," replied Mamba.

Emin tried to shake them off angrily and shouted: "What is the meaning of this? Is this a foolish jest? How dare you hold my arms? What do you hope to get by killing me? Who are you that you should dare condemn a man to death?"

Kinena answered: "The order is not mine. Kibonge sent it. He is my master and I must obey him."

Emin was struggling desperately to reach his revolver, which lay on the table. One of the Arabs snatched it away. The death warrant written in Arabic was held close to Emin's eyes so he could read it.

When he knew his death was inevitable, he faced it without any sign of fear, but he warned his assassins that the government would seek them out and execute them. He made no resistance as Kinena's men lifted him from the chair. His last words were that it was all a mistake. Kibonge had given him a safe-conduct to his village.

Four men held him down upon the floor while Mamba slit his throat. His head was cut off, put in a box and sent to Kibonge. His grave was

never discovered. His men were killed and eaten by the Manyuema.
Ismaili, when caught, gave in a deposition the details of the murder.
All the guilty, including Kibonge, were eventually caught and executed.

Farida was taken to Germany by a German deaconess and welcomed
into Emin's home at Neisse. There, after her unconventional childhood, she was baptised and educated as befitted a well-born German
girl.

All the appreciation of Emin in the German Press, the mention of
wealth, ivory and power, had roused much interest in a lady who had not
seen him for sixteen years. Madame Hakki Pasha had remarried but
this did not prevent her declaring herself Emin's widow and heir. She
claimed the fortune in ivory said still to be stored in Equatoria. Her
case, however, was not strong—she had remarried, she had widely
accused Emin of deserting her without marrying her and she could give
no proof of marriage to him. Apart from this, the ivory had not been
Emin's personal property.

Casati, whom Emin had left with a power of attorney, spent many
months trying to recover from the Egyptian Government the salary
due to Emin since 1883. The amount of the salary had never been
fixed, and as Emin had not agitated for a sum, the Egyptian Government had let the matter drift on. Casati's claims met with indifference.
Only after long litigation, the government fixed the salary at £600 a
year, but wished to pay only two-thirds of the total sum due. Casati
fought on until at last the government reluctantly agreed to pay about
£5,200. Some of this Emin had willed to Madame Hakki Pasha, the
rest went to Farida.

For Stanley the future held the first real happiness he had ever
known. In July, 1890, he married Dorothy Tennant, daughter of a
Member of Parliament, and by her devotion she changed his whole
mental outlook. Resuming his British nationality, he five years later
was elected to Parliament himself.

A tamed and kindly Stanley paid one more visit to Africa, this time
to the south, an area popularly supposed to be more civilised than those
he had visited before. He died of a stroke in 1904.

Ten years before, a formal protectorate had been declared over
Uganda and the territory expanded to include countries east and west.
Fadl-el-Mulla, who a year earlier had taken service with a Congo

State expedition, was killed fighting Mahdist troops. A remnant of his men was found by a British officer drifting about the Albert Nyanza in search of food, and was taken back under British protection to Uganda.

Following the Franco-Congolese Treaty of 1894, two British officers were sent to Dufilé, where they planted the British flag on January 15th, 1895. To-day the boundary of Uganda runs some miles north of Wadelai while the rest of Equatoria and Bahr-el-Ghazal are included in the Anglo-Egyptian Sudan.

As for the Sudan itself, its rescue had to be left to a new generation of heroes. The young Lieutenant Kitchener of the early 'eighties had by 1896 become Sirdar of the Egyptian army and in a campaign that lasted four years, he destroyed the power of the Mahdists in the southern provinces. The cost of the reconquest was borne by the British and Egyptian Governments, and to-day they wrangle over the profits.

BIBLIOGRAPHY

Rearranged and expanded for the new edition, 1985. (Additional entries are marked with an asterisk.)

Baker, Sir Samuel White, *The Egyptian Question: Letters to 'The Times' and 'Pall Mall Gazette'*. London, Macmillan, 1884.

*Barttelot, W.G., ed., *The Life of Edmund Musgrave Barttelot*, from his letters and diary. London, Richard Bentley, 1890.

Butler, William F., *Charles George Gordon*. London, Macmillan, 1889.

Casati, Gaetano, *Ten Years in Equatoria, and the Return with Emin Pasha*. 2 vols. London and New York, Frederick Warne & Co., 1891 (English translation of *Dieci Anni in Equatoria*, Milan, 1891.

Egerton, Admiral the Hon. F., W. Rathbone, C.M. Norwood, *Great Britain, Egypt and the Suez Canal*. London, Chapman & Hall, 1884.

Fox-Bourne, H.R., *The Other Side of the Emin Pasha Relief Expedition*. London, Chatto & Windus, 1891.

*Gray, Simon, *The Rear Column*, a play first performed at the Globe Theatre, London, on 22 February 1978.

Jameson, James S., ed. Mrs James S. Jameson, *The Story of the Rear Column of the Emin Pasha Relief Expedition*. London, Pater, 1890.

Jephson, A.J. Mountenay, *Emin Pasha and the Rebellion at the Equator*. London, Sampson Low, 1890.

*Jones, Roger, *The Rescue of Emin Pasha: The Story of Henry M. Stanley and the Emin Pasha Relief Expedition, 1887–1889*. London, Allison & Busby, 1972.

Marston, E., *How Stanley wrote 'In Darkest Africa'*. London, Sampson Low, 1890.

*Middleton, Dorothy, ed., *The Diary of A.J. Mountenay Jephson: Emin Pasha Relief Expedition 1887–1889*. Cambridge University Press for the Hakluyt Society, 1969.

*Moorehead, Alan, *The White Nile*. London, Hamish Hamilton, 1960.

*Parke, Thomas Heazle, *My Personal Experiences in Equatorial Africa as Medical Officer of the Emin Pasha Relief Expedition*. London, Sampson Low, 1891.

Paul, E., *The Future of Egypt from a French Point of View*. London, Norgate, 1884.

Peters, Carl, *New Light on Dark Africa*. London, Ward, Lock & Co., 1891. (English translation of *Die Deutsche Emin-Pasha Expedition*. Munich and Leipzig, R. Oldenbourg, 1891.)

Pimblett, W., *Emin Pasha: His Life and Work*. London, Methuen & Co., 1890.

Report of the Egyptian Provinces of the Sudan, Red Sea and Equatoria. London, War Office, 1882.

Schweinfurth, G., F. Ratzel, R.W. Felkin, G. Hartlaub, eds., *Emin Pasha in Central Africa*, being a collection of his letters and journal, translated by Mrs R.W. Felkin. London, George Philip & Son, 1888.

Schweitzer, Georg, *Emin Pasha: His Life and Work*, compiled from his journals, letters, scientific notes and from official documents. 2 vols. London, Constable, 1898. (English translation of *Emin Pasha: Eine Darstellung seines Lebens und Wirkens*... Berlin, Hermann Walther, 1898.)

*Smith, Iain R., *The Emin Pasha Relief Expedition 1886–1890*. Oxford, Clarendon Press, 1972.

Stanley, H.M., Lecture by, *Across Africa and the Rescue and Retreat of Emin Pasha*. London, Clowes & Sons, 1890.

Stanley, Henry M., *In Darkest Africa or The Quest, Rescue and Retreat of Emin, Governor of Equatoria*. 2 vols. London, Sampson Low, 1890.

Stanley, H.M., lecture by, *The Great Forest of Central Africa, its Cannibals and Pigmies*. London, Clowes & Sons, 1890.

Stanley, H.M., *Incidents of the Journey through the Dark Continent*. London, Clowes & Sons, 1886.

Stanley, H.M., lecture by, *The Rescue of Emin Pasha and our March athwart Darkest Africa*. London, Clowes & Sons, 1890.

Stanley, H.M., *The Story of Emin's Rescue as told in Stanley's Letters*. London, Sampson Low, 1890.

Stone, William, *Shall We Annex Egypt?* London, Sampson Low, 1884.

Stuhlmann, Franz, *Mit Emin Pasha ins Herz von Afrika*. Berlin, Dietrich Reimer, 1894.

*Stuhlmann, Franz, ed., *Die Tagebücher von Dr Emin Pascha*. 5 vols. Braunschweig, Berlin, Hamburg, Westermann, 1917–27.

Symons, A.J.A., *Emin, the Governor of Equatoria*. London, The Fleuron, 1928.

*Symons, A.J.A., *H.M. Stanley*. London, Duckworth, 1933.

*Troup, J. Rose, *With Stanley's Rear Column*. London, Chapman & Hall, 1890.

Ward, Herbert, *My Life with Stanley's Rear Guard*. London, Chatto & Windus, 1891.

Wauters, A.J., *Stanley's Emin Pasha Expedition*. London, Nimmo, 1890.

Wills, J.T., 'Emin Bey: Gordon's Lieutenant in Central Africa' in *The Fortnightly Review*, December 1887.

INDEX

OLIVIA MANNING

Olivia Manning spent much of her childhood in North Ireland and subsequently lived in Rumania, Greece, Egypt, Cyprus, Transjordan and Palestine during the years of the second world war. She was the author of a number of novels and three volumes of short stories, in addition to *The Remarkable Expedition,* for which she received the highest acclaim. She died on 23 July, 1980.